IFIP Advances in Information and Communication Technology   523

Editor-in-Chief

Kai Rannenberg, Goethe University Frankfurt, Germany

IFIP – The International Federation for Information Processing

IFIP was founded in 1960 under the auspices of UNESCO, following the first World Computer Congress held in Paris the previous year. A federation for societies working in information processing, IFIP's aim is two-fold: to support information processing in the countries of its members and to encourage technology transfer to developing nations. As its mission statement clearly states:

> IFIP is the global non-profit federation of societies of ICT professionals that aims at achieving a worldwide professional and socially responsible development and application of information and communication technologies.

IFIP is a non-profit-making organization, run almost solely by 2500 volunteers. It operates through a number of technical committees and working groups, which organize events and publications. IFIP's events range from large international open conferences to working conferences and local seminars.

The flagship event is the IFIP World Computer Congress, at which both invited and contributed papers are presented. Contributed papers are rigorously refereed and the rejection rate is high.

As with the Congress, participation in the open conferences is open to all and papers may be invited or submitted. Again, submitted papers are stringently refereed.

The working conferences are structured differently. They are usually run by a working group and attendance is generally smaller and occasionally by invitation only. Their purpose is to create an atmosphere conducive to innovation and development. Refereeing is also rigorous and papers are subjected to extensive group discussion.

Publications arising from IFIP events vary. The papers presented at the IFIP World Computer Congress and at open conferences are published as conference proceedings, while the results of the working conferences are often published as collections of selected and edited papers.

IFIP distinguishes three types of institutional membership: Country Representative Members, Members at Large, and Associate Members. The type of organization that can apply for membership is a wide variety and includes national or international societies of individual computer scientists/ICT professionals, associations or federations of such societies, government institutions/government related organizations, national or international research institutes or consortia, universities, academies of sciences, companies, national or international associations or federations of companies.

More information about this series at http://www.springer.com/series/6102

Marcelo Götz · Gunar Schirner
Marco Aurélio Wehrmeister
Mohammad Abdullah Al Faruque
Achim Rettberg (Eds.)

System Level Design from HW/SW to Memory for Embedded Systems

5th IFIP TC 10 International
Embedded Systems Symposium, IESS 2015
Foz do Iguaçu, Brazil, November 3–6, 2015
Proceedings

Editors

Marcelo Götz
Federal University of Rio Grande do Sul
Porto Alegre
Brazil

Gunar Schirner
Northeastern University Boston
Boston, MA
USA

Marco Aurélio Wehrmeister
Federal University of Technology Parana
Curitiba
Brazil

Mohammad Abdullah Al Faruque
University of California at Irvine
Irvine, CA
USA

Achim Rettberg
Carl von Ossietzky University
Oldenburg
Germany

ISSN 1868-4238   ISSN 1868-422X (electronic)
IFIP Advances in Information and Communication Technology
ISBN 978-3-030-07917-8   ISBN 978-3-319-90023-0 (eBook)
https://doi.org/10.1007/978-3-319-90023-0

Printed on acid-free paper

This Springer imprint is published by the registered company Springer International Publishing AG part of Springer Nature
The registered company address is: Gewerbestrasse 11, 6330 Cham, Switzerland

Preface

This book presents the technical program of the International Embedded Systems Symposium (IESS) 2015. A broad discussion on the design, analysis, and verification of embedded and cyber-physical systems is presented in a complementary view throughout the chapters of this book, including design methodologies, verification, performance analysis, and real-time systems design. The book includes real-world application case studies discussing challenges and realizations of embedded systems.

The advances in technology over recent years have provided a resourceful infrastructure to embedded systems in terms of an enormous amount of processing power and storage capacity. Formerly external components can now be integrated into a single System-on-Chip. This tendency has resulted in a dramatic reduction in the size and cost of embedded systems. Such a hardware infrastructure has led to an increasing number of services provided, allowing embedded systems to enter numerous application areas (including cyber-physical applications). As a unique technology, the design of embedded systems is an essential element of many innovations.

Embedded systems meet their performance goals, including real-time constraints, through a combination of special-purpose hardware and software components tailored to the system requirements. Both the development of new features and the reuse of existing intellectual property components are essential to keeping up with ever-demanding customer requirements. Furthermore, design complexities are steadily growing with an increasing number of components that have to cooperate properly. Embedded system designers have to cope with multiple goals and constraints simultaneously, including timing, power, reliability, dependability, maintenance, packaging and, last but not least, price.

The significance and importance of these constraints vary depending on the application area a system is targeted for. Typical embedded applications include consumer electronics, automotive, avionics, medical, industrial automation, robotics, communication devices, and others.

The International Embedded Systems Symposium (IESS) is a unique forum to present novel ideas, exchange timely research results, and discuss the state of the art and future trends in the field of embedded systems. Contributors and participants from both industry and academia take active part in this symposium. The IESS conference is organized by the Computer Systems Technology committee (TC10) of the International Federation for Information Processing (IFIP), especially the Working Group 10.2 "Embedded Systems."

IESS is a true interdisciplinary conference on the design of embedded systems. Computer Science and Electrical Engineering are the predominant academic disciplines concerned with the topics covered in IESS, but many applications also involve civil, mechanical, aerospace, and automotive engineering, as well as various medical disciplines.

In 2005, IESS was held for the first time in Manaus, Brazil. In this initial instalment, IESS 2005 was very successful with 30 accepted papers ranging from specification to embedded systems application. IESS 2007 was the second edition of the symposium held in Irvine (CA), USA, with 35 accepted papers and two tutorials ranging from analysis and design methodologies to case studies from automotive and medical applications. IESS 2009 took place in the wonderful Schoß Montfort in Langenargen, Germany, with 28 accepted papers and two tutorials ranging from efficient modelling to challenges for designers of fault-tolerant embedded systems. IESS 2013 was held in Paderborn, Germany, at the Heinz Nixdorf Museums-Forum (HNF) with 22 full papers and eight short papers.

IESS 2015 was held in Foz do Iguaçu, Brazil, close to the beautiful Iguaçu Falls. The articles presented in this book are the result of a thorough review process implemented by the Technical Program Committee. Out of 25 valid submissions, 12 full papers were accepted yielding an acceptance rate of 48%. In addition, six short papers are included, yielding an overall acceptance rate of 72%.

The technical program of IESS 2015 included sessions with complementary and interdisciplinary themes, e.g., cyber-physical systems, system level design, multi/many-core systems design, memory systems design, and embedded hardware and software design and applications. Very interesting keynotes on diverse topics, such as the Internet of Things, real-time operating systems, ubiquitous computing infrastructure, and adaptive systems design based on COTS, were also included in the technical program.

With our strong technical program, we had a successful IESS 2015 conference with fruitful discussions.

First and foremost, we thank our sponsors Hella KGaA Hueck & Co. and the Carl von Ossietzky University Oldenburg for their generous financial support of this conference. Without these contributions, IESS 2015 would not have been possible in its current form. Very special thanks to the co-located conference team from SBESC 2015, who supported mainly the local arrangements with the Golden Tulip Conference Hotel where the event was hosted.

We would also like to thank IFIP for the promotion and support of the IESS conference.

Last but not least, we thank the authors for their interesting research contributions and the members of the Technical Program Committee for their valuable time and effort in reviewing the articles.

November 2015   Marcelo Götz
                                                                Gunar Schirner
                                                            Marco Wehrmeister
                                                    Mohammad Abdullah Al Faruque
                                                                Achim Rettberg

IFIP TC10 Working Conference: International Embedded Systems Symposium (IESS) November 3–6, 2015 Golden Tulip Conference Hotel, Foz do Iguacu, Brazil

General Chairs

Gunar Schirner	Northeastern University Boston, USA
Marcelo Götz	Federal University of Rio Grande do Sul, Brazil

General Co-chair

Achim Rettberg	Hella KGaA Hueck & Co./Carl von Ossietzky, University Oldenburg, Germany

Program Co-chairs

Marco Wehrmeister	Federal University of Technology Parana, Brazil
Mohammad Al Faruque	University of California at Irvine, USA

Steering Committee

Achim Rettberg	Hella KGaA Hueck & Co./Carl von Ossietzky, University Oldenburg, Germany
Mauro C. Zanella	ZF Friedrichshafen AG, Germany
Franz J. Rammig	University of Paderborn, Germany

Local Arrangements Chair

Marcio Kreutz	Federal University of Rio Grande do Norte, Brazil

Publicity Chair

Hamed Tabkhi	Northeastern University Boston, USA

Review System Chair

Ina Podolski	Carl von Ossietzky University Oldenburg, Germany

Web Chair

Tayfun Gezgin   Lufthansa Cargo, Germany

Finance Chair

Achim Rettberg   Hella KGaA Hueck & Co./Carl von Ossietzky,
                          University Oldenburg, Germany

Technical Program Committee

Samar Abdi   Concordia University Montreal, Canada
Christian Allmann   Audi Electronics Venture, Germany
Michael Amann   ZF Friedrichshafen, Germany
Richard Anthony   The University of Greenwich, UK
Jürgen Becker   University of Karlsruhe, Germany
Alecio Binotto   IBM Research, Brazil
Christophe Bobda   University of Arkansas, USA
Luigi Carro   Federal University of Rio Grande do Sul, Brazil
Florian Dittmann   Kromberg & Schubert GmbH & Co. KG, Germany
Rainer Doemer   University of California at Irvine, USA
Cecilia Ekelin   Volvo Technology Corporation, Sweden
Rolf Ernst   Technical University of Braunschweig, Germany
Danubia B. Espindola   Federal University of Rio Grande, Brazil
Mohammad Al Faruque   University of California at Irvine, USA
Masahiro Fujita   University of Tokyo, Japan
Andreas Gerstlauer   University of Texas Austin, USA
Tayfun Gezgin   Lufthansa Cargo, Germany
Marcelo Götz   Federal University of Rio Grande do Sul, Brazil
Kim Grüttner   OFFIS, Germany
Andreas Hein   Carl von Ossietzky University Oldenburg, Germany
Joerg Henkel   University of Karlsruhe, Germany
Stefan Henkler   University of Applied Science Dortmund, Germany
Carsten Homburg   dSPACE, Germany
Uwe Honekamp   Vector Informatik, Germany
Michael Huebner   Ruhr-University Bochum, Germany
Marcel Jackowski   University of Sao Paulo, Brazil
Ricardo Jacobi   University of Brasilia, Brazil
Michael Keckeisen   ZF Friedrichshafen, Germany
Timo Kerstan   Vector Informatik, Germany
Amin Khajeh   Intel, USA
Doo-Hyun Kim   Konkuk University, South Korea
Hermann Kopetz   Technical University Vienna, Austria
Marcio Kreutz   Federal University of Rio Grande do Norte, Brazil
Horst Krimmel   ZF Friedrichshafen, Germany
Thomas Lehmann   HAW Hamburg, Germany

Armin Lichtblau	Mentor Graphics, Germany
Patrick Lysaght	Xilinx Research Labs, USA
Roger May	Altera, UK
Adam Morawiec	ECSI, France
Wolfgang Nebel	Carl von Ossietzky University Oldenburg, Germany
Markus Oertel	Vector Informatik, Germany
Mike Olivarez	Freescale Semiconductor, USA
Carlos Pereira	Federal University of Rio Grande do Sul, Brazil
Edison Pignaton de Freitas	Federal University of Rio Grande do Sul, Brazil
Franz Rammig	University of Paderborn, Germany
Achim Rettberg	Hella KGaA Hueck & B Co./Carl von Ossietzky, University Oldenburg, Germany
Stefan Schimpf	ETAS, Germany
Juergen Schirmer	Robert Bosch GmbH, Stuttgart, Germany
Gunar Schirner	Northeastern University Boston, USA
Aviral Shrivastava	Arizona State University, USA
Joachim Stroop	dSPACE, Germany
Hamed Tabkhi	Northeastern University Boston, USA
Hiroyuki Tomiyama	Ritsumeikan University, Japan
Flavio R. Wagner	Federal University of Rio Grande do Sul, Brazil
Marco Wehrmeister	Federal University of Technology Parana, Brazil
Marilyn Wolf	Georgia Institute of Technology, USA
Mauro Zanella	ZF Friedrichshafen, Germany
Jianwen Zhu	University of Toronto, Canada

Co-organizing Institution

IFIP TC 10, WG 10.2 and WG 10.5

Sponsors

Hella KGaA Hueck & Co.
Carl von Ossietzky University Oldenburg

Contents

Cyber-Physical Systems

Ontological User Modeling for Ambient Assisted Living Service Personalization

Maurício Fontana de Vargas$^{(\boxtimes)}$ and Carlos Eduardo Pereira

Automation Engineering Department, Federal University of Rio Grande do Sul,
Porto Alegre, Brazil
mauricio.vargas@ufrgs.br, cpereira@ece.ufrgs.br

Abstract. Given that the population is aging, it is crucial to develop technologies which will not only help the elderly to *age in place*, but also *live in place* with independent and healthy lifestyle. Ambient Assisted Living (AAL) environments can help the elderly and people with functional diversity by anticipating their needs in specific situations and acting proactively in order to properly assist them in performing their activities of daily living (ADLs). Since the users needs tend to be very diverse in regard to functioning and disability levels, it is crucial to have personalized services capable of providing tailored assistance to a user based on their unique preferences, requirements, and desires. This paper introduces the ontology named AATUM (Ambient Assistive Technology User Model), to be adopted by systems whose goal is to enhance user quality of life within ALL environments through service personalization. Its main feature is the use of The International Classification of Functioning, Disability and Health (ICF) to model the user's functioning and disability levels in a consistent and internationally comparable way. The use of the proposed ontology is illustrated through its application in two different case studies.

Keywords: Ontology · Context-aware · Functioning · User centered
World Health Organization

1   Introduction

The percentage of global population aged 60 or older is expected to be 22% by 2050 [8]. As a result, there is an expected increase of chronic illnesses and disability associated with old age. This demographic change toward an aging society results in many social and health care system challenges to ensure that our infrastructures can support the needs of the elderly, enabling them to have an independent and healthy lifestyle.

Given the fact that 64% of older adults prefer to stay in the comfort of their own homes, and given the costs of nursing home care, it is crucial to develop technologies that help older adults not only to *age*, but also *live in place* i.e., independently and comfortably in their home [2].

© IFIP International Federation for Information Processing 2017
Published by Springer International Publishing AG 2017. All Rights Reserved
M. Götz et al. (Eds.): IESS 2015, IFIP AICT 523, pp. 3–14, 2017.
https://doi.org/10.1007/978-3-319-90023-0_1

In recent years, researchers have developed a variety of assistive technologies based on a the paradigm called "ambient intelligence", where the ambient anticipates users needs in specific situations and acts proactively in order to properly assist the user to perform his/her activities of daily living (ADLs). Assisted living technologies based on ambient intelligence are called Ambient Assisted Living (AAL) tools and can be used for preventing, healing, and improving quality of life of the elderly and people with functional diversity.

Since these users tend to be greatly variable in regards to functioning and disability levels, service personalization is crucial [7]. A personalized service is a service capable of providing tailored assistance to a user based on their unique preferences, requirements, and desires. Therefore, service personalization within AAL environments can help elderly people or people with functional diversity to increase their independence and quality of life.

The need for service personalization has led to the use of ontologies as a means to provide a correct user model in a machine understandable format. This model is generally represented in the form of a user profile which captures the personal aspects in terms of user's behaviors, goals, capacities, likes and dislikes. Therefore, the user model can be seen as an abstract entity and the user profile represents an instantiation of the user model for a specific user [1].

This work focuses on user modeling using an ontology to enhance user quality of life within ALL environments through service personalization. Section 2 presents related work within user modeling and service personalization. The third section presents the Ambient Assistive Technology User Model (AATUM) ontology and its structure, highlighting the main covered aspects and describing its functionality. Then, in the fourth section, two use cases are presented showing real life situations; these are used in the fifth section in order to demonstrate the ontology usage. The last section includes conclusions and future research work.

2   Related Work

As mentioned before, one of the core aspects in service personalization is user modeling. Ontology-based user modeling has been previously proposed in many research areas like knowledge management systems [12], semantic web search [6] and digital museum guides [4]. The increasing attention of ontological modeling is mostly due to its interoperability feature and ability to enable knowledge sharing and reuse over several application domains [5].

One important issue is that user preference and needs may change depending on the user context. Thus, the system has to be able to infer which context the user is in and consequently adapt the ambient to provide the appropriate assistance. The UPOS (User Profile Ontology with Situation-Dependent Preferences Support) [16] introduced the concept of dynamic user profiles. The ontology supports the creation of a subset of conditional user profiles associated with the user context. According to a condition (e.g. if the context of user Bob equals the MyOffice location), the matching process tries to find the correspondent sub-profile. If a match happens, the found user profile is applied for service personalization.

Another relevant concern within AAL service personalization is the need of having information about the user's health condition and his/her limitations performing daily activities. Without the correct representation of the user's needs and capabilities, it's unlikely that the ambient will properly adapt itself to provide optimum assistance for the elderly and for people with special requirements.

Kadouche *et al.* [7] proposed the Semantic Matching Framework (SMF) capable of providing an appropriate middleware for delivering personalized assistive services according to the user's needs and capabilities. The main feature of SMF is based on the semantic matching between the user model and the environment model. The user model describes user information, preferences and capabilities while the environment model defines the available devices (e.g. door) and their attributes (e.g. required force to open the door). Using a reasoning mechanism, the SMF analyzes user capabilities and the environment and deduces the "handicap situation" in order to deliver personalized services.

The PCEICL (Person Centered Environment for Information, Communication and Learning) [3] platform aims to offer a better assistance to elderly people using context aware and personalizable services. They have proposed an ontology where the user is the central concept and is described by their characteristics such as their health condition, capabilities and preferences. In order to have an exact and correct description of the user's health condition, they have used the International Code for Diseases (ICD) [11].

Another approach of service personalization in the field of AAL is the MobileSage [15]. The main purpose of their work is to provide help on-demand services as the user moves between mobile environments. Based on the user's characteristics and his/her location, the system can personalize services in order to assist the user in his/her daily activities like outdoor navigation and the use of devices such as ticket vending machines. As in [3], MobileSage ontology models the user as a central concept of the system as well as his/her environment. The user profile is composed by a set of sub profiles like a capability profile, a health profile and an interest profile.

The main issue of the aforementioned works is the lack of a uniform and consistent representation of user health condition, functioning and disability. The representation of this information is usually designed in order to meet the requirements of a specific application. Thus, the main feature of using an ontology, i.e. the knowledge sharing and reuse, is not fully utilized.

3   The AATUM Ontology

In order to prevent common mistakes and make the best modeling decisions while developing the ontology, we have taken into account the design method proposed by [9]. Using a traditional top-down approach, both static and dynamic high-level concepts related to the user were selected and further broken down into specialized concepts. The AATUM ontology has been implemented in OWL, the Ontology Web Language that is a xml-based semantic web language proposed by the World Wide Web Consortium (W3C). To help with the process of creating, editing and viewing the ontology, the *Protégé-OWL Editor*[1] was selected. A brief explanation of the ontology main classes is depicted in Table 1. To illustrate the ontological structure and the relationship between its classes, a graphical representation is presented in Fig. 1.

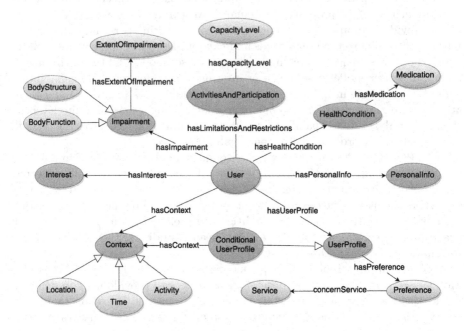

Fig. 1. An overview of the AATUM ontological structure

Basic information such as address, date of birth, telephone number and family contacts is stored in the class `PersonalInfo`. Though this information may not seem to be very useful, it could be used for important purposes in terms of ALL. For example, this information could be used to send an ambulance to a user's house after a heart attack or in a statistical report documenting the health conditions of a neighborhood's residents.

The class `Interest` holds information about personal interests related either to a hobby or work. Every interest has a weight associated in order to measure how much the user is interested in that specific subject. Moreover, additional information like descriptions or schedules can be stored. This class is useful for recommendations or content-filtering applications and can help people to have a higher quality of life. For example, the task of choosing a movie on television would be much easier for an elderly person if only desirable options were presented.

The class `Context` is used to represent user's context such as the location, the time, and the activity the user is performing. One key advantage of defining

---

[1] Protégé-OWL Editor: Available at http://protege.stanford.edu/.

Table 1. AATUM ontology main classes

Concept	Description	Example values
User	The user of the system	"User_John"
User profile	Default profile associated to preferences of one particular user	"John_DefaultProfile"
User conditional profile	Conditional profile associated to the user's context describing situation-dependent preferences	"John_SleepingProfile", "John_WeekendsProfile", "Noel_LivingRoomProfile"
Context	Environmental information related with the user such as location, time or activity	"Sleeping", "In the kitchen", "Evening"
Personal info	Basic user information like address, contacts, age and e-mail	"59 Homewood st." "37 year old", "Son's Tel.: 800-876-5380"
Interest	Hobbies or work-related interests	"Cooking", "Hockey", "Science news"
Preference	Individual preferences related to a service	"Room temperature = 75 °F", "Text size = LARGE", "Preferred media = AUDIO"
Health condition	A disorder, disease or injury diagnosis	"Cerebral palsy", "Back pain", "Diabets"
Medication	Medication used in the disorder, disease or injury treatment	"Lisinopril', "Simvastatin", "Hydrocodone"
Impairment	Problems in body function and structure such as significant deviation or loss	"Pancreatic dysfunction", "Respiratory dysfunction", "Reduced mobility joint"
Extent of impairment	The degree of the impairment of function or structure	"Mild impairment", "Severe impairment"
Activities and participation	Difficulties the user may have in executing activities or in involvement in life situations	"Walking", "Reading", "Relating with strangers"
Capacity level	Individual's ability to execute a task or an action	"Mild difficulty", "Severe difficulty"

the context this way is the possibility of inferring additional information from a small amount of sensor data. For example, using only the information that the user is located in his bedroom and it is 01:00 AM, the system can infer that the user is sleeping and then adapt the ambient in order to give the user a better night sleep.

The user's behavior and preferences depend on the temporal and environmental context the user is in. For example, the user's smartphone should be set to silent mode during a meeting and to loud mode when the user is at home; the shower water temperature is likely to be higher in the winter compared to the summer; the desired ambient luminosity may be set to *high* in the evening and to *none* during sleep time. Thus, it's crucial to have different profiles related to different contexts. This is done through the class `ConditionalUserProfile` that is linked to the class `Context`. The preferences that are unlikely to change according to the context are linked to a default profile represented by the class `UserProfile`, which is the superclass of `ConditionalUserProfile`.

The most important concepts of the ontology are the classes related to the user's health condition and capabilities. Having a complete, uniform, and consistent model of the user's functioning and disability levels allows correct service tailoring, and thus a better quality of life for impaired and elderly people.

Information about user health condition, i.e., the disease or disorder diagnosis is stored in `HealthCondition` class. As in [3], this information is composed by the disease/disorder level, its related medication, and its ICD, which is a worldwide used code. Also, additional information relevant to medical accompaniment or treatment can be stored. This information could be used, for instance, to give an analysis of the general health situation of a population group or to prompt the user about his/her medication schedule.

According to [10], diagnosis of a disease or disorder by itself does not predict service needs, length of hospitalizations, level of care, or functional outcomes. If a person cannot perform an activity it may be related to any of various different health conditions. In other words, it is very hard to infer participation in everyday life from medical diagnosis alone. This implies that without data about levels of functioning and disability, we will not have the information needed to properly assist the user in his daily activities. Therefore, we used The International Classification of Functioning, Disability and Health (ICF) to model the user's functioning and disability levels in a consistent and internationally comparable way. An excerpt of the class describing user impairments is shown in Fig. 2 while Fig. 3 presents an excerpt of the class that describes user limitations performing activities and participation restrictions.

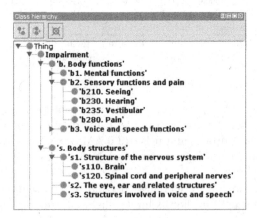

Fig. 2. An excerpt of the `Impairment` class as shown within Protégé

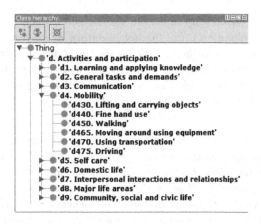

Fig. 3. An excerpt of the `ActivitiesAndParticipation` class as shown within Protégé

We also have used the ICF qualifiers to record the presence and severity of a problem in functioning at the body, person and societal levels. For the classifications of body function and structure, the qualifier `ExtentOfImpairment` indicates, on a five point scale, the degree of the impairment of function or structure. The possible values are: no impairment, mild, moderate, severe and complete. In the case of the Activity and Participation list of domains, the `Capacity` qualifier describes an individual's ability to execute a task or an action using the same five point scale.

4 Use Case Study

Based on the elderly and people with functional diversity most important requirements presented in [13,14], two use cases where the ontology can be used in order to properly assist the user to perform his/her activities of daily living were defined. First, a short description of the users is given:

Mr. John: *Mr. John is a 63 year old retired Professor living alone is his apartment. Though he left his job recently, he still reads scientific news on his personal computer or tablet. He started to cook as a hobby and a few weeks ago he started to follow a foreign documentary about Asian cuisine that is broadcast every Wednesday night. He has a high level of myopia which makes it hard to read small or distant texts.*

Mr. Noel: *Mr. Noel is a 81 year old widower living with his daughter. Because he suffers from cardiac arrhythmia, his heart rate needs to be checked constantly. His daughter used to assist him with the daily care needs such as giving the medicines and checking his heart rate, but since she got a new job, Mr. Noel will have to stay by himself during weekday afternoons.*

Use case 1: *Every Wednesday night the system will show a notification in Mr. John's smartphone telling him that the documentary is about to start. Moreover, additional information about the specific episode is shown. If Mr. John confirms he's going to watch the documentary, the system will turn on the TV, switch to the correct channel, set the subtitles to English and adjust its size in order to make it possible for Mr John to read it comfortably. Also, the room lights are turned off.*

Use case 2: *While Mr. Noel is by himself at home, his heart rate is obtained by a wearable sensor and transmitted wirelessly to the system. This data is compared with values determined safe by his doctor, and in case of an emergency, both his daughter and medical staff are notified. Since Mr. Noel takes two different medications, the system attends to his medicine schedule and prompts him when medication is required. This is done through the closest electronic device, such as the living room television or his personal computer.*

5 Ontology Usage

Once we have the user model ontology, we need a infrastructure capable of delivering customizable services available in the ambient. Figure 4 presents an overview of a service-oriented architecture (SOA) within a smart home that aims to assist the user with special requirements to have a safe and independent lifestyle using a combination of context-awareness, user modeling and service personalization. This architecture is part of our ongoing research and will be further discussed in future papers.

The data needed for populating the ontological user model is gathered in several ways. Context invariant data such as personal information, interests and health condition is acquired during the system initialization by the user or the caregiver. On the other hand, information such as preferences can be deduced from previously given information. For example, if the user has a mild hearing impairment, his preference for volume level should automatically be set to *high*.

Specifically for collecting the health and disability information, the system can use one of the two application instruments proposed by the World Health Organization (WHO). This is another compelling benefit of using the ICF as part of the ontology. The first one is a checklist with the most relevant ICF categories which allows the identification and qualifications of the individuals functioning profile in a straightforward manner. The second one, named WHODAS (WHO Disability Assessment Schedule), is a generic assessment instrument designed from a comprehensive set of the ICF items that are sufficiently reliable and precise for providing a standardized method for measuring health and disability across different cultures [17]. A unique feature of WHODAS, that distinguishes it from other disability measures, is its direct association to the ICF. According to the WHO, the WHODAS 12-item version has an average interview time of only five minutes, what it makes it a very affordable strategy to collect all necessary user's health and disability information.

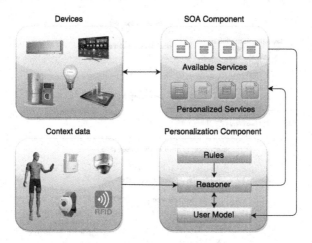

Fig. 4. System architecture for service personalization in a smart home

The next subsections depict how the proposed AATUM ontology and the system architecture are used to provide user optimal assistance with the use cases introduced in Sect. 4.

5.1 Use Case 1

Mr. John's interest about the Asian cuisine documentary is stored as an instance of the class `Interest` and the documentary's hours and channel is saved as the class's property `AdditionalInformation`.

Knowing the current day and time, the system searches on the Internet additional information about the episode and sends to John's smartphone. After Mr. John confirms he's going to watch the episode, the living room television is turned on and set to the documentary's channel.

Using the information about his seeing impairment stored as an instance of the ICF class `b210. Seeing` along his context information `Watching TV`, the system infers the preference `Subtitle size: large` and saves it as an instance of the class `Preference` that is linked to his conditional profile `John_WatchingTvProfile`.

In the last times Mr. John watched TV, he turned off the room's lights. This pattern was learned by the system reasoner using a predefined rule and stored as the preference `Room lightning: dark` that is also linked to his conditional profile `John_WatchingTvProfile`.

An excerpt of the ontology classes instances describing this use case is presented in Fig. 5.

5.2 Use Case 2

Mr. Noel's heart disease is stored as an instance of the class `HealthCondition`, as it's ICD code (I49.9) and medication schedule. The heart rate values determined

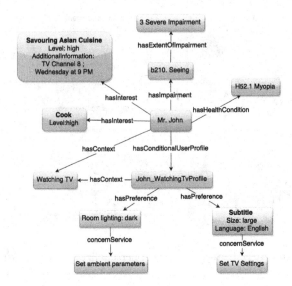

Fig. 5. Ontology classes instances for Use case 1

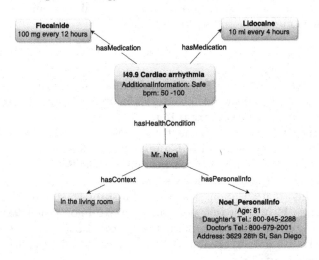

Fig. 6. Ontology classes instances for Use case 2

safe by his doctor are stored as the class' property `AdditionalInformation`. His daughter's and hospital's telephone number, as his address, are saved in the class `PersonalInfo`. This way, when his body sensor detect unsafe values, the system sends a text message notifying his daughter and calls an ambulance to his house. After attending his medicine schedule, the system determines the device where the notification should be displayed using his context information stored in `Location`, that was obtained through presence sensors.

An excerpt of the ontology classes instances describing this use case is presented in Fig. 6.

6   Conclusion

In this paper we have presented the AATUM, a novel ontology for user modeling in the field of AAL. We have demonstrated, through two case studies, how the proposed ontology is used to properly assist the elderly with their activities of daily living in a smart home, achieving a safe and independent lifestyle.

The use of ontologies for user modeling within AAL is not new, but the related works fail in the representation of user health condition, functioning, and disability, which are essential components to properly provide optimum assistance for the elderly and for people with special requirements. In the AATUM ontology, the user is the central concept and is described by his/her static and dynamic properties such as personal information, interests, health condition, etc. The AATUM ontology main feature is the use of the ICF, the World Health Organization's framework for health and disability, to model the user's functioning and disability levels in a consistent and internationally comparable way. Also, the ICD code is used to properly describe the disease or disorder diagnosis. Another compelling feature is the use of a conditional user profile related to the user's context to describe situation-dependent preferences.

Future work will aim to develop the reasoning mechanism to provide personalized services according to the user profile described by the AATUM ontology and his/her context. Further evaluation will involve the total implementation and integration of the service personalization component with a smart home based on a service-oriented and context-aware architecture.

Acknowledgment. This research work has been funded by the CAPES PROCAD project (071/2013), whose support is gratefully acknowledged.

References

1. Bhowmick, P.K., Sarkar, S., Basu, A.: Ontology based user modeling for personalized information access. IJCSA **7**(1), 1–22 (2010)
2. Centers for Disease Control and Prevention (CDC): The State of Aging and Health in America 2013. US Department of Health and Human Services, Centers for Disease Control and Prevention, Atlanta (2013)
3. Fredrich, C., Kuijs, H., Reich, C.: An ontology for user profile modelling in the field of ambient assisted living. In: Sixth International Conferences on Advanced Service Computing, SERVICE COMPUTATION 2014, pp. 24–31 (2014)
4. Hatala, M., Wakkary, R.: Ontology-based user modeling in an augmented audio reality system for museums. User Model. User-Adap. Inter. **15**(3–4), 339–380 (2005)
5. Heckmann, D., Schwartz, T., Brandherm, B., Schmitz, M., von Wilamowitz-Moellendorff, M.: GUMO – the general user model ontology. In: Ardissono, L., Brna, P., Mitrovic, A. (eds.) UM 2005. LNCS (LNAI), vol. 3538, pp. 428–432. Springer, Heidelberg (2005). https://doi.org/10.1007/11527886_58

6. Jiang, X., Tan, A.H.: Learning and inferencing in user ontology for personalized semantic web search. Inf. Sci. **179**(16), 2794–2808 (2009)
7. Kadouche, R., Mokhtari, M., Giroux, S., Abdulrazak, B.: Personalization in smart homes for disabled people. In: Second International Conference on Future Generation Communication and Networking, FGCN 2008, vol. 2, pp. 411–415. IEEE (2008)
8. Lutz, W., Sanderson, W., Scherbov, S.: The coming acceleration of global population ageing. Nature **451**(7179), 716–719 (2008)
9. Noy, N.F., McGuinness, D.L., et al.: Ontology development 101: a guide to creating your first ontology (2001)
10. World Health Organization: International classification of functioning, disability and health: ICF. World Health Organization (2001)
11. World Health Organization: International classification of diseases (ICD) (2012). http://www.who.int/classifications/icd/en/. Retrieved June 2015
12. Razmerita, L., Angehrn, A., Maedche, A.: Ontology-based user modeling for knowledge management systems. In: Brusilovsky, P., Corbett, A., de Rosis, F. (eds.) UM 2003. LNCS (LNAI), vol. 2702, pp. 213–217. Springer, Heidelberg (2003). https://doi.org/10.1007/3-540-44963-9_29
13. Rusu, L., Cramariuc, B.: A conceptual approach for innovative home care solution. J. Appl. Comput. Sci. Math. **17**(17), 22–26 (2014)
14. de Ruyter, B., Zwartkruis-Pelgrim, E., Aarts, E.: Ambient assisted living research in the carelab. GeroPsych: J. Gerontopsychol. Geriatr. Psychiatr. **23**(2), 115 (2010)
15. Skillen, K.-L., Chen, L., Nugent, C.D., Donnelly, M.P., Burns, W., Solheim, I.: Ontological user profile modeling for context-aware application personalization. In: Bravo, J., López-de-Ipiña, D., Moya, F. (eds.) UCAmI 2012. LNCS, vol. 7656, pp. 261–268. Springer, Heidelberg (2012). https://doi.org/10.1007/978-3-642-35377-2_36
16. Sutterer, M., Droegehorn, O., David, K.: UPOS: User profile ontology with situation-dependent preferences support. In: First International Conference on Advances in Computer-Human Interaction, pp. 230–235. IEEE (2008)
17. Üstün, T.B.: Measuring Health and Disability: Manual for WHO Disability Assessment Schedule WHODAS 2.0. World Health Organization, Geneva (2010)

Multi-Agent Based Implementation of an Embedded Image Processing System in FPGA for Precision Agriculture Using UAVs

Érico Nunes, Lucas Behnck$^{(\boxtimes)}$, and Carlos Eduardo Pereira

Federal University of Rio Grande do Sul - UFRGS/ DELET, Av. Osvaldo Aranha,
103, Porto Alegre, RS 90035-190, Brazil
emnunes@inf.ufrgs.br, lucas.pluceno@ufrgs.br, cpereira@ece.ufrgs.br
http://www.ufrgs.br

Abstract. This work proposes a framework and design-space exploration on possible implementations for Multi-Agent based embedded systems for precision agriculture applications using image processing. For
this application, we evaluate both purely software-based implementations
on different embedded processors, as well as implementations which feature dedicated peripherals for image processing implemented in FPGA.
All of the implementations feature agent capabilities provided through
the JADE Framework. The proposed Reconfigurable hardware Agent
framework features capabilities which allow it to offer high performance
for applications such as high resolution image processing. We consider
the impact of JADE agent migration to an FPGA platform and evaluate
the impact of partially reconfiguring the FPGA in this application. The
proposed framework is evaluated in an application of use of UAVs for
precision agriculture. A faster execution for the image processing algorithms and detection of points of interest (POI) allows for processing
images of higher resolution, which may help the accuracy of POI detection. It may also allow for processing an increased number of images in
real-time or improve the autonomy of the UAVs.

1 Introduction

Multi-Agent Systems (MAS) are currently a technology targeted for applications
which require flexibility, robustness and reconfigurability [12]. Due to their characteristics, there is interest in application and research about MASs in several
fields, such as industrial applications [8], area surveillance [11], Unmanned Aerial
Vehicle (UAV) missions [17], security [10], smart grids [18], among others.

While this technology is already finding its way into the industry, there are
still a drawbacks that hinder large scale application of Agent concepts in industry, such as lack of development tools and standards, lack of skilled design, engineering and maintenance personnel, and many others [8]. Another issue regarded

© IFIP International Federation for Information Processing 2017
Published by Springer International Publishing AG 2017. All Rights Reserved
M. Götz et al. (Eds.): IESS 2015, IFIP AICT 523, pp. 15–26, 2017.
https://doi.org/10.1007/978-3-319-90023-0_2

as a challenge for MASs is real-time control [13]. There have been recent studies in this area as described in [5,7].

One common method for implementation of agents is the Java Agent Development Framework (JADE) framework. JADE is a well known Agent framework which simplifies the implementation of MAS through a middleware that complies with the Foundation for Intelligent Physical Agents (FIPA) specifications, among other features [2]. JADE allows the agent to be developed in a high level language (Java), provides management and debugging features and allows easy agent migration.

Another recent topic in Agent development in the implementation of Agents in hardware and communication of hardware and software agents. Some works discuss implementations of MASs with hardware Agents, such as in [1,3,15]. Most of the work in this area results in implementation proposals which allow only communication between Agents of the same implementation nature (hardware or software) or allow communication between Agents among different implementation natures only through the use of a custom protocol. Usually, the topic of migrating agents from software to hardware is also out of scope.

The work described in [3] details an architecture proposal for implementing hardware Agents and allowing communication and migration between hardware and software Agents. Hardware agents are composed of an field-programmable gate array (FPGA) to implement the Agent hardware functionality and a host processor to provide the bridge between JADE messages and hardware execution. In this work, a middleware is proposed for managing the FPGA reconfiguration during Agent migration. Through the use of the JADE framework for both implementation natures, it enables hardware agents to communicate through a well known interface and to provide faster Agent execution times.

Some limitations discussed in [3] are that complete FPGA reconfiguration can be costly and that an external host processor has to be provided. This also brings the limitation that only one Agent is considered to exist in the FPGA at a time. FPGA partial reconfiguration was cited as an alternative but was left as future work. Adding FPGA partial reconfiguration to this work is expected to reduce FPGA reconfiguration time and increase flexibility, such as in the number of coexisting hardware agents in a same FPGA.

A further contribution which can be made to [3] is the use of higher performance methods of communication between the host processor and the Agent function in FPGA. The proposed middleware relies on Programmed Input/Output (PIO) register accesses, which becomes suboptimal when transferring larger amounts of data such as high resolution video or images. Through the use of Direct Memory Access (DMA) communication, for instance, high performance image processing capabilities can be added to the proposed architecture.

This work can be regarded as an extension to [3], and proposes a new framework, through the addition of higher performance methods of communication between the host processor and the FPGA.

The proposed framework is evaluated through a study case regarding the use of UAVs on a precision agriculture application. Aerial images obtained by UAV are processed using a segmentation algorithm which executes the segmentation of crop and soil pixels. The execution time is evaluated on different platforms through the framework to evaluate the possibility of executing it on an embedded hardware on board the UAV.

This paper is organized as follows: Sect. 2 presents the proposed framework and discusses the proposed implementation in detail. Section 3 further discusses the applications and challenges of using UAV for precision agriculture. Section 4 presents experimental results for the evaluated implementation options. Section 5 presents conclusions and discusses future works.

2   Reconfigurable Hardware Agent Framework

This work proposes an architecture in order to allow image processing Agents to be implemented in hardware through the use of an FPGA. The Agent is composed of a host processor which is capable of running the Agent framework, as well as the FPGA.

This architecture is targeted at embedded systems which have reconfigurable hardware capabilities such as an FPGA. The high performance capabilities are targeted to applications which need to transfer large amounts of data between host processor and FPGA, which is a requirement in applications such as high resolution image processing. Figure 1 shows a detailed view of the architecture inside the FPGA, where the hardware Agent is implemented.

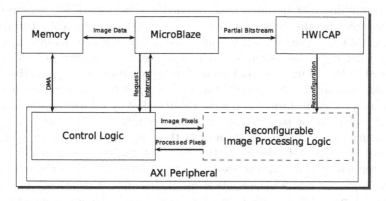

Fig. 1. Hardware components block diagram. Note that besides memory, all of the other components are logic instantiations on the FPGA.

This architecture makes use of a soft core processor inside the FPGA itself. MicroBlaze is a soft core processor provided by Xilinx, which is easily extended with peripherals through the Xilinx Embedded Development Kit (EDK), so it is a suitable option for this architecture. MicroBlaze offers limited processing power for processor intensive algorithms such as image processing, however it can be used for this architecture as the expensive algorithms can be implemented in FPGA and interfaced easily with it. The use of a lower end processor for this application is also more advantageous as it demands less resources to perform its function, which is to only provide a bridge interface between the framework and the FPGA.

Through the use of the Xilinx EDK, custom peripherals can be added to the MicroBlaze peripheral bus. There are a few different ways to connect custom peripherals to the MicroBlaze, however the recommended way is to add devices to MicroBlaze is through the Advanced eXtensible Interface (AXI) [20]. AXI is part of the Advanced Microcontroller Bus Architecture (AMBA) specification and is currently a standard specification for implementing peripheral devices. These devices can be either AXI4, AXI4-Lite or AXI-Stream, each of which has its own application.

In order to provide high performance for image processing, the architecture features the transfer of images to the FPGA through DMA transfers. An option would be to implement it using PIO (or register-based accesses), but that is very inefficient to transfer data such as an image to the FPGA.

Performance can be maximized if the peripheral is able to read the image from the buffer and write it back without software intervention at all. For example if the peripheral does not interrupt the processor after the whole read/write process. The current implementation uses full AXI with burst capability, in order to provide the best performance.

Figure 2 demonstrates the operations which can be made by the Agent application to the driver in order to perform image processing in FPGA. The first step is to obtain an mmap buffer from the driver. The application must use the mmapped buffer because it is allocated by the kernel as a physically contiguous buffer in DMA'able memory. For example, the device may need a physically contiguous buffer it if does not support scatter-gather functionality, and the driver is responsible for ensuring this in behalf of the application. The application must then load the image to be processed to the mmapped buffer. If the image came packed in an image file format and must be unpacked by a file format library, the mmapped buffer can be passed directly to the file format API to avoid an additional memory copy. The application must then request to the driver to initiate the processing step in the device. In this proposal, the same input buffer will be overwritten with the output processed image, in order to reduce the amount of DMA memory reserved for the application. If the application intends to use the unprocessed image later, it must perform a copy before the processing step. The driver must provide a way to tell the application when the processing is done. This can be implemented as a state which can be polled or through a blocking operation such as a blocking read which will only return when the operation is done. When the driver returns that the operation is finished, the application can read the processed image back from the same buffer. After working with the processed image, the application can unmap the memory mapped buffer (munmap) and finish.

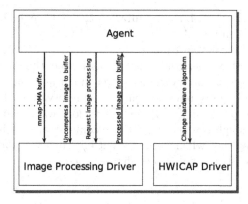

Fig. 2. Operations performed by the Agent application in the driver in order to perform image processing in FPGA.

As also demonstrated by Fig. 2, the Agent application is also given the possibility to reconfigure the FPGA by sending an alternate bitstream to a reconfigurable region, through the Hardware Internal Configuration Access Port (HWICAP) driver.

Another performance boost can be obtained if the peripheral can be designed to match the image encoding format that software uses, so that it eliminates further image manipulation by software later. If the peripheral is able to work with images as they are output by the software encoding/decoding libraries, this makes software implementations much simpler and faster.

If the peripheral supports only contiguous memory buffers for DMA, a large DMA buffer may be required for the image to be read from and written to by the peripheral. Recent Linux kernel versions provide the Contiguous Memory Allocator (CMA) for large buffer allocation. Nevertheless the memory is going to be locked and be unavailable for the rest of the system. Note that this might not be a problem for an application specific embedded system.

An alternative to large DMA buffers is the addition of scatter-gather functionality to the peripheral. Scatter-gather makes use of a descriptor in memory which tells the peripheral the location and size of scattered DMA buffers in memory, allowing the peripheral to use a set of smaller, non-contiguous buffers.

The architecture also includes the possibility of using FPGA partial reconfiguration in order to dynamically change the image processing algorithm in the peripheral. Note that inside the FPGA, there can be as many reconfigurable regions as necessary, but a first thing to note is that there must be a bitstream for each reconfigurable region for each netlist. That is, even if more than one reconfigurable partition is expected to use a same netlist description, each physical reconfigurable partition must have a bitstream specifically generated for it. Each partial reconfiguration bitstream depends on the size of the partition only.

As will be shown in Sect. 4, reconfiguration time for partial bitstreams can be considerably lower than reconfiguring a whole FPGA, so this is another advantage of using partial reconfiguration.

Another benefit of using partial bitstreams is that the static logic only has to be implemented once, and dynamically reconfigurable modules can later be added to the design by only reimplementing the reserved block.

JADE offers the possibility of Agent migration, which can be exploited in this architecture through the use of partial reconfiguration. Initially, JADE can be used in such a way that whenever an Agent migrates to a platform containing a free reconfigurable block, that it reconfigures the block to perform its function in hardware.

3   Case Study: UAV in Precision Agriculture

The case study presented on this paper is a precision agriculture application using UAVs. These UAVs are used as low altitude sensing platforms, used to acquire images from crops in order to identify crops characteristics. The main advantage of such systems is their low cost and easy deployment, compared to other solutions such as satellite based sensing. However, using commercial UAVs on such applications may require new processing units in addition to the existing ones, which are usually responsible for flight control and navigation. These processing units may be part of mission control system, allowing the execution of more sophisticated tasks such as image processing or path planning onboard the UAV [4]. An example of such a mission control module which can be attached to an UAV is presented on Fig. 3.

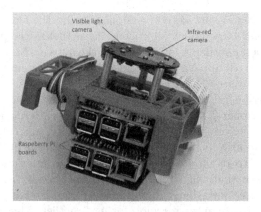

Fig. 3. A sample mission control module composed by two Raspberry Pi computers with visible light and infrared cameras.

Crop images acquired from UAVs may have high spatial and temporal resolution, and each flight mission may yield a large quantity of high resolution images that need to be analyzed in order to obtain useful data [21], such as points of infestation or drought. In order to obtain such information about the crop condition, image processing algorithms are widely employed. However, these algorithms may demand a large amount of computational power, and executing them on hardware onboard the UAV may impact its energy consumption. The execution time of these algorithms may also be of critical importance if time constraints exist during a given flight mission (for example, a mission where the image processing output is being used as input on the UAV flight path planning). If the execution time of the image processing algorithm is to be considered as the main concern, it is important to note that this sort of algorithm is a typical task that can usually be accelerated when implemented on hardware, and so it is interesting to study if the use of FPGA alongside the mission control system leads to interesting results.

3.1 UAV and Multi-Agent Systems

Scenarios with multiple UAVs may benefit from MAS implementations. For instance, some authors tackle the coordination of UAVs swarms during search or sensing missions using Agents [6,14]. In this paper scenario, an Image Processing Agent is studied, which may be onboard an UAV and provide information to other Agents with different roles (such as path planner Agent or another sensing Agent). Some studied features of this Agent are its migration capability and the possibility of it carrying out a partial FPGA reconfiguration, when this Agent is implemented on a platform containing such processing unit. Agent migration may perform an interesting role, where a given UAV may be substituted (due to low battery or failure, for example) and a new UAV may continue to perform its tasks. FPGA reconfiguration, alongside Agent migration, allows the existence of multiple hardware Agents on a single FPGA.

The Agent is implemented using the JADE [2] framework due to its characteristics: the Agent is developed using a high level language (Java), it is a well known framework for Agent development with management and debugging features, and allows easy Agent migration.

3.2 Image Processing Algorithm

The example algorithm used to evaluate the framework proposed on this work executes the segmentation of a young wheat crop image by discriminating between soil and wheat crop. The first step of the algorithm is the conversion from the RGB colorspace to the excess green index [19], based on Eq. 1,

$$ex_g = 2g - r - b, \tag{1}$$

where r, g and b are the red, green and blue channels. After the index calculation, a 5×5 Finite Impulse Response (FIR) filter with a homogeneous weight mask is convoluted with the image in order to smooth it. Finally, crop and soil are segmented through the application of a simple threshold.

 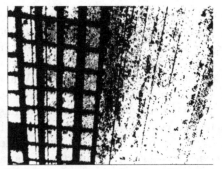

(a) Sample crop image. On the left, wheat (b) Result of the segmentation algorithm.
rectangular wheat patches. On the right,
a continuous wheat crop with degraded
regions.

Fig. 4. Segmentation algorithm example. (Color figure online)

This simple algorithm could be used to detect low developed wheat plants among crops. The ratio between the total number of "green pixels" and "soil pixels" would be able to give an indicator of the vegetal coverage of the frame, with low ratios indicating possible problems at a given location. Figures 4(a) and (b) represent an obtained image and its corresponding post processed version.

4   Results

This section presents and discusses results of a few different implementations of the algorithm described in Sect. 3. Three target systems were considered: A mainstream Desktop Personal Computer (PC), a Raspberry Pi B+ computer, and a Xilinx ML605 board with a Virtex-6 FPGA. These results were obtained by running the algorithms separately but still not in the JADE environment. All of the experiments were run on the specified target systems in order to obtain the presented results.

A Raspberry Pi B+ computer [16] was considered as a viable processing unit on the case study of this paper, so it is important that its characteristics are presented on this section. A Raspberry Pi is a credit card sized computer with integrated 5MP camera that is suitable for use along UAVs due to its low weight and small dimensions. The model used on this paper is a Raspberry Pi B+ model with an ARM1176JZF-S at 700 MHz. A notable feature of the Raspberry Pi for this application is the ARM NEON extension, which provides the processor with Single instruction, multiple data (SIMD) instructions which may accelerate vector operations such as image processing. It is presented as a mission control module on Sect. 3.

The second target is a Xilinx ML605 board, has at its core a Xilinx Virtex-6 FPGA (XC6VLX240T). Inside the FPGA, the board was loaded with a Xilinx

MicroBlaze soft core processor. The MicroBlaze version used is 8.40.a from Xilinx EDK 14.2, running at 100 MHz. The MicroBlaze processor communicates with its peripherals through an AXI interconnect which also runs at 100 MHz. The board provides 512 MB of DDR3 memory which is also used by the soft core processor. The soft core processor is configured with a full Memory Management Unit (MMU), which allows it to run Linux. On top of Linux, it runs the JamVM Java Virtual Machine (JVM) through which it is capable of running JADE. JamVM is an open-source JVM that aims to support the latest version of the Java specification, while at the same time being compact [9].

In order to have a reference for performance evaluation, the algorithm was also tested on a Desktop PC with an Intel Core I5-2450M processor at 2.50 GHz, with Ubuntu 14.04 as operating system.

The image processing algorithm was implemented primarily in the MATLAB environment. The same MATLAB model was used to generate both HDL and C code. In the Raspberry Pi and PC systems, the software version of the code was executed. In the ML605 system, the HDL code was inserted inside an AXI peripheral through the Xilinx EDK and the algorithm was executed in hardware through the FPGA.

Table 1 present the execution time of the image processing algorithm on the different systems. The measured time corresponds to the image process-ing algorithm execution time, excluding the time used for image capture or image file opening. Three versions of the algorithm with different image resolu-tions were tested in all of the three targets. Images were tested in resolutions 256×256, 1920×1080 and 2592×1944. The 2592×1944 resolution was chosen as it matches the resolution of the 5MP camera provided by the Raspberry Pi.

Table 1. Execution time for different resolutions of the image processing algorithm, excluding the time used for image capture or image file opening.

Resolution	Processing time (ms)		
	Desktop PC	Raspberry Pi	ML605 (FPGA)
256×256	4	110	7.99
1920×1080	131	4290	21.87
2592×1944	333	10510	42.01

The software implementations were run as simple Linux applications and therefore may include noise coming from multi-tasking. It should come off as no surprise that the execution in FPGA is faster, but a few more observations can be made about these results.

The Raspberry Pi results show that it is capable of performing image pro-cessing relatively fast for low to medium resolution sizes, and would be able to handle a low rate of images to process in real time.

It is notable that the FPGA times are smaller even than the Desktop PC results for the higher resolution, even considering that the FPGA peripheral runs at only 100 MHz. It must be considered that the AXI peripheral is capable of performing large bursts to memory and to perform the whole operation in a single cycle after the pipeline is full, in parallel with memory accesses. It is reasonable that the Desktop PC performs better for the small resolution image as it can also provide high performance through SIMD instructions. For the higher resolution, the software execution may suffer from issues such as cache misses and scheduling in the processor, which may add to the total time.

Table 2. Resource requirements and reconfigurable partition size for different resolutions of the image processing algorithm.

Resource	Available	256 × 256		1920 × 1080		2592 × 1944	
		Required	% util	Required	% util	Required	% util
LUT	12480	1651	14	4367	35	4481	36
FD_LD	24960	711	3	1372	6	1378	6
SLICEL	1680	221	14	586	35	602	36
SLICEM	1440	193	14	506	36	520	37
RAMBFIFO36E1	36	2	6	5	14	10	28

The JADE framework also provides the Agent migration capability, which can be further exploited in the ML605 platform through the use of partial FPGA reconfiguration. For this experiment, the algorithm was implemented in such a way that the Agent application is able to switch the hardware in the reconfigurable region between the three different image resolution implementations of the algorithm. One additional interesting result regarding this is the reconfiguration time required to change this algorithm. As stated in Sect. 2, the reconfiguration time is only dependent of the reconfigurable partition and partial bitstream size. For a partition size which is roughly three times larger than our larger image processing algorithm, the average reconfiguration block time was measured as 500 ms. This was measured on the ML605 board by performing partial reconfiguration on the block described by Table 2, using the HWICAP driver on the board. Table 2 shows the results in resource requirements and partition size.

The similar work presented in [3] shows times in the order of 20 s for a full agent migration to hardware including dynamic FPGA configuration, so 500 ms can be considered as a reasonable gain. Given that this is a relatively large partition with a large portion of the FPGA reserved for it, it is probably acceptable for Agent applications to perform this reconfiguration on-the-fly. An example application is as demonstrated by this work, where the hardware can be reconfigurated to operate optimally with a given image resolution for image processing.

5   Conclusion

In this work, an architecture proposal for a MAS involving reconfigurable hardware was presented. The architecture was detailed from a practical perspective and it was validated in a case study of an embedded image processing system for precision agriculture using UAVs. The case study algorithm was also described and experiments implementing the case study algorithm were performed in three different platforms, of which one is the reconfigurable hardware architecture. The use of partial reconfiguration in this case study was also implemented and evaluated. The proposed framework and experiments are modeled considering the JADE framework. The JADE framework is able to run on all of the presented platforms however it is still not considered in the presented results.

The experiments were performed with both low and high resolution images, and have shown performance gains for the implementation in FPGA even at a relatively low frequency of operation. The use of DMA operations with the AXI bus has shown to be efficient for transferring images to the image processing algorithm implemented in FPGA, and this is a key factor to allow the architecture to maximize performance. The increased performance of the proposed architecture may also allow for processing an increased number of images in real-time or to improve the autonomy of the UAVs.

The proposed architecture is able to communicate with JADE agents through the use of its host processor, which is a soft core processor. The use of the soft core processor has proven to be worthy as it provides enough resources to run the Agent framework and to interface to the FPGA in an easy and efficient way.

Measurements of reconfiguration time were performed and it is noted that reconfiguration time is low even for reconfiguring a significative area of the FPGA. The addition of partial reconfiguration also adds the possibility for multiple hardware agents to coexist independently in the same FPGA platform, which enhances the previous work where the entire FPGA had to be reconfigured. The JADE framework can take advantage of reduced FPGA partial reconfiguration time in order to provide better agent migration from and to hardware.

Further advancements in this work include evaluation of the energy consumption of these implementations in an embedded target. This work has evaluated the performance of the image processing algorithm itself, however end-to-end tests including the JADE framework and actual deployment of the FPGA in the UAV must still be performed.

References

1. Belkacemi, R., Feliachi, A., Choudhry, M., Saymansky, J.: Multi-agent systems hardware development and deployment for smart grid control applications. In: Power and Energy Society General Meeting, pp. 1–8. IEEE, July 2011
2. Bellifemine, F., Poggi, A., Rimassa, G.: JADE-A FIPA-compliant agent framework. In: Proceedings of PAAM, London, vol. 99, p. 33 (1999)
3. Cemin, D., Gotz, M., Pereira, C.: Reconfigurable agents for heterogeneous wireless sensor networks. In: 2012 Brazilian Symposium on Computing System Engineering (SBESC), pp. 1–6, November 2012

4. Doering, D., Benemann, A., Lerm, R., Freitas, E.P., Muller, I., Winter, J.M., Pereira, C.E.: Design and optimization of a heterogeneous platform for multiple UAV use in precision agriculture applications. In: World Congress, vol. 19, pp. 12272–12277 (2014)
5. Filgueiras, T., Lung, L.C., de Oliveira Rech, L.: Providing real-time scheduling for mobile agents in the JADE platform. In: 2012 IEEE 15th International Symposium on Object/Component/Service-Oriented Real-Time Distributed Computing (ISORC), pp. 8–15, April 2012
6. Kingston, D., Beard, R.W., Holt, R.S.: Decentralized perimeter surveillance using a team of UAVs. IEEE Trans. Rob. **24**(6), 1394–1404 (2008)
7. Krol, D., Nowakowski, F.: Practical performance aspects of using real-time multi-agent platform in complex systems. In: 2013 IEEE International Conference on Systems, Man, and Cybernetics (SMC), pp. 1121–1126, October 2013
8. Leitao, P., Marik, V., Vrba, P.: Past, present, and future of industrial agent applications. IEEE Trans. Ind. Inform. **9**(4), 2360–2372 (2013)
9. Lougher, R.: JamVM - a compact Java virtual machine. http://jamvm.sourceforge.net/. Accessed Feb 2015
10. Megherbi, D., Kim, M., Madera, M.: A study of collaborative distributed multi-goal & multi-agent-based systems for large critical key infrastructures and resources (CKIR) dynamic monitoring and surveillance. In: 2013 IEEE International Conference on Technologies for Homeland Security (HST), pp. 687–692, November 2013
11. Mustapha, K., Mcheick, H., Mellouli, S.: Modeling and simulation agent-based of natural disaster complex systems. Procedia Comput. Sci. **21**, 148–155 (2013). 4th International Conference on Emerging Ubiquitous Systems and Pervasive Networks (EUSPN-2013) and 3rd International Conference on Current and Future Trends of Information and Communication Technologies in Healthcare (ICTH)
12. Pereira, A., Rodrigues, N., Leitao, P.: Deployment of multi-agent systems for industrial applications. In: 2012 IEEE 17th Conference on Emerging Technologies Factory Automation (ETFA), pp. 1–8, September 2012
13. Pereira, C.E., Carro, L.: Distributed real-time embedded systems: recent advances, future trends and their impact on manufacturing plant control. Annu. Rev. Control **31**(1), 81–92 (2007)
14. Schlecht, J., Altenburg, K., Ahmed, B.M., Nygard, K.E.: Decentralized search by unmanned air vehicles using local communication. In: IC-AI, pp. 757–762 (2003)
15. Schneider, J., Naggatz, M., Spallek, R.: Implementation of architecture concepts for hardware agent systems. In: 7th IEEE International Conference on Computer and Information Technology, CIT 2007, pp. 823–828, October 2007
16. Upton, E., Halfacree, G.: Raspberry Pi User Guide. Wiley, Hoboken (2014)
17. Ure, N., Chowdhary, G., Toksoz, T., How, J., Vavrina, M., Vian, J.: An automated battery management system to enable persistent missions with multiple aerial vehicles (2014)
18. Vrba, P., Marik, V., Siano, P., Leitao, P., Zhabelova, G., Vyatkin, V., Strasser, T.: A review of agent and service-oriented concepts applied to intelligent energy systems (2014)
19. Woebbecke, D., Meyer, G., Von Bargen, K., Mortensen, D.: Color indices for weed identification under various soil, residue, and lighting conditions. Trans. ASAE **38**(1), 259–269 (1995)
20. Xilinx Inc.: EDK Concepts, Tools, and Techniques UG683 (v14.1), April 2012
21. Zhang, C., Kovacs, J.M.: The application of small unmanned aerial systems for precision agriculture: a review. Precis. Agric. **13**(6), 693–712 (2012)

Combining Service-Oriented Computing with Embedded Systems - A Robotics Case Study

Alexander Jungmann$^{(\boxtimes)}$, Jan Jatzkowski, and Bernd Kleinjohann

C-LAB, University of Paderborn, Fuerstenallee 11, 33102 Paderborn, Germany
{global,janj,bernd}@c-lab.de

Abstract. In this paper, we introduce an approach for combining embedded systems with Service-oriented Computing techniques based on a concrete application scenario from the robotics domain. Our proposed Service-oriented Architecture allows for incorporating computational expensive functionality as services into a distributed computing environment. Furthermore, our framework facilitates a seamless integration of embedded systems such as robots as service providers into the computing environment. The entire communication is based on so-called recipes, which can be interpreted as autonomous messages that contain all necessary information for executing compositions of services.

Keywords: Embedded systems · Service-oriented Computing
Service-oriented Architecture · Services · Behaviour-based robotics
Mobile robots

1 Introduction

Embedded Systems such as mobile robots are usually restricted in their computational capabilities. Although technology is progressing and computing capacities for embedded systems are gradually increasing, algorithms applied to embedded systems usually have to be highly specialized in order to ensure feasibility. Furthermore, although sophysticated algorithms may already exist for a problem at hand, those algorithms might be too computationally expensive. Consider, e.g., an autonomous robot that has to navigate based on visual information in a non-deterministic environment. Camera images have to be processed (at least in soft real-time), natural or artificial landmarks have to be detected, and a robust localization mechanism has to estimate the robot's pose.

In our work, we investigate to what extend techniques from Service-oriented Computing (SOC) can be applied to the field of embedded systems in order to overcome these limitations and consequently increase the functionality of computationally restricted embedded systems. SOC represents a new generation distributed computing platform [4]. It is a cross-disciplinary paradigm for distributed computing that gradually changes the way software applications

© IFIP International Federation for Information Processing 2017
Published by Springer International Publishing AG 2017. All Rights Reserved
M. Götz et al. (Eds.): IESS 2015, IFIP AICT 523, pp. 27–37, 2017.
https://doi.org/10.1007/978-3-319-90023-0_3

are designed, delivered, and consumed. For our work, that means, that computational expensive functionalities are outsourced into a distributed computing environment and provided as services to all entities in this environment. At the same time, we investigate how embedded systems can be integrated as service providers into the entire environment, so that distributed applications can make use of them.

In this work, we make use of a concrete application scenario in the robotics domain: autonomous, mobile robots have to accomplish an objective, which they could not solve under normal circumstances due to their limited computational capabilities. Apart from the robots, the realized system makes use of several servers for computational expensive tasks. That is, functionality for tasks such as an Extended Kalman Filter (EKF) [8] based localization are provided as services. The whole system builds upon a Service-oriented Architecture (SOA), which handles the overall communication.

The remainder of this paper is organized as follows. Section 2 introduces the case study including the BeBot as embedded system and the concrete application scenario. Section 3 introduces our SOA framework as basis for the entire system. The node-based architecture that enables a BeBot to act autonomously is described in Sect. 4. Section 5 presents the integration of the BeBot into the SOA and briefly describes the overall system that realizes the application scenario. Section 6 finally concludes the paper.

2   Case Study

The main purpose of our case study is to provide a concrete application context for identifying promising application possibilities of techniques from Service-oriented Computing to the field of embedded systems.

Embedded System: Miniature Robot BeBot. The BeBot is a miniature chain driven robot, which has been developed at the Heinz Nixdorf Institute of the University of Paderborn [5]. Despite its small size (approximately $9\,cm \times 9\,cm \times 8\,cm$), it is equipped with modern technology such as an ARM Cortex-A8 CPU with a maximum frequency of 600 MHz accessing up to 256 MB RAM of main memory for running an embedded Linux environment. By illuminating its so-called light guide in arbitrary colours during runtime, the miniature robot can express its current state to human observers and other robots. The network based TCP/IP communication is enabled by an integrated W-LAN module.

In order to extend the field of view for our application scenario, we replaced the built-in camera by a Firefly MV USB camera attached on top of the BeBot. Furthermore, we additionally replaced the integrated W-LAN chip by a customary W-LAN USB stick, resulting in a significantly higher network performance (117 kb/s vs. 2 mb/s). Attaching all devices on top of the BeBot finally leads to the rather unconventional construction depicted in Fig. 1a.

(a) BeBot   (b) Environment   (c) Landmarks   (d) Object

Fig. 1. Ingredients and setting of the application scenario. (Color figure online)

Application Scenario. The objective to be solved in the application scenario is (i) to utilize BeBots as mobile physical sensors in order to locate artificial objects (henceforth simply referred to as objects) in a predefined yet partially non-deterministic environment and to (ii) reconstruct 3-dimensional models of these objects based on images taken by BeBots. Figure 1b shows the setup of the scenario environment. The system may use several BeBots to fulfil the task stated above. In order to facilitate the localization process of the BeBots, the playground contains several artificial, colour-coded landmarks (cf. Fig. 1c).

The objects consist of fixed sized cubes with blue and magenta coloured faces on the sides. The top and bottom face are coloured in black (cf. Fig. 1d). Furthermore, the edges of the cubes are also coloured in black to allow a better distinction between separate cubes next to each other.

3   Service-Oriented Architecture

The main goal of our Service-oriented Architecture (SOA) is to provide a distributed computing framework for all participating *entities* such as BeBots or dedicated servers. The framework enables the BeBots to outsource computationally expensive tasks, while it simultaneously enables the entire system to make use of the BeBots as physical sensors in the environment.

Overview. The key concept of our framework are *services*. Services are distributed and usually stateless components that encapsulate distinct functionality [3]. For addressing a composition of services, we developed a uniform and data-driven protocol based on so-called *recipes*. Recipes are autonomous messages travelling through the network containing all information and data to complete a complex task step by step. The main idea is that a service receives a recipe, extracts the required data, processes this data, appends the processed data (i.e., the result) to the recipe, and finally forwards the updated recipe to the next services defined in the recipe. Please note that we use the terms recipe and message synonymously in this work.

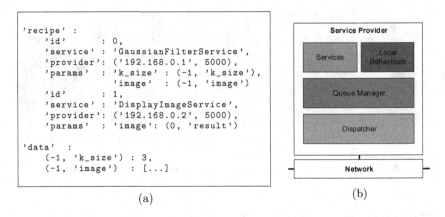

```
'recipe' :                                      
    'id'          : 0,                          
    'service'  : 'GaussianFilterService',       
    'provider': ('192.168.0.1', 5000),          
    'params'   : 'k_size' : (-1, 'k_size'),     
                    'image'   : (-1, 'image')    
    'id'          : 1,                           
    'service'  : 'DisplayImageService',          
    'provider': ('192.168.0.2', 5000),          
    'params'   : 'image': (0, 'result')         
                                                 
'data'   :                                       
    (-1, 'k_size') : 3,                          
    (-1, 'image')   : [...]                      
```

(a)   (b)

Fig. 2. (a) Exemplary recipe. (b) Fundamental components of our SOA.

Another building block of our SOA are *service providers*, which realize the environment for executing services. Service providers are interconnected via network and take care of the recipe packing, unpacking, and parsing, execution management, as well as the routing and transmission of a recipe to the next service-provider (if necessary). In fact, our SOA corresponds to a network of loosely coupled service providers. That is, each entity (BeBot or server) participating in the overall system features a local management unit in terms of a service provider instance.

Recipes. A recipe is a data driven construct to define (i) an order in which specific services have to be executed and (ii) how input and output parameters of the services have to be connected to achieve a certain goal. That is, a recipe defines and describes an orchestration of services. Initial input as well as intermediate and final result values are stored in a dedicated data section of the recipe.

Figure 2a shows an excerpt of an exemplary recipe. The 'recipe' section contains two services. The first service ('id': 0) is provided by a service provider located at IP 192.168.0.1 and accessible via port 5000. The service implements a Gaussian filter for reducing image noise. The input parameters (kernel size 'k_size' and 'image' to be processed) are stored in the 'data' section. The second service ('id': 1) displays the processed image on a different entity in the network. The corresponding input data 'image' is not yet available in the recipe, but will be stored with key (0, 'result') by the first service in the data section.

Service Provider. A service provider resides directly on top of the network and consists of multiple components on three different levels of abstraction (cf. Fig. 2b). The *dispatcher* implements the application-level protocol for sending and receiving messages over the network. On top of this, the *queue man-*

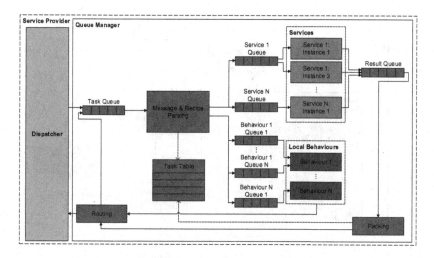

Fig. 3. Internal processes of a service provider.

ager handles parsing of recipes, manages local services, and acts as intermediary between them. The top layer consists of individual services and so-called *local behaviours.*

Figure 3 gives a detailed overview of the processes within a service provider. The dispatcher is responsible for the communication between different service provider instances among the network. Each message is serialized before it is sent across the network, and is de-serialized after it was received. In order to allow concurrent message processing, each message reception and sending task is handled in an individual thread. After de-serialization, the dispatcher puts the respective recipe into the task queue of the queue manager.

The queue manager is the heart of a service provider: Recipes are parsed and processed. That is, the next service to be executed and the associated input parameters are extracted from the recipe. The extracted information is put into the input queue of the corresponding service type. Service instances of the same type are polling on this queue. Whenever data is available in a queue, one service instance takes the data, processes it, and puts the result data into a public result queue. The queue manager appends the computed result value to the corresponding recipe. In order to keep track of which result belongs to which recipe, unique task ids are generated and stored in a so-called task table. In this way, the execution of services is strictly separated from any recipe parsing.

After being repacked, a recipe is processed by the routing component of the queue manager in order to determine the next recipe-specific processing step. If the next service is located at the same service provider, the recipe is put into the task queue of the queue manager again. Otherwise, the recipe is forwarded to the dispatcher, which takes care of sending the recipe to the respective service provider in the network.

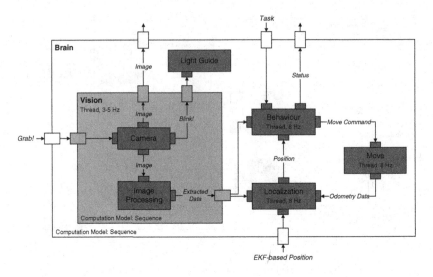

Fig. 4. Node-based software architecture of a BeBot. Ports are not labelled.

Services vs. Local Behaviours. Within our SOA, there are two main types of computation units: services and local behaviours. These modular units provide a standardized way of computation steps that can be accessed and combined by means of recipes. They form the main logic of every application that uses our SOA for distributed computing.

According to the design principles of Service-oriented Computing [3], services provide a stateless execution of a predefined task. However, in order to cope with inherent stateful tasks such as localization, we introduce so-called local behaviours as "stateful services". In contrast to services, which are only executed if input data is available, local behaviours can be executed periodically. Furthermore, local behaviours may have multiple input queues and have full control over them. That is, behaviours are not automatically executed when new recipes are available, but recipes are explicitly taken out of the input queues by the behaviour according to its application logic. Finally, in comparison to services, local behaviours can make use of other services by creating and emitting recipes. That is, local behaviours access the routing component of the queue manager (cf. Fig. 3) and directly inject new recipes into the overall system. This concept allows to seamlessly integrate stateful and more complex functionality into the SOA framework.

4   BeBot - Basic Node-Based Architecture

The robot's software system for autonomous behaviour is built based on a node-based software framework that facilitates the periodic execution of tasks. Figure 4 gives an overview of the node hierarchy of the system. Ports and port interconnections implement the data flow between nodes. The control flow corresponds to the applied computation model such as sequential execution. Furthermore, nodes can be initialized as a Thread with a distinct frequency. That is, executing a node's application logic can be decoupled from other nodes. Copying the data from one port to another, however, always depends on the defined computation model of the corresponding parent node.

Brain: The *Brain* node is the root node of the hierarchy. The Brain node's own input and output ports serve as a connection between node architecture and the SOA framework of the overall system. The computation model corresponds to the following sequence: [Vision, Localization, Behaviour, Move, Light Guide]. That is, data is copied among the ports based on the defined port interconnections according to the order of the nodes in this list. The Brain node itself is not a Thread. Its compute handler is explicitly called by a *Wrapper* that glues together node architecture and SOA framework (cf. Sect. 5).

Vision, Camera, and Image Processing: The functionality for capturing and processing images is split up into three nodes: Camera node, Image Processing node, and Vision node. The Camera node implements the image acquisition step. Captured images are sent to the Image Processing node. However, if triggered by its input port, single snapshots are additionally sent to the Brain node. In this manner, whenever necessary, images can be provided to services. The Image Processing node extracts scenario specific information from captured images by means of a colour-based segmentation algorithm [7] and creates landmark- and cube-data. Also, the intersection points that are used for the collision avoidance are calculated in this node.

The Vision node implements no application logic but encapsulates the distinct functionalities of the Camera node and the Image Processing node. Furthermore, the Vision node is running threaded to decouple the vision functionality from other functions such as localization. This is necessary, since the vision node is the slowest node within the hierarchy: It runs with 3–5 Hz, depending on the amount of features that were detected within an image.

Light Guide: The Light Guide node implements the interface to the robot's light guide and offers different functions. For example, the light guide gives a visual feedback to indicate that a BeBot has captured an image for the 3D reconstruction process: After an image was taken, the robot blinks three times.

Localization: The Localization node provides the currently estimated position of the robot to the Behaviour node. Due to the high computational effort of the necessary algorithms, an EKF-based estimation of the robot position cannot be done on the BeBot. As a consequence, the functionality is outsourced into a local behaviour within the SOA (cf. Sect. 3). The Localization node gathers the data coming from the Vision node and the odometry data from the Move node and transmits it to the localization provider.

Behaviour and Move: The Behaviour node coordinates the robot's behaviour. In each computation cycle, it executes one step of a behaviour state machine [1] according to the currently assigned task in order to obtain the next move command. A move command is composed of a translational velocity and a heading direction, and is subsequently passed on to the Move node. The Move node implements an abstraction layer for the actuator's related functionality by mapping a move command to the actual chain speeds. It also incorporates collision avoidance techniques based on an efficient occupancy grid map approach [2]. Furthermore, the Move node gathers the raw odometry data and transmits the data to the Localization node in order to make a local pose prediction.

5   Integration: Service-Oriented Robotics

So far, we presented the application scenario, our proposed SOA framework, and the BeBot with its node-based software architecture for autonomous behaviour. We now describe how BeBot architecture and SOA framework are integrated. Furthermore, we briefly describe the overall system that realizes the application scenario.

BeBot Wrapper: A Local Behaviour. A BeBot is offering services such as "drive to position" and demanding services such as EKF-based localization at the same time. To enable a BeBot to interact with the SOA, a so-called *BeBot Wrapper* is introduced as adapter. It allows for passing messages from the SOA framework to the node hierarchy and offers an interface to the nodes for emitting recipes into the system (e.g., a recipe that contains gathered data for the EKF-based localization process). More precisely, the Wrapper implements a local behaviour in the SOA and explicitly invokes the compute handler of the BeBot's Brain node. The wrapper encapsulates the entire node-architecture as a local behaviour, which runs on a BeBot within the scope of a service provider instance. After each execution cycle, a blocked service is unblocked if data was produced for it.

A BeBot (i.e., the service provider instance running on a BeBot) also offers services. These services can pass data to the input ports of the Brain node by calling the Wrapper's delegate methods. For example, if the system wants a BeBot to drive to a specific position in the environment, the corresponding service is executed with the desired position as input values. Internally, the service uses the wrapper to delegate the task to the Brain node and blocks until it is informed by the wrapper that the task terminated.

Overall System. Figure 5 shows a schematic overview of the basic functional components. Please note, that only local behaviours are depicted. Stateless services (e.g., for image processing) are not displayed. The entire system corresponds to a network of loosely coupled service providers, which are either located on BeBots or dedicated servers. The application logic is distributed in terms of

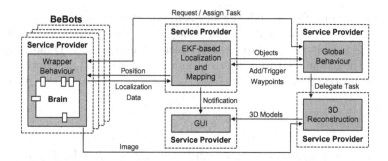

Fig. 5. Overview of the entire system.

services and local behaviours among the service providers. The entire communication is based on recipes. We already introduced the Wrapper behaviour which integrates the node-architecture of the BeBot into the overall system. For that reason, let us take a closer look at the other functional components.

EKF-Based Localization and Mapping: The localization and mapping behaviour encapsulates the EKF-based localization methods and maintains a global map of the scenario. For each BeBot in the system, a dedicated instance of the EKF is created. Each instance receives localization data (e.g., detected landmarks) from the corresponding BeBot. More concretely, the localization node of a BeBot gathers the localization data and emits a recipe by using the interfaces provided by the Wrapper behaviour. After the computation step, the localization and mapping behaviour emits a recipe with the newly estimated position to the service provider instance of the corresponding BeBot. Furthermore, a notification recipe is sent to the GUI behaviour for updating the visualization, and the global behaviour is notified about newly tracked objects.

GUI: The GUI behaviour is created for monitoring the localization and mapping process. The behaviour receives notification updates from the localization and mapping behaviour and visualizes the current state in a two dimensional map. The actual GUI is running in a separate Thread created by the behaviour. Furthermore, the GUI provides some convenient control elements, e.g., in order to reset the EKF of a BeBot or to manually move a BeBot to a certain position in the environment.

Global Behaviour: This behaviour is responsible for coordinating the BeBots and delegating the 3D reconstruction process. It sends recipes including tasks such as "explore environment and discover objects" or "capture image of side X of object Y" to a selected BeBot, which adjusts its strategy accordingly. Whenever the global behaviour receives a notification about a newly tracked object, it organizes the reconstruction process. That is, four waypoints for taking images from each side of the object are created. The waypoints are subsequently used for assigning tasks to the BeBots. Furthermore, the waypoints are also integrated into the global map for enabling BeBots to identify waypoints in their direct surroundings.

3D Reconstruction: This local behaviour is responsible for the actual reconstruction process. If four images of the same object (an image from each side) are available, the reconstruction process takes place. The resulting 3D model is subsequently sent to the GUI in order to visualize it. A detailed description of the concrete reconstruction process, however, is beyond the scope of this paper.

6   Conclusion

In this work, we introduced an approach for combining embedded systems with techniques from SOC. That is, computational expensive as well as coordination tasks are outsourced as services and so-called local behaviours, and integrated into a distributed computing environment. While services correspond to stateless functional components, local behaviours allow for integrating statefull, periodically executed functionality into a distributed application. Furthermore, the presented approach allows for a seamless integration of embedded systems into a distributed application in order to provide distinct functionalities as services to other entities.

In the future, starting from our latest results in the On-The-Fly Computing project [6], we want to investigate to what extend processes such as service composition (recipe generation) and service integration and deployment can be automated in our SOA framework.

Acknowledgments. This work was partially supported by the German Research Foundation (DFG) within the Collaborative Research Center "On-The-Fly Computing" (SFB 901) and by the German Ministry of Education and Research (BMBF) through the project "it's OWL Intelligente Technische Systeme OstWestfalenLippe" (02PQ1021) and the ITEA2 project AMALTHEA4public (01IS14029J).

The authors gratefully acknowledge the contribution of Mouns R. Husan Almarrani, Maarten Bieshaar, Dominik Buse, Dominic Jacobsmeyer, Simon Merschjohann, Florian Pieper, and Christopher Skerra to the project "SoPhysticated - Service-oriented Cyber Physical Systems".

References

1. Arkin, R.C.: Behavior-Based Robotics. MIT Press, Cambridge (1998)
2. Borenstein, J., Koren, Y.: Histogramic in-motion mapping for mobile robot obstacle avoidance. IEEE Trans. Robot. Autom. **7**(4), 535–539 (1991)
3. Erl, T.: Service-Oriented Architecture: Concepts, Technology, and Design. Prentice Hall, Upper Saddle River (2005)
4. Erl, T.: SOA Principles of Service Design. Prentice Hall, Upper Saddle River (2008)
5. Gausemeier, J., Schierbaum, T., Dumitrescu, R., Herbrechtsmeier, S., Jungmann, A.: Miniature robot BeBot: mechatronic test platform for self-x properties. In: Proceedings of the 9th IEEE International Conference on Industrial Informatics, pp. 451–456 (2011)

6. Jungmann, A., Mohr, F.: An approach towards adaptive service composition in markets of composed services. J. Internet Serv. Appl. **6**(1), 1–18 (2015)
7. Jungmann, A., Schierbaum, T., Kleinjohann, B.: Image segmentation for object detection on a deeply embedded miniature robot. In: Proceedings of the International Conference on Computer Vision Theory and Applications, pp. 441–444 (2012)
8. Thrun, S., Burgard, W., Fox, D.: Probabilistic Robotics (Intelligent Robotics and Autonomous Agents). MIT Press, Cambridge (2005)

Integration of Robot Operating System and Ptolemy for Design of Real-Time Multi-robots Environments

Luis Feliphe Silva Costa, Alisson V. Brito[✉][iD], Tiago P. Nascimento,
and Thiago Henrique Menezes Bezerra

Federal University of Paraiba (UFPB), Joao Pessoa, Brazil
`luis.feliphe@dce.ufpb.br`, {`alisson,tiagopn`}`@ci.ufpb.br`
`http://laser.ci.ufpb.br`

Abstract. This work presents a technique for designing of real-time systems embedded applied to multi-robots scenarios, exploiting High-Level Architecture (HLA) standard for interoperability and simulation platforms, and Robot Operating System (ROS) with Robot-in-the-Loop simulations. The goal is to integrate existing consolidated standards and tools, rather than separately design and later hardly integrate. Through HLA, heterogeneous simulations can be synchronously co-simulated, enabling the joint execution of consolidated embedded system design tools for dedicated tasks, like, network simulation, circuits and algorithms design, etc. In parallel, ROS simplifies the task of creating complex robots across a wide variety of platforms. A bridge has been developed to provide an interface among HLA and ROS, exchanging data and keeping both synchronized. As proof of concept, the Ptolemy framework for Embedded System design has been integrated to Stage, a ROS compatible robotic simulator for 2D environments. This innovative integration has been successfully developed and validated, which enables future generalizations and opens opportunities to co-simulation of diverse tools for designing of embedded and robotics systems.

Keywords: Co-simulation · Robotics · Embedded systems
Real-time systems

1 Introduction

Robotics is a multidisciplinary field, which demands cooperation of expertises and technologies from different research fields, i.e., Mechanics, Electronics, Artificial Intelligence, Embedded Systems. Each one brings consolidated methodologies and technologies that must perfectly work together.

Integration of different design tools, simulators and physical devices are not an easy task. Different efforts mainly formed by large communities of industrial and academic partners have successfully developed standards and tools to fill this gap.

© IFIP International Federation for Information Processing 2017
Published by Springer International Publishing AG 2017. All Rights Reserved
M. Götz et al. (Eds.): IESS 2015, IFIP AICT 523, pp. 38–47, 2017.
https://doi.org/10.1007/978-3-319-90023-0_4

When Embedded System Design is applied to Robotics normally gather different components with heterogeneous Models of Computation (MoC). Thus, tools with higher abstraction power are necessary in order to model, simulate and test all such MoCs, e.g., Finite State Machines (FSM), Synchronous Data Flow (SDF), Discrete Events (DE) and Continuous Time (CT). The Ptolemy II framework [1] is an example of a simulation and modeling tool intended to support system designs that combine different MoCs.

In 2007, a group of scientists, industries and engineers created an open-source robotic framework called Robot Operating System (ROS) [2]. It is a flexible framework for designing robots, providing a collection of tools, libraries, and conventions that aim to simplify the task of creating complex and robust robot behavior across a wide variety of robotic platforms. There are many other initiatives for merging different robot platforms [3].

Even more, high performance, availability and reliability of robots have turn them into increasingly complex computing systems. Dealing with such complexity requires most effective designing approaches, for example, using Hardware-in-the-loop (HIL) simulation, which means to add the real device in the simulation loop. This can enhance the quality of testing, reduce design time and anticipate usability tests immersed in the environment. Although its relevance, combine specific architecture designs and protocols with design tools is always a hard task. Some approaches, like in [4], present some methods to assist designers with hardware and simulation integration.

Thus, how would be possible to co-simulate different design standards and tools to form a unique simulation platform for designing of multi-robots scenarios? Aiming at filling this lack of tools and techniques, we have developed a simulation platform that combines Ptolemy (for Embedded System design), ROS (for robot design and real robots) and HLA (for synchronization and coupling of heterogeneous simulators). As proof of concept, a 2D robotic simulator called Stage was integrated to Ptolemy. A real robot also was integrated to provide an Robot-in-the-loop (RiL) simulation, this kind of simulation consists in using real robot in simulations to provide more realistic results. It is useful when it is not possible simulate an specific environment or when there is not enough robots to perform some experiment [5].

The remaining of this paper is organized as follows. Related works is presented in Sect. 2, the proposed architecture is presented in Sect. 3, while the experimental results are presented in Sect. 4. Finally, Sect. 5 tackles the main discussions and concluding remarks.

2   Related Works

This work uses co-simulation environment where is possible test embedded systems and robotics. Works that perform only co-simulations of homogeneous models often are unable to implement the heterogeneity due to the great effort that is employed for adaptation to different hardware platforms, communication and synchronization protocols. Such characteristics like heterogeneity, synchronization and testing with different Models of Computation are provided in this work through the integration of Ptolemy and ROS through HLA standard.

In [6] is presented the integration of heterogeneous simulators through HLA. A framework was developed for rapid integration of different simulators. A car-to-car communication application was presented, were SystemC is used to model the electronic controller of a car, and Omnet++ and Sumo were used to simulate network communication and car traffic, respectively. Present work also will provide interoperation between simulators using HLA, however to integrate Stage and Ptolemy.

An Architecture for Robot-in-the-loop is present in [7]. It proposes to separate sensors/actuators from decisions models of robots using an interface that allows different kinds of sensors to decision models. Also it cites the mainly steps to develop simulations: to develop a conventional simulation in which all robots are simulated; to develop an mixed environment with simulated and real robots; and make an experiment with real system were all real robots execute on real environment and have real sensors and actuators. We create a similar environment, where developer choose which sensors/actuator want to use.

In citeartigoExemploTresRiL is proposed a continuation of [7]. It is presented three examples of how Hardware-in-the-loop can be use on different situations. It uses an Management Model that is parted in two: Time manager and space manager. In first example, one robot was used to avoid obstacles, the second one evolves robots formation with two robots where each robot try find other one. In this experiment robots have not interconnections between themselves. When they meet each other, an software named manager running on laptop creates an connection between themselves and they work like a team. On experiment one robot is leader and the other one is an follower. One is real and other is simulated. In third scenario, an robotic patrol is used starting with an undefined number of robots ($n > 1$). These robots stay on line, each one with two neighborhoods: one forward and other backward. This experiment shows that is possible to use more than one real robot on RiL simulation. This system does not use global coordination. We develop a similar experiment, but to make a real robot avoid simulated obstacles on Stage simulator, providing a Hardware-in-the-loop Simulation.

This work represents a considerable advance compared to the last works, were multiple instances of Ptolemy were integrated to performance improvement [8] and, specially, hardware devices were integrated to Ptolemy for verification [9].

3   Architecture

The proposed architecture can be seen in Fig. 1. The environment is divided in two parts, the first one is the ROS environment (in yellow) with ROS Robot Nodes, the Bridge ROS Interface, and ROS Core, which is responsible for communication between ROS nodes. The second part is the HLA environment (in blue) with the RTI, the Bridge Ambassador and the Ptolemy Ambassador.

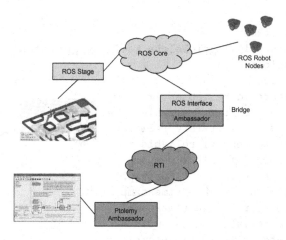

Fig. 1. Proposed architecture (Color figure online)

The intersection point between these environments is the Bridge. It is possible because the Bridge is an ROS Node and also implements an Ambassador. To became a ROS node, bridge uses Rospy library [10] that allows a Python application subscribe and publish on ROS topics. The ROS topics are responsible to share an specific information from ROS environment (e.g., speed, position, data from sensors, etc.). The Ambassador is an interface with methods used by HLA to share information and manage time simulation, it was developed using Pyhla library [11]. Thus, it make possible to have multiple robots in ROS sharing their data with any others simulators that implements an HLA Ambassador, like Ptolemy.

3.1   Robot Description

In HLA an object-oriented paradigm is used to describe data, called Federate Object Model (FOM). There, it is possible to describe classes, objects, attributes and hierarchy of classes. Once configured, the Bridge maps all necessary ROS Topics and attributes to objects and members of HLA. Both ROS and HLA may use the publish-subscribe protocol, the Brigde must just know for each subscribed variable from one side, to which variable it must publish in the other side.

The description of these variables is presented following. For more details about Federation Object Model (FOM) rules and syntax, refer to [12].

```
(FED
  (Federation TestFed)
  (FEDversion v1.3)
  (spaces)
```

```
(objects
  (class ObjectRoot
    (attribute privilegeToDelete reliable timestamp)
    (class RTIprivate)
    (class robot
      (attribute id reliable timestamp)
      (attribute battery reliable timestamp)
      (attribute temperature reliable timestamp)
      (attribute sensor1 reliable timestamp)
(attribute sensor2 reliable timestamp)
(attribute sensor3 reliable timestamp)
(attribute position reliable timestamp)
(attribute compass reliable timestamp)
(attribute goto reliable timestamp)
(attribute rotate reliable timestamp)
(attribute activate reliable timestamp)))))
  (interactions))
```

With conclusion of FED file, an Ptolemy Actor was necessary to provide communication with HLA using this FED file, making possible to Ptolemy create or join on federation. Previous works already develop this kind of actor [13,14], so they were modified to work with new FOM.

The Slave Federate actor was changed to manage new variables of fed file. The Fig. 2 shows old Slave Federate Actor and the new one.

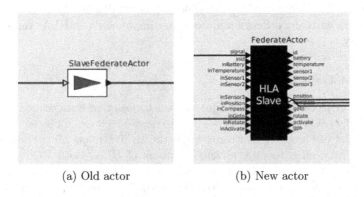

(a) Old actor   (b) New actor

Fig. 2. Actors that allows communication between Ptolemy and HLA

The Ptolemy Actors, like the bridge, implements an Ambassador. This make possible to models from Ptolemy communicate with High Level Architecture, sharing data and managing time simulation. To change the Object Model and allows communication with stage, new ports were used to each specific information from fed file. To send and receive data the inputs and outputs ports were used respectively.

3.2 General Architecture

According to HLA specification, individual simulators, called Federates, inter-operate with each other through a Runtime Infrastructure (RTI), forming a Federation. The RTI is responsible for data exchanging and synchronization. Each Federate must implement an Ambassador, which translates the data and timing policies of the specific simulator to a common standard used by all other Federates. In this one we have used the implementation of a project named CERTI [15].

As it can be seen in Fig. 3, two federates were used. The Ptolemy Federate, which provides the interface among RTI and Ptolemy. On the other side is the ROS Federate that interfaces with ROS environment.

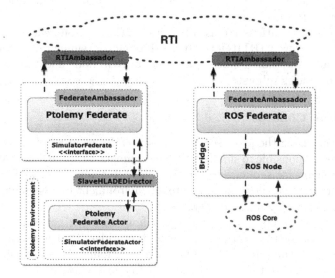

Fig. 3. General architecture

In the Ptolemy side, a specific Director is responsible for coordinate the simulation, send data to RTI when necessary and, when data arrives from there, send them to specific actors also developed in this project. As proof of concept we have integrated the Stage Robot Simulator (http://rtv.github.io/Stage), Ptolemy and a real robot.

4   Methodology

To develop this environment, an Model was created on Ptolemy. The proposed model must to contain the Slave Federate Actor to interact with federation and other actors to process data from robot and generate commands to control the robot. These commands also are send to ROS using the Slave Federate Actor.

The model uses an DE Director, an extension of Discrete Events (DE) Director from Ptolemy. It is responsible to manage the time in the Ptolemy simulation and to communicate with Ptolemy Ambassador.

An Algorithm to control the robots was developed using Ptolemy. It receive data from distance sensor of avatar robot and send command to avatar and real robot go on, stop or go on slowly to wait mobile obstacles out of way. The algorithm was created using the Python Actor, that allow Ptolemy use Python Applications.

To use the Stage simulator, an world file is necessary. This file have information of starting position of all robots and objects on Simulator. It was configured to have three robots used as obstacles on simulations, one additional robot that represent a real robot and a wall. A Real Turtlebot also is used on simulation to compare behavior with the simulated robot. This make the simulation became an Hardware-in-the-Loop simulation.

Some other applications are used to perform the environment. The Runtime Infrastructure Gateway (RTIG), that is used to manage simulation and exchange of messages and a python application that is an ROS node and is responsible to control the obstacles robots.

4.1   Proof of Concept

An experiment using the proposed tools was perform as proof of concept. Stage simulator was responsible to simulate the environment with the robots and obstacles, and Ptolemy for simulate the control algorithm for avatar and real robot. With this environment possible to create an environment for co-simulation with Robot-in-the-loop to increase reality.

Figure 4 presents how components are communicating between themselves. Blue side is composed by three components: the bridge, Ptolemy simulator running control algorithm, and RTIG. On green side, four robots are simulated on Stage simulator, where three are virtual robots and the avatar.

On Stage simulator, three virtual robots are used as obstacles to avatar robot. They do the same path going from left to right side crossing way of avatar robot. Avatar robot has to pass by the robots without collide until it arrives at the wall. Figure 5 shows the disposition of the robots on map, where the black square is the avatar robot and the other squares are the obstacle robots.

On simulation, the virtual robots on Stage, walk right side for left side crossing the avatar way. The Avatar must to go to wall and stop before clash with it. The Ptolemy Control Algorithm will make Avatar stop walk or walk slowly when the distance sensor of avatar detect some obstacle. When the obstacle move out of range, avatar back to walk normally. Then Ptolemy subscribes the distance sensor of avatar and publish linear and angular velocities on avatar and real robot.

The model used by Ptolemy present on Fig. 6. Is possible see many components, the clock is responsible to generate events that are used by other actors, the HLA Actor receive information from RTI and send it to output ports, the

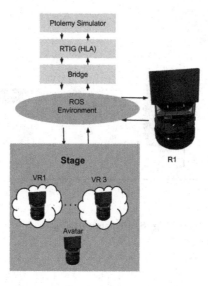

Fig. 4. Experiment (Color figure online)

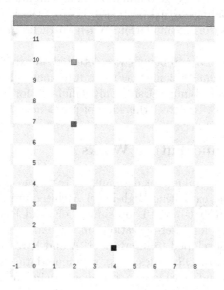

Fig. 5. Disposition of the robots on map

inputs values from HLA Actor are published to RTI. Control is the Python Actor with algorithm that receives data from sensor, and generate output converted into string and send to input of HLA Actor.

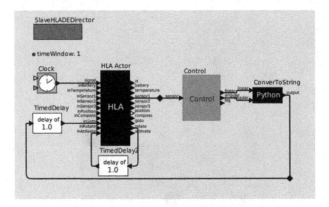

Fig. 6. Ptolemy model

4.2   Results

The proof of concept was perform. The Ptolemy Simulator received information from robotic environment (Stage Simulator), and generate outputs to move real robot and avatar avoiding virtual obstacles. Both, avatar and real robot stops to avoid the obstacles during simulation. When obstacles moves out range, they back to walk.

One Hardware-in-the-Loop benefit was detected on experiment. During simulation was detected that Ptolemy was using too much velocity and was necessary decrease it to avoid bumps. Using only simulator for development process it would not be possible to detect this kind of problem.

5   Conclusions and Future Works

This work presents a technique for designing of real-time embedded systems in multi-robots scenarios, exploiting High-Level Architecture (HLA) standard for interoperability and Robot-in-the-Loop simulation, and Robot Operating System (ROS) framework for inter-operation among real robots and simulations. Then, a Bridge was developed to interface HLA and ROS components, or Federate Ambassadors and ROS Nodes. Also, a unique data model was defined to represent robot ports and attributes, and new actors in Ptolemy to send/receive data to/from these ports and attributes were developed.

The presented technique make possible perform experiments with many robots merging virtual and real robots. A benefit is when many robots are necessary to perform a simulation but just one is available. So, the real robot can be used to check characteristics from real world and the simulated robots can interact with the real robot. Also is useful when an environment is hard to create on real world, then it can be simulated.

Furthermore, other specific simulators could also be integrated and more detailed outputs could be collected, like power consumption, data traffic in the network over different technologies and protocols, electro-mechanical and thermal analysis, etc. These possibilities will be explored in future works.

References

1. Ptolemaeus, C. (ed.): System Design, Modeling, and Simulation using Ptolemy II. Ptolemy.org, Berkeley (2014). http://ptolemy.org/books/Systems
2. Quigley, M., Conley, K., Gerkey, B., Faust, J., Foote, T., Leibs, J., Wheeler, R., Ng, A.Y.: ROS: an open-source robot operating system. In: ICRA Workshop on Open Source Software, vol. 3, no. 3.2, p. 5 (2009)
3. Kerr, J., Nickels, K.: Robot operating systems: bridging the gap between human and robot. In: 2012 44th Southeastern Symposium on in System Theory (SSST), pp. 99–104, March 2012
4. Bacic, M.: On hardware-in-the-loop simulation. In: 2005 44th IEEE Conference on Decision and Control and European Control Conference, CDC-ECC 2005, pp. 3194–3198, December 2005
5. Hu, X., Zeigler, B.P.: Measuring cooperative robotic systems using simulation-based virtual environment. In: Performance Metrics for Intelligent Systems Workshop (PerMIS), August 2004
6. Roth, C., Bucher, H., Brito, A., Sander, O., Becker, J.: A simulation tool chain for investigating future v2x-based automotive e/e architectures, vol. 1, no. 1, pp. 1739–1748, February 2014
7. Hu, X.: Applying robot-in-the-loop-simulation to mobile robot systems. In: 2005 Proceedings of the 12th International Conference on Advanced Robotics, ICAR 2005, pp. 506–513, July 2005
8. Brito, A.V., Negreiros, A.L.V., Roth, C., Sander, O.: Development and evaluation of distributed simulation of embedded systems using Ptolemy and HLA. In: 17th IEEE/ACM International Symposium on Distributed Simulation and Real Time Applications (2013)
9. Júnior, J.C.V.S., Brito, A.V., Nascimento, T.P.: Verification of embedded system designs through hardware-software co-simulation. Int. J. Inf. Electron. Eng. 5(1) (2015). http://www.ijiee.org/index.php?m=content&c=index&a=show&catid=49&id=548
10. ROS: Rospy wiki, November 2014. http://wiki.ros.org/rospy
11. Nongnu: Pyhla - python bindings for M&S HLA, November 2014. http://www.nongnu.org/certi/PyHLA/
12. IEEE: IEEE standard for modeling and simulation - high level architecture (HLA) - federate interface specification. IEEE Std 1516.1-2010 (Revision of IEEE Std 1516.1-2000), pp. 1–378 (2010)
13. Brito, A., Negreiros, A., Roth, C., Sander, O., Becker, J.: Development and evaluation of distributed simulation of embedded systems using Ptolemy and HLA. In: 2013 IEEE/ACM 17th International Symposium on Distributed Simulation and Real Time Applications (DS-RT), pp. 189–196, October 2013
14. de Negreiros, A.L.V., Brito, A.V.: Analise da aplicacao de simulacao distribuida no projeto de sistemas embarcados. In: Simposio Brasileiro de Sistemas de Informacao (2013)
15. Savannah: CERTI resumo, November 2014. http://savannah.nongnu.org/projects/certi

System-Level Design

Bit-Precise Formal Verification for SystemC Using Satisfiability Modulo Theories Solving

Lydia Jaß and Paula Herber[(✉)]

Technische Universität Berlin, Berlin, Germany
{lydia.jass,paula.herber}@tu-berlin.de

Abstract. Hardware/software codesigns are often modeled with the system level design language SystemC. Especially for safety critical applications, it is crucial to *guarantee* that such a design meets its requirement. In this paper, we present an approach to formally verify SystemC designs using the UCLID satisfiability modulo theories (SMT) solver. UCLID supports finite precision bitvector arithmetics. Thus, we can handle SystemC designs on a bit-precise level, which enables us to formally verify deeply integrated hardware/software systems that comprise detailed hardware models. At the same time, we exploit UCLID's ability to handle symbolic variables and use k-inductive invariant checking for SystemC designs. With this inductive approach, we can counteract the state space explosion problem, which model checking approaches suffer from. We demonstrate the practical applicability of our approach with a SystemC design that comprises a bit- and cycle-accurate model of a UART and software that reads data from the UART.

1 Introduction

Embedded systems are ubiquitous in today's everyday life, and they are often used in safety-critical applications, e.g. in airplanes or cars. A failure of such a system can lead to high financial losses and even human injuries or deaths. This makes it crucial to verify their correctness under all circumstances.

One of the main challenges for embedded systems verification is that the systems usually consist of deeply integrated hardware and software components. There already exists a large variety of validation and verification techniques for integrated HW/SW systems. However, the validation techniques are mostly non-systematic and incomplete, such as simulation and testing. These techniques cover neither the whole design nor all possible input scenarios. Opposed to that, formal methods have the advantage of covering all possible input scenarios and all possible behaviors of a given system. However, most of the existing formal verification techniques for hardware/software codesigns are either tailored to hardware or to software verification and can not cope well with designs that contain both bit-precise hardware models and high-level software.

© IFIP International Federation for Information Processing 2017
Published by Springer International Publishing AG 2017. All Rights Reserved
M. Götz et al. (Eds.): IESS 2015, IFIP AICT 523, pp. 51–63, 2017.
https://doi.org/10.1007/978-3-319-90023-0_5

In this paper, we present an approach to overcome this problem by using the UCLID verification system. The UCLID system is used to specify and verify systems modeled at the term level, and thus provides adequate abstractions for the representation of high-level software. At the same time, it supports the theories of bitvector arithmetics and of arrays. As underlying verification technique, UCLID uses a powerful Satisfiability Modulo Theory (SMT) solver supporting both eager and lazy SMT solving and the constructed formulas can be checked with any state-of-the-art SAT solver. Together, this makes UCLID a powerful tool for (bit-precise) system level design verification.

Our main contribution is a fully-automatic transformation of digital HW/SW co-designs that are modeled in SystemC into the UCLID specification language. The transformation enables us to apply the UCLID SMT solver to SystemC designs and thus to prove important properties like reliable safety and timing behavior. UCLID has the potential to cover most of the expressiveness of SystemC, including discrete time, static and dynamic sensitivity, inter-process communication and bit-vector arithmetics. Our representation of SystemC designs in UCLID and UCLID's symbolic simulation mechanism enable scalable verification using k-inductive invariant checking. By using inductive verification, we avoid the state space explosion problem that model checking approaches typically suffer from. We demonstrate the scalability and practical applicability of our approach with two case studies. The first is a simple producer-consumer example, where we use varying buffer sizes. The second case study is a typical industrial HW/SW codesign, namely a bit- and cycle-accurate model of a UART together with a software component that reads data from the UART.

The paper is structured as follows: In Sect. 2, we briefly introduce SystemC, UCLID, and k-inductive verification. In Sect. 3, we discuss related work. We present our transformation from SystemC to UCLID in Sect. 4. We discuss experimental results in Sect. 5 and conclude in Sect. 6.

2   Preliminaries

2.1   SystemC

SystemC is a system-level design language and a framework for HW/SW co-simulation. The semantics of SystemC is informally defined in an IEEE standard [11]. It is implemented as a C++ class library, which provides language elements for the description of hardware and software, and allows for modeling of both hardware and software components on various levels of abstraction. It also features an event-driven simulation kernel, which enables the simulation of the design. A SystemC design consists of a set of communicating processes, triggered by events and interacting through channels. Modules and channels represent structural information. SystemC also introduces an integer-valued time model with arbitrary time resolution. Listing 1.1 shows an excerpt of a SystemC *producer* module that writes to a FIFO buffer. The *produce* method (which is executed within an *SC_THREAD* process) contains an infinite loop where the producer writes a value between 0 and 32 to the fifo port at every clock cycle.

The execution of SystemC designs is controlled by the SystemC scheduler. Like typical hardware description languages, SystemC supports the notion of delta-cycles, which impose a partial order on parallel processes. Note that the order in which processes are executed within a delta-cycle is not specified in [11], i. e., it is inherently *non-deterministic*.

```
1   SC_MODULE(producer) {
2       ...
3       sc_port<myfifo_if> fifo;
4       void produce(void) {
5         int c = 0;
6         while(true) {
7           wait();
8           c = (c + 1) % 32;
9           fifo->write(c);
10      } }
11  };
```

Listing 1.1. A SystemC Module

2.2 UCLID

UCLID is a verification system developed in a joint project by Carnegie Mellon University and University of California, Berkeley [13]. It incorporates a decision procedure to verify (possibly infinite) state systems. The specification language supports uninterpreted functions, bit-vector arithmetic and lambda expressions. UCLID can handle symbolic simulation, which allows a design to be verified for an arbitrary start state and thus enables an inductive verification approach.

A UCLID module consists of inputs, variables, constants, macros, and assign expressions. The assign expressions define the state variables and the transition relation of the underlying labeled transition system. UCLID interprets the model together with the property to be verified as one formula and supports eager and lazy Satisfiability Modulo Theories (SMT) solving.

2.3 K-Inductive Invariant Verification

For k-inductive invariant checking [16], two models are needed. One explicit model representing the system from its initial state, and one symbolic model that represents the system in an arbitrary state. Desired properties are expressed as a predicate $P(x)$, which determines whether a requirement P holds in simulation step x of a given model. k-inductive invariant checking is done in two steps:

1. **Base case:** Simulate the explicit model k steps from its initial state and check $P(0) \wedge ... \wedge P(k)$.
2. **Induction:** Symbolically simulate the symbolic model from an arbitrary initial state for $k + 1$ steps. Then check $P(0) \wedge ... \wedge P(k) \implies P(k + 1)$.

If there exists a k so that both base cases can be shown, then the property under verification holds in all reachable system states. If the property under verification does not hold, the system is unsafe and we get a counter example. Note that the counter example may be spurious if k is too small.

3   Related Work

There exist several approaches to the automated formal verification of SystemC designs. For example, in [8], the authors propose program transformations from SystemC into state machines, but they ignore time, the transformation is performed manually, and hardware data types are not explicitly considered. Karlsson et al. [12] verify SystemC designs using a petri-net based representation and the PRES+ model checker. However, the petri-net based approach introduces a huge overhead because interactions can only be modeled by introducing additional subnets. As it is based on model checking, the approach also suffers from the state space explosion problem. Bit-precise hardware data types are not explicitly considered. In [10,14], an approach for the formal verification of SystemC designs using the model checker UPPAAL is presented. A large subset of SystemC is supported. However, UPPAAL does not support inductive verification techniques and thus suffers from the state space explosion problem. Furthermore, it is not well-suited to support hardware data types.

In [7], bounded model checking is used on untimed SystemC TLM designs. They use k-inductive invariant checking using CBMC [4] and Boolector [15] as underlying SMT solver. This work is very close to our approach. The main idea is to transform a given SystemC TLM design into a sequential C program and perform loop unwinding to achieve a complete model. However, compared to our approach, they only support a small subset of untimed SystemC TLM designs and disregard time and complex process interactions. Furthermore, bit-precise hardware data types are not explicitly considered.

In [6,9], an encoding from SystemC into the verification toolbox CADP is proposed. This approach is based on a manual definition of callback functions, which are then used to natively execute SystemC/C++ code in the CADP verification system. Still, the transformation has to be done manually. Furthermore, bit-precise hardware data types are not explicitly considered. In [3], Cimatti et al. generate three different verification models from a given SystemC design, each tailored to a specific aspect of the SystemC semantics on different levels of abstraction, and use software model checking techniques. While this approach is capable of handling the most important SystemC constructs including time and communication, it can not handle bit-precise hardware data types. Furthermore, by using model checking techniques, it also suffers from the state space explosion problem. In [5], the authors present an approach for the verification of SystemC designs using the software model checker SPIN. Again, by using a software model checker, they suffer from the state space explosion problem.

Note that there also exist some approaches to automated formal verification of other system level design languages. For example, in [2], the authors present an approach for formal deadlock analysis of SpecC models using SMT. However, they only consider the timing relations in a given design by formulating assertions over time stamps, which are assigned to executable code. This is sufficient for a deadlock analysis but does not allow for checking of other functional or nonfunctional properties.

4   Transformation from SystemC to UCLID

The key idea of our approach for the bit-precise verification of SystemC designs using satisfiability modulo theories solving is to transform a given SystemC design into a semantically equivalent UCLID specification. Our transformation preserves the (informally defined) bit-precise semantics of a given SystemC designs. The main challenges are to preserve the sequential simulation semantics of SystemC in a synchronous target language, i.e., to model the nondeterministic execution semantics of the SystemC scheduler, and to respect the bit-precise semantics of all data operations. The basic idea of our transformation is to translate all SystemC processes into UCLID state machines, and to control the execution of these processes by modeling the SystemC scheduler and SystemC events as UCLID state machines. To capture the simulation semantics of SystemC, our UCLID model of the scheduler interprets the operational sequences of the SystemC kernel, which manages process scheduling and channel updates.

The transformation result is a UCLID interpretation of the semantics of the given SystemC design. This can then be automatically verified using the UCLID verification system. The main advantage of our approach is that the formal semantics we define for SystemC by translating it into the formal specification language of UCLID is bit-precise, and that the underlying verification engine is based on SMT solving and thus enables inductive proofs.

4.1   Assumptions

The following assumptions on a SystemC design define our supported subset.

1. No dynamic variable or process creation.
2. No recursion.
3. No inheritance nor pointers, no side effects.
4. No external code or library calls.
5. For division and modulo operations the divisor is an integer power of 2.
6. So far, we only support Boolean and integer variables with fixed bit width, and arrays and structs thereof.

If all of these assumptions are fulfilled, we can transform a given SystemC design automatically into a semantics-preserving UCLID representation and verify it using the UCLID verification system.

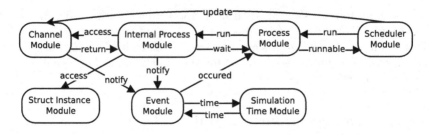

Fig. 1. Structure of a SystemC design in UCLID

4.2   Representation of SystemC Designs in UCLID

Our representation of a SystemC design in UCLID interprets the simulation semantics of SystemC. This means that not only all the SystemC modules of the design are represented in UCLID, but also the scheduler, processes, events and primitve channels, which altogether define the execution semantics.

SystemC modules contain processes, events and member variables. Module ports are connected to channels, which provide communication methods between modules. Before simulation, the SystemC kernel creates the module hierarchy in its elaboration phase and performs instantiation and binding. In this phase, all module, channel, and process objects are created and bound together. Because UCLID does not support dynamic module creation, we recreate the SystemC design after elaboration. This means we create UCLID modules for all module and channel instances and their connections. As a preprocessing step for our transformation from SystemC to UCLID, we flatten the design. The hierarchical structure is kept transparent in the UCLID specification using prefixes. To capture the state of a given SystemC design, we use the following state variables: (1) All local and global variables, including all module and all channel variables, (2) the state of each process (including its current program counter), (3) the state of each event, (4) the state of the SystemC scheduler. The structure of our representation of SystemC designs in UCLID is shown in Fig. 1. To capture the static part of a design, we create modules for each channel and module (or, more general, struct) instance. The communication methods provided by a channel are placed within the corresponding UCLID module that represents the channel instance. To capture the simulation semantics, we create modules for the scheduler and the simulation time, and for all processes and events of a given design. We distinguish between an *internal process module*, which keeps track of the program counter and performs event notifications and channel accesses, and a *process module*, which determines the state of the process, and reacts to events to implement static and dynamic sensitivity.

Scheduler and Simulation Time. We have defined two separate UCLID modules for the scheduler and simulation time. The scheduler module non-deterministically chooses the next runnable process and defines the phase the system is in (initialize, evaluate, update, or advance time). The simulation time module manages the advancement of time. In the advance time phase, the simulation time module advances time to the earliest pending timed notification.

Processes. Processes are SystemC's units of execution. For each process, we introduce two modules. The internal process module *ipm* keeps track of the program counter, notifies events and accesses channels. The process module *pm* determines the state the process is in, and reacts to events to implement static and dynamic sensitivity. When the scheduler chooses a process to be running, its process module changes its state to running. This triggers the internal process module, which runs until it reaches a wait statement or the process terminates.

An excerpt of the internal process module *ipm* is shown in Listing 1.2. It realizes a state machine that keeps track of the program counter and evaluates control flow conditions. The internal state *istate* is first set to *initialized*. As soon as the state of the process module *pm* is set to running, *istate* is set to the first program counter label *line9_while_loop* where a while loop is entered. Then, *istate* is set to the label *line11_call_wait*. Next, the process is suspended and waits to become runnable again. Function calls are realized by a similar mechanism. For example, the *write* method of the channel module *fifo* is started if the internal state is set to *line13_call_write*. It returns control to the produce process by setting its program counter to *fifo_done*.

```
1   ASSIGN
2   init[istate] := not_initialized;
3   next[istate] := case
4       ((istate = not_initialized) & (scheduler.state = initialize)) : initialized;
5       ((istate = initialized) & (pm.state = running)) : line9_while_loop;
6       ((istate = line9_while_loop) & true) : line11_call_wait;
7       ((istate = line11_call_wait)) : line11_wait_return;
8       ((istate = line11_wait_return) & (pm.state = running)) : line13_call_write;
9       ((istate = line13_call_write)) : line13_wait_for_write;
10      ((istate = line13_wait_for_write) & (fifo.write = fifo_done)) : line9_while_loop;
11      ((istate = line9_while_loop) & ˜(true)) : done;
12      default : istate;
13  esac;
```

Listing 1.2. Excerpt of the Internal Process Module *ipm*

Note that we did not include a program counter label for each line of code in the *istate* state machine. Instead, we reduced the set of program counter labels to represent the necessary atomic blocks. An atomic block comprises a sequence of states in the control flow without branches or process suspension. As SystemC uses a cooperative scheduler, atomic blocks can never be interrupted. Thus, it is possible to abstract from some intermediate steps and to combine multiple sequential actions in one (synchronous) simulation step as long as we ensure that no data race may occur. So far, we just exclude cases where a potential data race may occur from this optimization. The benefit of the reduction is a smaller UCLID model while preserving the execution semantics of SystemC.

An excerpt of the process module *pm* is shown in Listing 1.3. It implements the process state, which may be one of *process_initialized, running, runnable, process_done, wait_t, wait_e,* or *wait_s* (the latter to wait for a given time, an event or for the sensitivity list, respectively). Note that *pm* makes use of the current state of *ipm*, the current process selected by the scheduler, and the current state of the FIFO channel. The latter is necessary because the process might be suspended by a wait call that occurs within the FIFO channel.

```
1   DEFINE
2   sensitivity_list_occurred := case clk_edge_event.occurred : true;
3                                      default : false; esac;
4   ASSIGN
5   init[state] := process_no_state;
6   next[state] := case
7     (ipm.istate = initialized) : process_initialized;
8     (state = process_initialized) : runnable;
9     ((scheduler.next = produce) & (scheduler.current = none)) : running;
10    ((state = wait_s) & sensitivity_list_occurred) : runnable;
11    (ipm.istate = done) : process_done;
12    (ipm.istate = line11_call_wait) : wait_s;
13    (ipm.istate = line13_wait_for_write & fifo.write = line31_call_wait) : wait_e;
14    (ipm.istate = line13_wait_for_write & r_event.occurred & state = wait_e) : runnable;
15    default : state;
16  esac;
```

Listing 1.3. Excerpt of the Process Module *pm*

Events. We create one UCLID module for each event. Additionally, we also create timeout event modules for processes that suspend themselves by calling a timed wait. Processes may notify events immediately, delta-delayed or timed. If a process performs an immediate notification of an event, the event immediately occurs and all processes that are sensitive to the event react by changing their states. For a delta-delayed notification, the notification is delayed until the next delta-cycle starts. If a process performs a timed notification, the event adopts the time value and waits until the simulation time is equal to the target time. If a process calls the wait function without any argument, its process module waits for one of the events from the processes sensitivity list to occur. New notifications overwrite pending notifications if they expire at an earlier target time.

An excerpt of a UCLID event module is shown in Listing 1.4. Initially, the event state *estate* is set to *no_notification*. Then, it reacts to all processes that might notify the event and sets the state to *immediate, delta* or *timed* accordingly. The event state is reset if *occurred* becomes true. This happens whenever an immediate notification occurs, if we have a pending delta-delayed notification and the scheduler starts a new delta cycle, or if we have a pending timed notification and the simulation time becomes equal to the target time.

```
1   DEFINE
2   occurred := case ((estate = immediate) | ((estate = delta) & scheduler.new_delta)
3                           | ((estate = timed) & (t = sim_time.time))) : true;
4                    default : false; esac;
5   ASSIGN
6   init[estate] := no_notification;
7   next[estate] := case
8      occurred : no_notification; (* reset the event state *)
9      process.notify_event_immediate : immediate;
10     ((estate != immediate) & process.notify_event_delta) : delta;
11     ((estate != immediate) & (estate != delta) & process.notify_event_timed) : timed;
12     default : estate;
13  esac;
14  init[t] := ...
```

Listing 1.4. Event Module

Channels. For each channel, we create a module that contains all channel variables and all communication methods for all process modules that might call those methods. If a channel method waits for an event to occur, the caller process module changes its state to also wait for the event. Primitive channels implement the request-update semantics. This means that they do not change the state of the channel directly. Instead, they request the channel to be updated during the update phase. For this purpose, primitive channels have a dedicated *update* method, which is executed in the update phase after all evaluations are finished. In UCLID, we represent this mechanism by setting a *request_update* variable in the channel module that activates an *update* state machine.

Variables. Beside process and event states, the state of a SystemC design comprises local and global variables. Using the program counter labels described above, we can decide for each variable at what points in the program it is manipulated. Using this information, we can construct one UCLID state machine for each variable of a given SystemC design. An example for a state machine that models the local variable c of our running example is shown in Listing 1.5.

Note that in UCLID, a declaration of a variable does not ensure that the given number of bits is used for its representation. Instead, UCLID always uses as few bits as possible. To ensure that the bit-precise semantics of SystemC is preserved, we use the correct bitwidth for all arithmetic and logic operations and we cast all expressions into the left hand side types within assignments.

So far, we support Boolean- and int-typed variables, sc_int and sc_uint, arrays, and structs. We represent Boolean types by UCLID's TRUTH type. The types int, sc_int and sc_uint are represented as bitvectors using UCLID's BITVEC-type with the specified length respectively. Arrays are modeled using lambda-expressions, as described in the UCLID documentation [1].

```
1   ASSIGN
2   init[c] := (0 +_32 0);
3   next[c] := case
4       (istate = line9_while_loop) : 0;
5       (istate = line13_call_write) : (c +_32 1);
6       default : c;
7   esac;
```

Listing 1.5. Variable Handling

4.3   Verification of SystemC Designs Using UCLID

With our representation of SystemC designs within UCLID as described above, we can automatically transform a given SystemC design into a UCLID specification. Then, it can symbolically be simulated and verified in UCLID using k-inductive invariant checking [16]. To adapt k-inductive invariant checking with UCLID, we create an explicit UCLID model and check the base case and a symbolic model for the induction, as described in Sect. 2.3. The explicit model starts in the same state as the SystemC design. For the symbolic model, we set all state variables to symbolic constants (for truth types, bitvectors and bitvector functions) or non-deterministic choice variables (for enum variables) respectively. If UCLID returns a counter example, it might be spurious, i.e. it might not be reachable by the original system. If UCLID returns that the induction step is valid, we can conclude that the system never violates the requirement and it is safe. There is no straightforward way to determine the value of k needed to prove or disprove a property. Thus, we incrementally increase k until we reach a predefined maximum value of k or the counter example is not spurious.

5   Evaluation

We have implemented our transformation from SystemC to UCLID in Java. The resulting framework is shown in Fig. 2. A given SystemC design is preprocessed and translated into our SystemC intermediate representation SysCIR. There, we flatten the design and resolve all port and channel connections. Our novel transformation engine then generates an explicit and a symbolic UCLID model. Those are then used for k-inductive invariant checking as described above.

To evaluate our approach, we use two case studies and compare the verification times with those achieved with UPPAAL [10,14]. In the first case study, two producers and one consumer communicate over a FIFO buffer (3 processes, 1 channel). The second case study is a more complex UART design that consists of a bit- and cycle-accurate UART model and software that reads data from the UART (7 processes, 9 channels). We ensure that we cover all possible input scenarios by modeling input data using selections in UPPAAL and symbolic constants in UCLID. Note that the UART case study could not be handled with

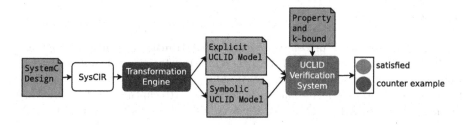

Fig. 2. Framework for verifying SystemC designs with UCLID

the approach presented in [7]. All experiments were performed on a 64 bit Linux system with an Intel Core i7-4770 with 3.2 GHz and 32 GB main memory. All designs are transformed into UCLID respectively UPPAAL in less than a second.

We have shown that the producer-consumer example does not cause a buffer over- or underflow with our k-inductive invariant checking approach. The requirement we check is $P(i) := \text{fifo}.n \leq BS \land \text{fifo}.n \geq 0$. To verify this, k must at least be *10*. This corresponds to the maximum number of steps until the desired property is restored from an arbitrary start state. To evaluate the scalability of our approach, we have varied the buffer size from 10 to 1000. As Table 1 shows, the time it takes UCLID to verify the model with growing buffer capacities stays nearly constant, while the verification time in UPPAAL increases exponentially.

Table 1. Verification times in [hh:]mm:ss

	Producer-consumer				UART system				
Buffer size/bitwidth	10	50	100	1000	4	8	16	24	32
BMC	<1	<1	<1	<1	10:30	10:25	10:03	10:07	10:03
k-induction	0:06	0:06	0:06	0:06	7:22:00	7:03:00	7:11:00	6:40:00	7:11:32
UCLID total	0:06	0:06	0:06	0:06	7:32:30	7:13:25	7:21:03	6:50:07	7:21:35
UPPAAL total	0:02	0:02	0:09	3:00:51	2:42:40	x	x	x	x

For the UART system, we verify that the software correctly reads all data that is sent over the UART. The requirement we check is $P(i) := sw.error\_cnt \leq 0$, where *error_cnt* is used in the software component *sw* to mark if the values differ. To verify the UART system, k must at least be *200*. We evaluated the scalability by varying the bitwidth of the transmitted data from 4 bit to 32 bit. Table 1 shows the runtimes of both bounded model checking and the induction step. Although the computational effort is considerable, we achieve a complete proof for all possible input scenarios, and the verification time is similar for varying bitwidths. UPPAAL is able to verify the 4-bit system in less time, but exceeds resources for all larger bitwidths[1].

---

[1] UPPAAL did not return results after 48 h while using 32 GB main memory.

6   Conclusion

In this paper, we have presented an automatic transformation from SystemC to the formal verification system UCLID. Our transformation is able to cover a large subset of SystemC including static and dynamic sensitivity, time, primitive channels, and bit-precise hardware data types. To capture the semantics of a given SystemC design, we translate all variables and processes into UCLID state machines, and we provide predefined state machines that model the execution semantics of SystemC and the event notification mechanism. The structure of the original design is kept transparent by using prefixing. This eases comprehensibility of counter examples. With the result of our transformation, we can use UCLID's powerful verification mechanisms and underlying SMT solver to verify a given SystemC design using k-inductive invariant checking.

To demonstrate the practical applicability of our approach, we have used a simple producer-consumer example taken from the SystemC reference implementation and an industrial UART system. We have shown that our approach scales well for increasing data ranges and bit widths, which is typically not the case for model checking based approaches. With the UART system, we have also shown the applicability of our approach to (small) industrial applications.

In future work, we plan to optimize our transformation by allowing parallel executions whenever we can safely assume that no data race may occur. We are confident that in doing so, we can significantly reduce the necessary k for k induction, which in turn will significantly reduce the verification effort.

References

1. Brady, B., Seshia, S., Lahiri, S., Bryant, R.: A user's guide to UCLID (2008)
2. Chang, C.-W., Dömer, R.: Formal deadlock analysis of SpecC models using satisfiability modulo theories. In: Schirner, G., Götz, M., Rettberg, A., Zanella, M.C., Rammig, F.J. (eds.) IESS 2013. IAICT, vol. 403, pp. 116–127. Springer, Heidelberg (2013). https://doi.org/10.1007/978-3-642-38853-8_11
3. Cimatti, A., Narasamdya, I., Roveri, M.: Software model checking SystemC. IEEE Trans. CAD Integr. Circuits Syst. **32**(5), 774–787 (2013)
4. Clarke, E., Kroening, D., Lerda, F.: A tool for checking ANSI-C programs. In: Jensen, K., Podelski, A. (eds.) TACAS 2004. LNCS, vol. 2988, pp. 168–176. Springer, Heidelberg (2004). https://doi.org/10.1007/978-3-540-24730-2_15
5. Elshuber, M., Kandl, S., Puschner, P.P., Choppy, C., Sun, J.: Improving system-level verification of SystemC models with SPIN. In: FSFMA, pp. 74–79 (2013)
6. Garavel, H., Helmstetter, C., Ponsini, O., Serwe, W.: Verification of an industrial SystemC/TLM model using LOTOS and CADP. In: MEMOCODE, pp. 46–55. IEEE Computer Society (2009)
7. Große, D., Le, H.M., Drechsler, R.: Proving transaction and system-level properties of untimed SystemC TLM designs. In: MEMOCODE, pp. 113–122. IEEE Computer Society (2010)
8. Habibi, A., Moinudeen, H., Tahar, S.: Generating finite state machines from SystemC. In: Design, Automation and Test in Europe, pp. 76–81. IEEE (2006)

9. Helmstetter, C.: TLM.open: a SystemC/TLM frontend for the CADP verification toolbox. Leibniz Trans. Embed. Syst. **1**(1) (2014)
10. Herber, P., Fellmuth, J., Glesner, S.: Model checking SystemC designs using timed automata. In: CODES+ISSS, pp. 131–136. ACM Press (2008)
11. IEEE Standards Association: IEEE Std. 1666–2011, Open SystemC Language Reference Manual. IEEE Press (2011)
12. Karlsson, D., Eles, P., Peng, Z.: Formal verification of SystemC designs using a petri-net based representation. In: DATE, pp. 1228–1233. IEEE Press (2006)
13. Lahiri, S.K., Seshia, S.A.: The UCLID decision procedure. In: Alur, R., Peled, D.A. (eds.) CAV 2004. LNCS, vol. 3114, pp. 475–478. Springer, Heidelberg (2004). https://doi.org/10.1007/978-3-540-27813-9_40
14. Pockrandt, M., Herber, P., Klös, V., Glesner, S.: Model checking memory-related properties of hardware/software co-designs. In: Schirner, G., Götz, M., Rettberg, A., Zanella, M.C., Rammig, F.J. (eds.) IESS 2013. IAICT, vol. 403, pp. 92–103. Springer, Heidelberg (2013). https://doi.org/10.1007/978-3-642-38853-8_9
15. Brummayer, R., Biere, A.: Boolector: an efficient SMT solver for bit-vectors and arrays. In: Kowalewski, S., Philippou, A. (eds.) TACAS 2009. LNCS, vol. 5505, pp. 174–177. Springer, Heidelberg (2009). https://doi.org/10.1007/978-3-642-00768-2_16
16. Sheeran, M., Singh, S., Stålmarck, G.: Checking safety properties using induction and a SAT-solver. In: Hunt, W.A., Johnson, S.D. (eds.) FMCAD 2000. LNCS, vol. 1954, pp. 127–144. Springer, Heidelberg (2000). https://doi.org/10.1007/3-540-40922-X_8

Timed Path Conditions
in MATLAB/Simulink

Marcus Mikulcak[✉][iD], Paula Herber, Thomas Göthel, and Sabine Glesner

Technische Universität Berlin, Ernst-Reuter-Platz 7, 10587 Berlin, Germany
marcus.mikulcak@tu-berlin.de

Abstract. MATLAB/Simulink is a widely-used industrial tool for the development of complex embedded systems. However, due to the complexity and the dynamic character of the developed models, their analysis is a difficult challenge, in particular if timing aspects are involved. In this paper, we present an approach for the construction of *timed path conditions* for MATLAB/Simulink models. Timed path conditions allow for fine-grained conclusions about the existence of possibly critical paths through a model containing time-dependent elements. With the help of timed path conditions, it is possible to identify interference and non-interference between model parts. Furthermore, they have the potential to reduce the complexity of models to improve verifiability, reason about compliance with security policies as well as generate feasible, efficient test cases. We demonstrate the applicability of our approach with a shared buffer for public as well as confidential data.

1 Introduction

In the area of safety-critical embedded software, such as in the automotive and aerospace domain, programming errors can lead to disastrous and, if occurring, often fatal accidents. At the same time, the complexity of such systems has increased dramatically over recent years. To cope with the steadily increasing complexity, current design processes rely more and more on models. One of the most widely-used tools for model-based design is MATLAB/Simulink[11] by MathWorks, which supports the graphical design and simulation of time-continuous as well as time-discrete systems using block diagrams. Simulink is very well-suited to grasp the structure of a design on high abstraction levels and to visualize its behavior by simulation. However, due to the complexity and the dynamic character of the developed models, the analysis of a given model is a difficult challenge, in particular if timing aspects are considered. At the same time, knowledge about the existence of certain paths and the conditions under which they are executed is highly desirable. In particular, if a Simulink model becomes the main artifact in a model-based design process, the analysis

Funded by the German Federal Ministry of Education and Research as part of the research project *CISMo*.

M. Götz et al. (Eds.): IESS 2015, IFIP AICT 523, pp. 64–76, 2017.
https://doi.org/10.1007/978-3-319-90023-0_6

of its properties becomes crucial for the correctness and reliability of the whole development process. With the help of (timed) path conditions, it is possible to identify interference and non-interference between model parts and, thus, to reason about compliance with security policies. Furthermore, (timed) path conditions can be used to compute areas of low dynamic coupling for subsequent model separation. With that, they have the potential to reduce the complexity of Simulink models and thus to improve verifiability and testability. Finally, they provide a basis for generating feasible, efficient test cases for quality assurance.

In this paper, we present an approach for the construction of timed path conditions in Simulink. The main challenge we face is that all dependencies in a given design must be considered. Thereby, dependencies might be indirectly introduced via control flow, or delayed, which introduces dependencies between signals from different time slices. In our approach, we start with a static over-approximation of all potential dependencies on a path between a timed output signal and a timed input signals and collect all control flow conditions. Then, for each path, we compute a set of constraints on all input signals by performing a backward propagation of control flow conditions, which also takes timing dependencies into account. The result of our analysis is a precise description of the timed dependencies between input and output signals, represented by timed path conditions that solely depend on model-wide input variables. We demonstrate the applicability of our approach by computing timed path conditions for a case study containing a shared buffer for public as well as confidential data.

2   Preliminaries

In this section, we describe the basic concepts and tools employed by our approach.

2.1   Path Conditions

In general, *path conditions* [9] describe sufficient conditions for paths to be executed. In [5,6], path conditions are used to capture all paths where information might flow from a source to a target. In contrast to static analyses, which consider all syntactically possible dependencies, path conditions take data and control flow conditions into account. With that, they exclude, for example, information flow which is only possible if disjoint control flow conditions are satisfied. Thus, a path condition based analysis is more precise than classical static analyses.

2.2   MATLAB/Simulink

MATLAB/Simulink[11] is an add-on to the MATLAB IDE by MathWorks that enables graphical modeling and simulation of reactive systems. In its data-flow oriented notation, Simulink employs *blocks* which are connected using *signals*. Additionally, each block and signal is assigned a set of *parameters*.

Simulation of Simulink models is performed using *solvers* which compute the output of each block according to its semantics. *Variable step* solvers aim at automatically finding a simulation step size for each block in the model to achieve a level of precision set by the model developer. *Fixed step* solvers use a fixed simulation step size at the expense of precision while increasing performance. The former class of solvers is commonly used for hybrid or purely time-continuous systems, while the latter is used for time-discrete models.

2.3   Information Flow Analysis

The protection of confidentiality of information inside a software system is a long-standing and increasingly important problem in the areas of general computing as well as embedded systems. Protecting not only the data itself but also the integrity of the functionality that produces and handles data is a goal of software non-interference policies [3]. Such policies, based on the assignment of security levels to data elements, describe rules between which levels information flow is allowed or forbidden [15]. When aiming at assuring *confidentiality*, data is prohibited to flow *to* inappropriate locations, while in the context of *integrity*, data is prohibited to flow *from* inappropriate sources. As non-interference refers to the absence of information flow, it ensures both confidentiality and integrity.

3   Related Work

Path conditions [9] are heavily used in the area of symbolic execution and automatic test generation. The use of path conditions to increase granularity of information flow analysis has first been proposed in [10]. In this work, the authors describe the combination of program slicing and *Constraint Logic Programming* (CLP) to increase the precision of slicing for C programs, implemented in the *VALSOFT* Slicing System. They consider purely static slicing as too conservative and propose the extraction of conditions on the edges of the generated *Program Dependence Graphs* (PDGs). Subsequently, the concatenation of these conditions along paths of interest are analyzed by a constraint solver. However, due to the inherent differences between C and MATLAB/Simulink, their approach cannot directly be transferred to Simulink. For example, their work does not take timing behavior into account. They report that the precision of slicing operations can be considerably raised by the use of path conditions.

In [14], the authors present an approach for slicing of Simulink models. Their algorithm identifies model parts that influence the computation of a given block. However, as their approach does not have the characteristics of an *Information Flow Analysis* (IFA), i.e., does neither consider conditions nor timing along model paths, it only provides a coarse-grained dependency analysis.

In [18], the authors present an adaptation of the concept of path conditions to MATLAB/Simulink. The authors describe the translation of Simulink models into *Lustre*, a synchronous data-flow programming language [4]. On this basis,

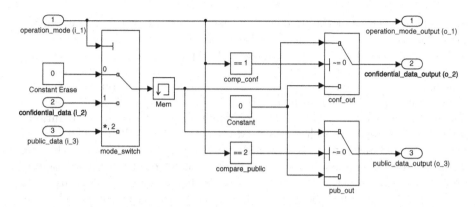

Fig. 1. A shared buffer for public as well as confidential data

they define an IFA notation and calculate path conditions on the translated models. Their approach has been implemented in the **Gryphon** tool suite and tested using the example shown in Fig. 1, which we adapted from their publication. With their approach, they are able to show non-interference between confidential and public data paths using path conditions. However, they assume that the timing dependencies do not influence the information flow. Although they discuss that this assumptions is violated in their own case study, they provide no solution that takes timing dependencies into account. Possible solutions to this problem have been presented in [7,12,17] via further translations of Simulink models into *Lustre*, *SIGNAL* and *UCLID*, respectively. However, as these approaches rely on a translation of models into a target language using different functional and timing semantics, properties of the original systems are lost. For example, the translation to *Lustre* maps Simulink signals onto mathematical data types, thereby losing the possibility to perform bit-precise analyses of data.

4   Timed Path Conditions in MATLAB/Simulink

In this section, we present our approach for the computation of timed path condition in MATLAB/Simulink. The main idea is to transfer the concept of path conditions from sequential programming languages like C to the Simulink modeling language. The main challenges are to take both data and control dependencies into account and to cope with timing dependencies. Data dependencies can simply be resolved by following signal lines where each connection corresponds to a direct dependency. Control dependencies are more difficult to compute as they introduce conditional dependencies which are locally resolved. To overcome this problem, we propagate control flow dependencies backwards through the model to the input signals. With that, we can decide whether a certain path actually exists on a very fine-grained level. For both data and control dependencies, we have to take timing dependencies into account. An output might only depend on an input at certain points of time, and sophisticated routing policies might even take advantage of timing delays to make sure that two signals can never interfere. A motivating example for this case is given in the following subsection and used as a running example throughout this paper.

In order to take timing dependencies into account, we introduce the concept of *time slices*, and incorporate timing dependencies into our approach for the computation of timed path conditions by expressing all dependencies with respect to relative time slices. For the computation of timed path conditions, we use a two-step approach: (1) We (statically) identify all paths in a given Simulink model and collect all path conditions on each path. (2) For each path, we propagate all local control flow conditions backwards through the model in order to compute timed path conditions that solely depend on input variables.

In the following subsections, we first present our running example. Then, we introduce assumptions that define a Simulink subset our approach is currently able to safely analyze. In Sect. 4.3, we present our notations. Then, we present the computation of path conditions in Sect. 4.4.

4.1 Running Example

To illustrate our approach, we use a simplified version of the shared buffer presented in [18] (see Fig. 1).[1] In this model, information of two different security levels (*public* and *confidential*) is fed into a shared buffer, which is implemented as a Mem block. According to the current operation mode, confidential (mode 1) or public (mode 2) information is saved in the buffer and passed to the corresponding output, or the contents of the buffer are erased (mode 0).

The most interesting aspect of this example is that it makes use of a sophisticated routing scheme to avoid security violations. Although confidential and public data share the same memory block as buffer, the routing conditions are intended to ensure that confidential input data can never flow to the public output. To this end, the operation mode defines which input should be routed to the output. The designer did, however, not take the timing behavior of the Mem block into account. When examining the timing of the output signals we discover that if the operation mode switches from *confidential* to *public*, the outputs register a spike of the data previously stored in Mem: the confidential contents are sent to the public output. By computing path conditions without taking timing dependencies into account, one would falsely assume that information flow is impossible, as the control flow conditions along the path from confidential input to public output are disjoint. This shows that we can only safely use path conditions for Simulink models if we take timing behavior into account.

4.2 Assumptions

In order to apply our approach for the computation of timed path conditions, a given Simulink model has to fulfill the following assumptions:

---

[1] Our simplified version does not contain the Stateflow controller used to set the operation mode present in the original.

1. It uses a *time-discrete, fixed-step* solver.
2. It does not contain algebraic loops or loop subsystems.
3. Only scalar signals are used.
4. So far, all blocks have to use the same sample time.
5. For conditional execution, we support `Enabled` and routing blocks so far.
6. Control signals only pass through simple arithmetic blocks without feedback.

The first two assumptions are acceptable as we target Simulink models from the field of discrete embedded controller design, where time-continuous solvers, loop subsystems, and algebraic loops are rarely used. Assumptions 3 to 5 are imposed due to the current state of our implementation, we are confident that our approach can easily be extended to vector or matrix signals, varying sample times, and other conditional subsystems. Assumption 6 is the most serious restriction regarding typical Simulink models of interest. However, many practical Simulink models only use simple control logics. An extension of our approach to support more complex blocks and subsystems is subject to future work.

4.3   Notations

We use the following notations: B denotes the set of *blocks* and S the set of *signals* in a given model. In addition, we use I and O as the sets of incoming and outgoing ports of a model, respectively. To describe paths, we use the set $P(b_l, b_k)$ that contains all paths between blocks b_l and b_k. On a path b_l to b_k, we denote the condition for information to flow through a block b_m as $c(b_m, b_l, b_k)$. While arithmetic blocks always establish a connection between all input and output signals ($c(b_i, *, *) = true$), routing blocks and conditional subsystems only establish a connection under certain conditions.

In order to take timing dependencies into account, we denote the dependency of an output signal to the set of input variables at a certain point of time as (note that $t_{\max}$ designates the maximum time slice depth over all paths):

$$o_n^t = d(i_1^t, \ldots i_1^{t-t_{\max}}, \ldots, i_k^t, \ldots i_k^{t-t_{\max}})$$

If a path starts at source block b_0 and passes through $b_1, \ldots, b_{n-1}$ to the target b_n, the timed condition for the complete path $p(b_0, b_n)$ is denoted by:

$$C\big(p(b_0, b_n)\big) = \bigwedge_{i=1}^{n-1} c(b_i, b_{i-1}, b_{i+1})^{t-t_i}$$

As described above, each atomic path condition applies to the connecting signals between two neighboring blocks and not to the complete set of input and output signals. Intersecting paths through the same *routing* block therefore create different sets of conditions.

4.4   Computation of Timed Path Conditions

In this section, we describe our approach to compute timed path conditions for Simulink models. As mentioned above, we propose a two-step approach where we first identify all paths and collect all path conditions on each path, and then propagate all local control flow conditions backwards through the model in order to compute timed path conditions that solely depend on input variables. In the following, we first describe how we compute the set of all (potential) paths using a backwards depth-first search. Then, we explain how we determine timing dependencies and how we extract (local) path conditions for each path. Finally, we present our approach for the backward propagation of the local path conditions to achieve the final timed path conditions that solely depend on input variables. We illustrate each step using our running example from Sect. 4.1.

Finding Paths. In the first step, we identify *all* potential paths between the model inports I and outports O. This is a first step to make it possible to analyze *confidentiality* of data as well as *integrity* of the model functionality, as data flowing *to* and *from* inappropriate sources can be detected (see Sect. 2.3). In order to find all paths $P(i_k, o_l)$, we traverse the model from o_l recursively.

Our path detection starts the model traversal with a given outport block o_l and implements a *depth-first* recursive search for all paths i_k to o_l while marking already visited blocks. This makes it possible to detect cycles along paths throughout the model. After completion of the path detection, the sets $P(i, o) \mid (i \in I, o \in O)$ contain all paths from all input and output ports and can be analyzed further.

Running Example. The results of the first step of our algorithm, the sets $P(i, o)$ of our example, are shown in Fig. 2.

$$P(i_1, o_1) = \{\langle i_1, o_1 \rangle\}$$
$$P(i_2, o_1) = P(i_3, o_1) = \varnothing$$
$$P(i_1, o_2) = \{\langle i_1, \texttt{comp\_conf}, \texttt{conf\_out}, o_2 \rangle, \langle i_1, \texttt{mode\_switch}, \texttt{Mem}, \texttt{conf\_out}, o_2 \rangle\}$$
$$P(i_2, o_2) = \{\langle i_2, \texttt{mode\_switch}, \texttt{Mem}, \texttt{conf\_out}, o_2 \rangle\}$$
$$P(i_3, o_2) = \{\langle i_3, \texttt{conf\_out}, \texttt{Mem}, \texttt{mode\_switch}, o_2 \rangle\}$$
$$P(i_1, o_3) = \{\langle i_1, \texttt{compare\_public}, \texttt{pub\_out}, o_3 \rangle, \langle i_1, \texttt{mode\_switch}, \texttt{Mem}, \texttt{pub\_out}, o_3 \rangle\}$$
$$P(i_2, o_3) = \{\langle i_2, \texttt{mode\_switch}, \texttt{Mem}, \texttt{pub\_out}, o_3 \rangle\}$$
$$P(i_3, o_3) = \{\langle i_3, \texttt{mode\_switch}, \texttt{Mem}, \texttt{pub\_out}, o_3 \rangle\}$$

Fig. 2. Detected paths through the model

Identifying Timing Dependencies. With the complete set of paths between all model inports and outports, the next step in our analysis is the determination of the timing dependencies on each path $p(i_k, o_l)$. Three different cases can occur:

(1) Untimed: The path neither contains time-dependent model elements nor is part of a feedback loop. (2) Fixed-Delay: The path contains time-dependent model elements but is not part of a feedback loop. (3) Feedback loop: The path is part of a feedback loop.

To compute the timing dependencies for a given set of paths, we iterate over each path and analyze it regarding time-dependent model elements and their parameters. If no timed element is found and the path is not part of a feedback loop, the untimed dependency relation $o_l^t = d(i_k^t)$ is established.

If the path is not part of a feedback loop but time-dependent model elements are encountered along the path during the iteration, a fixed-delay relation can be established and type and parameters of the blocks decide its magnitude. As explained above, we only consider discretely timed models with a fixed simulation step size so far. The behavior of a `Delay`, `UnitDelay` and a `Mem` block is therefore similar. Each time a `Mem` block is encountered, the magnitude of the fixed delay for the current path is increased by 1. When encountering a `Delay` block, after confirming the correct sampling time, its `DelayLength` parameter is read and added to the delay magnitude m of the current path, which yields $o_l^t = d(i_k^{t-m})$.

A path that is part of a feedback loop presents an *infinite* delay relation.

Running Example. The result of the application of this step to our running example is shown in Table 1. As illustrated, information from the data inputs does never arrive at the outputs in the same time slice, as there are no paths between i_{2t}, i_{3t} and o_{2t}, o_{3t}. Only information from the previous time slice arrives at the outports. This also presents an indicator for the existence of a security violation between the confidential data input and the public data output. At each time t, confidential information from the previous time slice $t-1$ is still held inside the system and is released in case of a change in mode of operation in the form of a spike. Note that we use the index c to denote indirect information flow through the control signal of routing blocks [1].

Table 1. Timing relations between ports of our shared buffer example

	i_1^t	i_1^{t-1}	i_2^t	i_2^{t-1}	i_3^t	i_3^{t-1}
o_1^t	$p(i_1^t, o_1^t)$	$\varnothing$	$\varnothing$	$\varnothing$	$\varnothing$	$\varnothing$
o_2^t	$p(i_1^t, o_2^t)_c$	$p(i_1^{t-1}, o_2^t)_c$	$\varnothing$	$p(i_2^{t-1}, o_2^t)$	$\varnothing$	$p(i_3^{t-1}, o_2^t)$
o_3^t	$p(i_1^t, o_3^t)_c$	$p(i_1^{t-1}, o_3^t)_c$	$\varnothing$	$p(i_2^{t-1}, o_3^t)$	$\varnothing$	$p(i_3^{t-1}, o_3^t)$

Extracting Path Conditions. After the identification of timing dependencies, in the next step of our analysis, we extract the conditions necessary for information to flow along paths. These conditions are dependent on the type of the block and its semantics. While it is *true* for blocks from the functionality and timing categories, routing blocks are analyzed further to extract their behavior. Thus, we iterate over each path in $P(I, O)$ to check for the existence of routing blocks and create a set $C\big(p(i_k^{t-c}, o_l^t)\big)$ that holds the extracted conditions. If a routing block b_r in time slice $t - d$ with inputs $s_{ctrl}, s_1, \ldots, s_n$, output s_{out} and neighboring blocks b_l and b_o is found, the necessary condition for the current path is extracted and saved for later analysis by the constraint solving tool. The condition is formed depending on the type of the encountered routing block.

Running Example. The goal of our running example, presented in Sect. 4.1, is to prove whether there is information flow between the confidential inport and the public outport. In the face of multiple routing blocks and a time-dependent model element, we will only consider one path in this example application of our approach: $p(i_2^{t-1}, o_3^t)$. After this step, the set of path conditions on this path is:

$$C\big(p(i_2^{t-1}, o_3^t)\big) = \big\{ s_{ctrl}(\texttt{pub\_out})^t \neq 0, s_{ctrl}(\texttt{mode\_switch})^{t-1} == 1 \big\}$$

Backward Propagation of Path Conditions. As shown above, a single condition is extracted for each routing block on each path. However, as these individual conditions only contain local information about a single control signal, we propagate these control flow signals backwards to the inports of the model. This requires to take the functionalities of each block between the control signal and the inports into account. It elevates the local information about control signals in path conditions to model-wide conditions for information flow, which solely depend on input signals. To accomplish this, we analyze each control signal separately and iterate over each path from the signal to its drivers while collecting the functionality of each block. We denote the resulting dependencies as:

$$s_{ctrl}(b_r) = d(i_1^t, \ldots, i_1^{t-t_{\max}}, \ldots, i_j^{t-t_{\max}}, \ldots, i_j^{t-t_{\max}})$$

For a single block b_l, we define its functionality as $s_o(b_l) = f_{b_l}(s_{i_1}, \ldots, s_{i_n})$. When considering a complete path $p(b_1, b_n)$, the resulting function f_p is formed by the composition of each output function along the path according to its structural connections. For example, a linear chain of blocks yields:

$$f_p := f_{b_1} \circ f_{b_2} \circ \ldots \circ f_{b_n}$$

Note that for each block type, a specific set of parameters is extracted and its resulting functionality is recorded. We currently support the following block types on control paths: `Bias`, `Gain`, `Abs`, `Compare`, `Add`, `Product`.

While we support untimed and fixed-delay timing relations over control paths, i.e., the existence of multiple time slices along these paths, we presently do not support feedback loops inside control flow paths, as no conclusion can be drawn under these circumstances. We plan to extend our approach with feedback loops and support for additional block types in control flow paths in future work.

Running Example. Using the previously created set of path conditions $C(i_2^{t-1}, o_3^t)$ as an input, this step of our analysis propagates the local path conditions of the routing blocks backwards and collects the functionality of each block along these paths. The model inports driving the control signals in C can be found in the first row of Table 1. There, untimed dependencies between i_1, the mode of operation and o_2^t as well as o_3^t leading through the control signals of the routing blocks can be found and the paths between the control signal and the inport i_1 are identified:

$$p(i_1^t, s_{ctrl}(\texttt{mode\_switch})) = \{i_1^{t-1}\}$$
$$p(i_1^t, s_{ctrl}(\texttt{pub\_out})) = \{\texttt{compare\_public}, i_1^t\}$$

Subsequently, we need to record the functionality of each block along these paths. The first path presents the trivial case that the control signal is directly connected to the inport of the model, we can therefore note its function as:

$$s_{ctrl}(\texttt{mode\_switch}) = f_{Inport}(i_1^{t-1}) = i_1^{t-1}$$

When collecting the functionality of the second path, we encounter a Compare block with a Const value of 2, which we translate into the following function:

$$s_{ctrl}(\texttt{pub\_out}) = f_{Compare} \circ f_{Inport}(i_1^t) = i_1^t == 2$$

With both extracted control flow relations, we have raised the scope of the path conditions from routing block-local to model-wide as path conditions are now presented as directly depending on a set of model inputs instead of local signals.

$$C\big(p(o_3^t, i_2^{t-1})\big) = \{(i_1^t == 2) \neq 0, i_1^{t-1} == 1\}$$

Translating and Solving Path Conditions. We can analyze our timed path conditions, which are expressed by sets of constraints, using a constraint solver. We chose a format that resembles a set of constraints on signals. To translate this representation into a set of constraints, we first declare all encountered signals as decision variables, then to extract each condition as a constraint on the signals. Finally, the solver is instructed to find an assignment to the decision variables that does not violate any constraints. If such an assignment can be found, we can conclude that the extracted conditions along the path overlap and there is indeed the possibility for information flow. If the constraint system is unsatisfiable, the path conditions prohibit information flow.

Running Example. The result from translating the path conditions extracted in the previous step into a constraint system is shown in Listing 1.1. Decision variables are declared first, then the two conditions extracted from the routing blocks along the path are shown. When solving the constraint system, we conclude that it is in fact satisfiable due to the timing annotation at the input signal i_1, allowing for information to flow from confidential to public signals.

```
1  % path condition variables
2  var int: i_1_t;
3  var int: i_1_t_sub_1;
4  % path conditions as depending on i_1
5  constraint (i_1_t == 2) != false;
6  constraint i_1_t_sub_1 == 1;
7  % find valid assignment
8  solve satisfy;
```

Listing 1.1. The translated constraint system

5   Evaluation

To evaluate our approach, we have implemented the analysis described above in Java. Our implementation uses an existing Simulink model parser originally developed for the *Methods of Model Quality* (MeMo) project [8]. We made our computation and implementation accessible via an Eclipse plug-in. While in its current state, our backward propagation algorithm only supports a small subset of simple blocks, we are confident that it still can be applied to a broad range of practical examples as this part of our approach must only be applied to the part of the design that models control signals. As a CLP language, we chose MiniZinc [13] for its simplicity and the possibility to be translated into multiple solver back ends. As a back end, we utilize the Gecode [16] constraint solver.

Table 2 shows the results of our analysis of the running example. With a complexity linear to the size of the model, our algorithm extracts the timed path conditions and passes them to the constraint solver. As can be seen in the table, both the extraction of path conditions as well as the solving of each constraint file by Gecode is performed in under 100 ms.

For the two paths $p(i_2^{t-1}, o_2^t)$ and $p(i_3^{t-1}, o_3^t)$ connecting the confidential and public inputs with their respective outputs, the satisfiable constraint system shows that their path conditions overlap and information flow is therefore possible. Additionally, their timing relation shows that information fed into the system at time t exits the corresponding output in the next time slice.

The constraint systems created for the two paths $p(i_2^{t-1}, o_3^t)$ and $p(i_3^{t-1}, o_2^t)$, on which confidential information crosses to the public output and vice versa, are satisfiable and therefore show that although the designer intended to use the

Table 2. Evaluation results

Path	Constraints	Sat	Time	
			Extraction	Solver
$p(i_1^t, o_1^t)$	$\varnothing$	-	73 ms	-
$p(i_2^{t-1}, o_2^t)$	$\{i_1^{t-1} == 1, (i_1^t == 1) \neq 0\}$	✓		38 ms
$p(i_2^{t-1}, o_3^t)$	$\{i_1^{t-1} == 1, (i_1^t == 2) \neq 0\}$	✓		29 ms
$p(i_3^{t-1}, o_2^t)$	$\{i_1^{t-1} == 2, (i_1^t == 1) \neq 0\}$	✓		27 ms
$p(i_3^{t-1}, o_3^t)$	$\{i_1^{t-1} == 2, (i_1^t == 2) \neq 0\}$	✓		33 ms

operation mode to ensure non-interference, information flow does indeed occur whenever the operation mode is changed. The security policy of non-interference between the confidential and public data flows is therefore violated.

6 Conclusion

In this paper, we have presented an approach to extract *timed path conditions* from Simulink models. These conditions can be used to reduce model complexity and as an IFA tool to argue about the existence of paths between arbitrary blocks in a model. We have shown how we find paths between inputs and outputs to the model and how we determine timing dependencies of signals along these paths. Further, we have demonstrated how we extract conditions from routing blocks on paths and how we identify control flow relations between blocks to be able to draw conclusions about the existence of paths using a constraint solving tool. Using the example of a shared buffer for confidential as well as public data, we have demonstrated the usability of our approach in the context of an IFA. Thereby, we have shown how timed path conditions can be used to both detect as well as rule out security policy violations.

To increase the precision of our approach, we are planning to extend its functionality to include more parts of the Simulink design library, such as `IndexVector` and `Selector` blocks to support non-scalar signals. Furthermore, we see high potential to increase the width of our approach by supporting State-flow [11], an extension to Simulink with functionality and semantics similar to state machines. Stateflow is widely-used to model control logic within Simulink, i.e., to drive the control signals of routing blocks within the model. Finally, we aim at extending our approach to support more Simulink-specific features used in industrial applications, such as bit-precise variable modifications and the TargetLink block set [2] used in the development of implementation-level Simulink models.

References

1. Denning, D.E., Denning, P.J.: Certification of programs for secure information flow. Commun. ACM **20**, 504–513 (1977)
2. dSpace: TargetLink Embedded Code Generator (2015). https://www.dspace.com
3. Goguen, J.A., Meseguer, J.: Security policies and security models. In: Symposium on Security and Privacy. IEEE (1982)
4. Halbwachs, N., Caspi, P., Raymond, P., Pilaud, D.: The synchronous data flow programming language LUSTRE. Proc. IEEE **79**, 1305–1320 (1991)
5. Hammer, C., Krinke, J., Snelting, G.: Information flow control for java based on path conditions in dependence graphs. In: International Symposium on Secure Software Engineering. IEEE (2006)
6. Hammer, C., Schaade, R., Snelting, G.: Static path conditions for Java. In: Workshop on Programming Languages and Analysis for Security. ACM (2008)
7. Herber, P., Reicherdt, R., Bittner, P.: Bit-precise formal verification of discrete-time MATLAB/Simulink models using SMT solving. In: EMSOFT (2013)

8. Hu, W., Wegener, J., Stürmer, I., Reicherdt, R., Salecker, E., Glesner, S.: MeMo-methods of model quality. In: MBEES (2011)
9. King, J.C.: Symbolic execution and program testing. ACM Commun. **19**, 385–394 (1976)
10. Krinke, J., Snelting, G.: Validation of measurement software as an application of slicing and constraint solving. Inf. Softw. Technol. **40**, 661–675 (1998)
11. MathWorks: MATLAB/Simulink (2015). www.mathworks.com/products/simulink
12. Messaoud, S.: Translating discrete time Simulink to SIGNAL. Ph.D. thesis, Virginia Tech (2014)
13. NICTA: The MiniZinc Constraint Programming Language (2014). http://www.minizinc.org/
14. Reicherdt, R., Glesner, S.: Slicing MATLAB/Simulink models. In: ICSE. IEEE (2012)
15. Sabelfeld, A., Myers, A.C.: Language-based information-flow security. IEEE J. Sel. Areas Commun. **21**, 5–19 (2003)
16. Schulte, C., Lagerkvist, M., Tack, G.: Gecode: generic constraint development environment. In: INFORMS Annual Meeting (2009)
17. Tripakis, S., Sofronis, C., Caspi, P., Curic, A.: Translating discrete-time Simulink to Lustre. ACM Trans. Embed. Comput. Syst. (TECS) **4**, 779–818 (2005)
18. Whalen, M.W., Hardin, D., Wagner, L.G.: Model checking information flow. In: Hardin, D. (ed.) Design and Verification of Microprocessor Systems for High-Assurance Applications. Springer, Boston (2010). https://doi.org/10.1007/978-1-4419-1539-9_13

Structural Contracts – Motivating Contracts to Ensure Extra-Functional Semantics

Gregor Nitsche[1](✉) (iD), Ralph Görgen[1], Kim Grüttner[1], and Wolfgang Nebel[1,2]

[1] OFFIS – Institute for Information Technology, 26121 Oldenburg, Germany
{nitsche,goergen,gruettner,nebel}@offis.de
[2] Carl von Ossietzky University Oldenburg, 26121 Oldenburg, Germany

Abstract. In our work we aim at a composable and consistent specification and verification of *contracts* for *extra-functional* properties, such as power consumption or temperature. To this end, a necessary precondition for the semantical correctness of such properties is to ensure the structurally correct modeling of their interdependences.

While this can be solved by a tailoring of the *Component Based Design (CmpBD)* frameworks, the resulting design constraints are specific to tools and viewpoints, not being sufficiently configurable for the designers. To solve this problem within the contract framework, *Contract Based Design (CBD)* with explicit port variables provides also no configurable but sound methodology for structurally relating the properties between different *components* and *views*. For that, we propose the idea of *structural contracts*. Using implicit *structural ports*, *structural guarantees* can be given according to the Component Based Design structure. Expressing structural design constraints by the means of *structural assumptions*, the CmpBD constraints can become part of the Contract Based Design framework and, thus, can be checked for compatibility and refinement.

As a result, structural contracts enable the contract based specification and verification of structural rules for the correct modeling of functional and extra-functional interdependences. Providing both, property specifications and Component Based Design constraints by contracts, the approach is flexible and sound.

Keywords: Contracts · Contract based design · Components
Component based design · Compositionality · Composability
Compatibility · Structure · Extra-functional · View · Aspect · Type
Semantics

1 Introduction

Following the increasing opportunities to integrate more functionality and improved performance in today's integrated microelectronic systems has lead

This work is supported by the ANCONA Project, funded by the German Federal Ministry of Research and Education (BMBF) under Grant Agreement 16ES021.

M. Götz et al. (Eds.): IESS 2015, IFIP AICT 523, pp. 77–87, 2017.
https://doi.org/10.1007/978-3-319-90023-0_7

to continuously growing design complexity and an increasing number and heterogeneity of design requirements. As a result, the specification, modeling and verification of such heterogeneous systems became a challenging task, requiring a reliable collaboration of specialists from different design and verification domains.

Following the paradigms of *encapsulation, divide and conquer* and *separation of concerns* the concepts of *components* and *viewpoints* have been introduced to master design complexity by *Component Based Design (CmpBD)* [9]. Commonly a component is considered to be a design element, which internally encapsulates its behavior, solely restricting its interaction with the environment to its well-defined *port interface*. Hence, a main precondition of Component Based Design is the components' behaviors to be *compositional*. That means, that for each point of time the interaction between connected components is clearly determined by solely one of the components, controlling the information exchange across this connection without being affected by undelayed influence from the environment.

Additionally, considering the further refinement and implementation of *subcomponents* to proceed independently, the *compatibility* of connected ports has to be ensured. To this end, *type systems* [6] are applied, to declare the *type* of the components' ports and to verify that connected ports have compatible types. Beyond the most common notion of untimed *static types*, such as *boolean, integer* etc., *Contract Based Design (CBD)* [3,11] enables a more dynamic notion of compatibility. By the means of the *contracts' assumptions* A all acceptable inputs of the components M are formally described by *timed traces*, declaring interconnections incompatible if the corresponding *environment* E is allowed to provide a timed sequence of outputs which violates the components' assumptions. Differently, when the assumptions are satisfied, the components provide outputs according to the *guarantee* G, which correspond to the satisfied assumption.

Nevertheless, static type and *compatibility checking* of contracts is not flexible enough to be applicable for the consistent specification and verification of the interactions between the properties from multiple *extra-functional* viewpoints, largely comprising physical properties w. r. t. power or temperature etc. Differently, a more flexible declaration of designer-defined types would be necessary, to allow for complex, derived and configurable types, which appropriately combine the value and time semantics of the ports with a viewpoint-specific physical interpretation, such as 'average power consumption per operation in μW'.

Considering viewpoint-specific models of a heterogeneous (multi-viewpoint) component to be viewpoint-specific components themselves, we assume that a sufficiently flexible but sound declaration and verification of designer-defined types can be achieved by extending the compatibility criteria of contracts to also structural properties, which constrain the basic design elements of the decomposition, such as the identifiers of components and ports. Since Contract Based Design allows contracts to constrain only the explicitly declared ports of components we propose a first concept of *structural contracts*. Based on an *introspection* of the component structure we implicitly instantiate a *decomposition component* plus *structural ports* and *structural nets*, to enable the contract based *reflection* of the component structure via these explicit ports. As a result, the usage of *structural assumptions* allows us to systematically constrain the instantiation and connection of subcomponents based on their component and port names.

To motivate our idea of structural contracts, Sect. 2 explains an artificial example, for which the extra-functional failure of the design becomes hidden – i.e. erroneously not visible – because of a semantically incorrect connection of extra-functional ports. Next, in Sect. 3 we summarize the related work, before we introduce the formal basics of components and contracts in Sect. 4. In Sect. 5 we present our approach of structural contracts based on the introspection, component extension and contract based reflection of the component structure. Then, in Sect. 6 we outline a first proof of concept, using our initial example to successfully invalidate the previously hidden false negative verification using structural contracts. In Sect. 7 we conclude and give an outlook to future work.

2   Motivating Example

To motivate structural contracts we consider the simplified, artificial example of a composed component M given in Fig. 1, which is specified to hold an average power consumption of at maximum $20\mu W$. The component has one functional *input port* x_0, indicating two different operating modes, and one extra-functional *output port* y_p, denoting the average power consumption per clock cycle.

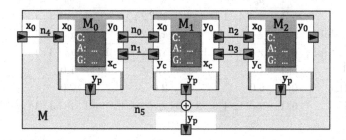

Fig. 1. Motivating example, composing a component M from subcomponents M_i, connecting their inputs $x_{(.)}$ resp. outputs $y_{(.)}$ from multiple extra-functional viewpoints (functional, capacitive load and power) by interconnecting nets $n_{(.)}$ to evaluate the composed system's power consumption.

Refining M by a composition of three different subcomponents, the subcomponents are M_0, M_1 and M_2, with all of them having one functional input x_0 and one functional output y_0, decoding their operating mode in one bit. Moreover, for the purpose of calculating the power consumption, the subcomponents provide inputs x_c and outputs y_c, which describe the components' input or load capacitance $\overline{C}_{sw}^{\ell}$, responsible for consuming a certain amount of power during the interaction of both components. Of course, in addition to that, each component consumes also an internal amount of power, based on the internally switched capacitance $\overline{C}_{sw}^{i}$. For simplification, the example contains no further ports for the supply voltage V_{DD} or clock frequency f_{clk}, considering both of them to be constant at $V_{DD} = 1.0\text{V}$ and $f_{clk} = 2.0\,\text{MHz}$ for components M_1 and M_2 and $M_0.V_{DD} = 1.0\text{V}$ and $M_0.f_{clk} = 6.0\,\text{MHz}$ for component M_0. Above that, following $\overline{P} = \frac{1}{2}V_{DD}^2 f_{clk}\overline{C}_{sw}$ the average power consumption $y_p = \overline{P}$ depends on the average switched capacitance $\overline{C}_{sw} = \overline{C}_{sw}^{i} + \overline{C}_{sw}^{\ell}$, internally resp. externally switched according to the functional activity of the component. Appropriately to these specifications, Table 1 outlines the functional and extra-functional behavior of the components w. r. t. their input resp. output ports. For example, the switched capacitance of M_1 is 3pF for $M.x_0 = 1$. This is because of $\overline{C}_{sw}^{i} = 2$ and $M_1.x_c = M_2.y_c = \overline{C}_{sw}^{\ell} = 1$, following from exchanging the functional and extra-functional information according to the interconnection of Fig. 1, so that $M_0.x_0 = 1$, $M_1.x_0 = 1$ and $M_2.x_0 = 0$. As a result of this evaluation, the given composition of M finally does not hold the specification of an average power consumption of at maximum $20\mu\text{W}$, consuming $23\mu\text{W}$ for the case of $M.x_0 = 1$.

Table 1. Overview of the example's functional and extra-functional component characteristics, which belong to the functional, capacitive load and power viewpoints. To consider the dependency on the functional inputs the expression $(x_0 ? a : b)$ shall logically denote $(x_0 \rightarrow a) \wedge (\neg x_0 \rightarrow b)$.

Viewpoint	$M.x_0$	M_0	M_1	M_2	$M.y_p$
fct	0/1	$y_0 = x_0$	$y_0 = \neg x_0$	$y_0 = x_0$	
$\overline{C}_{sw}^{i}\backslash[\text{pF}]$	0/1	$x_0 ? 4 : 1$	$x_0 ? 2 : 1$	$x_0 ? 3 : 1$	
$y_c = \overline{C}_{sw}^{\ell}\backslash[\text{pF}]$	0/1	–	$x_0 ? 2 : 1$	$x_0 ? 1 : 1$	
$\overline{C}_{sw}^{i} + \overline{C}_{sw}^{\ell}\backslash[\text{pF}]$	0/1	$x_0 ? 4 + 2 : 1 + 1$	$x_0 ? 2 + 1 : 1 + 1$	$x_0 ? 3 : 1$	
$V_{DD}\backslash[\text{V}]$	0/1	1.0	1.0	1.0	
$f_{clk}\backslash[\text{MHz}]$	0/1	6.0	2.0	2.0	
$\overline{P}\backslash[\mu\text{W}]$	0/1	$x_0 ? 12 + 6 : 3 + 3$	$x_0 ? 2 + 1 : 1 + 1$	$x_0 ? 3 : 1$	$x_0 ? 23 : 10$

Contrary to this, the same calculation of the power consumption asserts 'valid' when during *refinement* the following – semantically inconsistent – connection error occurs as given in Fig. 2. Refining M with n_6 and n_7 instead of n_1 and n_3, the externally switched capacitances $M_0.y_0$ and $M_1.y_0$ are interchanged, leading to the erroneous power calculation $M.y_0 = (x_0 ? 20 : 11)$ in Table 2.

Erroneously refining M with n_6 and n_7 instead of n_1 and n_3, the semantical meaning of the capacitive loads, corresponding to the real worlds functional interconnections n_0 and n_2 gets violated. Without the possibility of strictly relating these ports by some concepts of derived complex types, such – and similar – semantic errors can easily remain unrevealed. As a solution to this, we propose structural contracts, to allow the designers to add *composition constraints*, and an introspection and reflection of the component structure, making the *structural decomposition* part of the contract-based specification and verification approach.

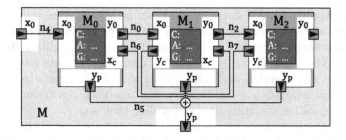

Fig. 2. Erroneous composition resp. refinement of M from the same subcomponents M_i, introducing semantically false connections n_6 and n_7 instead of n_1 and n_3, which violate the physical semantics of allocating the capacitive loads in correspondence with the real worlds functional interconnections n_0 and n_2, falsely verifying $M.\overline{P} < 20\mu W$.

Table 2. Extra-functional characteristics of the erroneously refined example, leading to a false negative verification of the power consumption, satisfying $M.\overline{P} < 20\mu W$.

Viewpoint	$M.x_0$	M_0	M_1	M_2	$M.y_p$
$\overline{C}_{sw}^i + \overline{C}_{sw}^e \backslash [\text{pF}]$	0/1	$x_0 ? 4 + 1 : 1 + 1$	$x_0 ? 2 + 2 : 1 + 1$	$x_0 ? 3 : 1$	
$V_{DD} \backslash [\text{V}]$	0/1	1.0	1.0	1.0	
$f_{clk} \backslash [\text{MHz}]$	0/1	6.0	2.0	2.0	
$\overline{P} \backslash [\mu W]$	0/1	$x_0 ? 12 + 3 : 3 + 3$	$x_0 ? 2 + 2 : 1 + 1$	$x_0 ? 3 : 1$	$x_0 ? 20 : 11$

3   Related Work

Considering the related work – to the authors' best knowledge – no other work aims at ensuring the *semantical consistency* of different components and viewpoints – i.e. a verifiable but flexible type system with complex, designer-defined types – by a contract based formulation of constraints for the logical decomposition structure.

The probably most common approach to support semantical consistency and compatibility would be to provide only a limited set of fixed types of components and ports resp. *design rules*, which are defined and checked by the component based design framework. While this *tailoring* may support complex type systems, as e. g. the polymorphic and *structured types* [12] in *Ptolemy II*, it lacks flexibility w. r. t. defining viewpoint-specific compatibility and refinement rules, meaning constraints on how these types can *bottom-up* be constructed resp. *top-down* refined, checking value-, causality- and time-aware construction rules.

In *interface theories* [1,2] the distinction between bottom-up components for *compositional abstraction* on the one hand, and top-down interfaces for *compositional design* on the other hand have lead to the general concepts of compatibility and refinement checking for component specifications using assumptions and guarantees. Applying timed languages to describe assumptions and guarantees, the contracts allow to specify and to verify the compatibility of the components' interaction protocols according to value and time resp. causality criteria. Nevertheless – while building the general foundation for contracts based design – without some introspection and reflection of the interface variables and their interconnection relations via additional ports, top-down constraints w. r. t. the logical decomposition structure are not possible that way.

Differently, to investigate and define behavioral types, in [4,5] the concepts of *glue operators* and *glue constraints* are defined for the *BIP (behavior, interaction, priority) framework*. Providing connectors with priorities and their own memoryless behavior the interaction between components connected by a connector can appropriately be synchronized w. r. t. to some timed or untimed causality relation. Hence, again compatibility is meant only in the sense of interaction protocols, not concerning extra-functional semantics of e. g. different viewpoints.

4   Formal Basics

As given in Fig. 1, Component Based Design allows to structurally compose the behavior of higher level components M from instantiating lower level subcomponents $M_i \in M_M^* = \{M_0, \ldots, M_j\}$, $j \in \mathbb{N}$. These subcomponents' behaviors can interact via the directed ports of the components' interface declaration $p_i \in \bigcup_m \chi_m$, $\chi_m = \chi_m^{in} \cup \chi_m^{out}$, $m \in \{M\} \cup M_M^*$. Its input ports are given by $x_i \in \chi_m^{in} = \{x_0, \ldots, x_j\}$, $j \in \mathbb{N}$ and its output ports are given by $y_i \in \chi_m^{out} = \{y_0, \ldots, y_j\}$, $j \in \mathbb{N}$. Their interconnection is denoted by directed nets $n_i = (p_{src}, p_{snk}) \in N_M = N_M^A \cup N_M^D = \{n_0, \ldots, n_j\}$, $j \in \mathbb{N}$. Among these, the *assembly nets* $n_i \in N_M^A = \{n_i | (p_{src} \in \chi_{M_M^*}^{out}) \wedge (p_{snk} \in \chi_{M_M^*}^{in})\}$ denote the connections between the different subcomponents M_M^* of M. In contrast, the *delegation nets* $n_i \in N_M^D = \{n_i | ((p_{src} \in \chi_M^{in}) \wedge (p_{snk} \in \chi_{M_M^*}^{in})) \vee ((p_{src} \in \chi_{M_M^*}^{out}) \wedge (p_{snk} \in \chi_M^{out}))\}$ denote the connections between subcomponents M_M^* and the composed component M. Assuming both, the behavior of the components as well as their communication, to be compositional, a top-down refinement resp. bottom-up *virtual integration* of the composed behavior becomes possible, reducing the design complexity by a – possibly hierarchical – structural decomposition.

Hence, we consider a component M as $M = (tp(M), \chi_M, S_M, D_M, B_M)$, with χ_M, S_M, D_M, B_M being tuples or sets and $tp(M)$ denoting a function to resolve the component's type name. For the top-level of a decomposition the type $tp(M) = `M`$ is also considered to represent the component's instance name, normally given by $id(M_i) = `M_i`$ for the lower levels of a decomposition. Similar to the notation in Sect. 2, the component's port interface is defined by the set $\chi_M = \chi_M^{in} \cup \chi_M^{out}$ of input ports $x_i \in \chi_M^{in}$ and output ports $y_i \in \chi_M^{out}$. Besides a function $id(\cdot)$ to resolve a port's name, the declaration of each port $(\cdot)$ defines also functions $\nu(\cdot)$ to resolve its *value domain* – e. g. boolean or integer – and $dir(\cdot) \in \{in, out\}$ to resolve its *direction* as input resp. output.

Using an extended linear temporal logic, contracts $C_i := (A_i, G_i)$ are used, to formally specify the assumptions A_i of a component M w. r. t. the timed behavior of its environment E, combined with its guarantees G_i, provided for the case that the corresponding assumptions A_i are satisfied. To this end, the assumptions describe expressions, which observe (read) only the *input* variables, while the guarantees are expressions, which control (write) only the *output* variables. Semantically, both expressions are interpreted as sets $[\![A]\!]$ resp. $[\![G]\!]$ of timed traces s_{x_i} resp. s_{y_i} with $[\![A]\!] = \{(s_{x_0},\ldots,s_{x_j})|(\bigcup_{i=0}^{j} x_i = \chi_M^{in}) \wedge ([\![A]\!] \models A)\}$, $[\![G]\!] = \{(s_{y_0},\ldots,s_{y_j})|(\bigcup_{i=0}^{j} y_i = \chi_M^{out}) \wedge ([\![G]\!] \models G)\}$, satisfying the corresponding assertions A resp. G, and with $s_{x_i} = \{e_0(x_i), e_1(x_i)\ldots\}$ resp. $s_{y_i} = \{e_0(y_i), e_1(y_i)\ldots\}$ describing the timed traces of x_i resp. y_i as possibly infinite sequences of *events* $e_\iota(x_i) = (v(x_i), t_\iota)$ resp. $e_\iota(y_i) = (v(y_i), t_\iota)$ with variable value $v(x_i) \in \nu(x_i)$ resp. $v(y_i) \in \nu(y_i)$, time $t_\iota : (t_\iota \in \mathbb{R}_0^+) \vee (t_\iota \in \mathbb{N})$ and $\iota \in \mathbb{N}_0^+$. Using the contracts' *saturated* interpretation $(A_i \to G_i')$, with $G_i' := (A_i' \to G_i)$ and $A_i' \subseteq A_i$, compositional assume/guarantee reasoning becomes possible to prove the compatibility and refinement within a component based decomposition.

Thus, we provide the component's contract based *specification* $S_M = \bigcup_i C_i$, which we onwards denote as behavioral specification. Accordingly, B_M describes the corresponding behavioral implementation, e.g. given as an executable program, automata or formula. Furthermore, the tuple $D_M = (M_M^*, N_M)$ describes the component's structural decomposition, either for the purpose of a structural top-down refinement of the initial specification as well as for the structural bottom-up *implementation* by instantiation and *integration* of available components. Finally, the norm $|\cdot|$ shall for all sets denote their number of elements and, if necessary for unambiguousness, we prefix identifiers and symbols by component identifiers M or M_i, using a dot as delimiter, as e.g. $M_0.C_0$, $M_1.C_0$, etc. For simplicity we identify components, contracts and ports by names equal to their symbols, so that $id(M) = 'M'$, $id(M_i) = 'M_i'$, $id(x_i) = 'x_i'$, $id(y_i) = 'y_i'$ etc.

5 Structural Contracts

In general, being based on interface theories, Contract Based Design is limited to such specifications S_M, declaring only the externally observable 'behavioral properties' of the component – meaning 'behavioral' in that sense, that its properties refer only to the components' explicitly declared ports. Differently, the component's inherently contained 'structural properties' can neither be specified nor verified that way – meaning 'structural' not necessarily w.r.t. the physical but w.r.t. the logical structure, such as available ports, the instantiated subcomponents or the interconnection of a structural decomposition D_M etc. As a solution, we suggest an introspection and reflection of these structural properties to introduce a structural point of view, enabling for structural contracts. According to the interface declaration $(\chi_M^{in}, \chi_M^{out})$ and the formal decomposition D_M we extract the available structural information and systematically add an implicit interface χ_M^{struc} of structural ports, which provide explicit access to the structural information. As a result, the component's decomposition structure becomes specifiable and verifiable via contract based constraints for its original interface declaration, structural decomposition resp. the instantiation and integration of the component within a hierarchical composition.

To explain our approach in detail, we follow its sequential steps according to:

1. extract structural information
2. build structural data types
3. insert introspection ports

4. add introspection components
5. add introspection subnets
6. add *structural guarantee*

First, the components' structural information $(tp(M), \chi_M, S_M, D_M, B_M)$ are derived from the component model, to build the data structure of M according to Sect. 4. In the second step – to avoid complete string analysis for the first approach – we generate *structural data types* according to the following enumerations:

dt_cId : set of all components identifiers $tp(M)$ and $id(M_i) \; \forall M_i \in M_M^*$
plus one additional 'open' symbol to denote ports without a connection

dt_pId : set of all port identifiers $id(p_i) \in \chi_m$ of M and $M_i \in M_M^*$
plus one additional 'open' symbol to denote ports without a connection

Based on these structural data types, we then introduce the structural introspection ports according to Fig. 3. That is, for each port $p_i \in \chi_{M_i}$ of each subcomponent $M_i \in M_M^*$ of the decomposition D_M two additional input ports of type dt_cId resp. dt_pId are added. For each input port $p_i = x_i \in \chi_{M_i}^{in}$ the ports are named $M_i.id(x_i)\_cSrc$ and $M_i.id(x_i)\_pSrc$ resp. $M_i.id(y_i)\_cSnk$ and $M_i.id(y_i)\_pSnk$ for each output port $p_i = y_i \in \chi_{M_i}^{out}$. Using these additional ports the components are enabled to receive information about the connections $n_i \in \{N_M, 'open'\}$ between their original ports, meaning the identifiers of the 'source component' and 'source port' resp. the 'sink component' and 'sink port' connected via the net n_i, resp. to receive 'open' if ports remained unconnected.

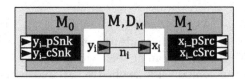

Fig. 3. Overview of the implicitly inserted structural introspection ports, extending the port interface of each subcomponent within a decomposition D_M of a component M.

In the fourth step, an additional introspection component M_{DM} is added to the decomposition structure – i.e. $M_M^* := M_M^* \cup M_{DM}$ – to reflect the component's structural information via the introspection ports. To this end, M_{DM} provides the structural output ports $M_{DM}.id(M_i.x_i)\_cSrc$, $M_{DM}.id(M_i.x_i)\_pSrc$, $M_{DM}.id(M_i.y_i)\_cSnk$ and $M_{DM}.id(M_i.y_i)\_pSnk$, building the corresponding counter part to the structural ports we introduced in step three.

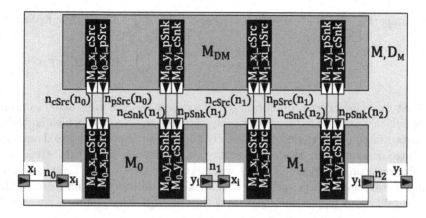

Fig. 4. Extension of a component's decomposition D_M by an introspection component M_{DM} and structural nets $n_{cSrc}(n_i)$, $n_{pSrc}(n_i)$, $n_{cSnk}(n_i)$, $n_{pSnk}(n_i)$, connecting the introspection component with the subcomponents.

In the fifth step, we complete the communication structure of the structural view according to Fig. 4, connecting the structural introspection ports of M_{DM} with the corresponding subcomponents $M_i \in M_M^*$. To this end, for all nets $n_i \in N_M$ additional subnets $N_{DM} = \bigcup_{n_i} n_{cSrc}(n_i) \cup \bigcup_{n_i} n_{pSrc}(n_i) \cup \bigcup_{n_i} n_{cSnk}(n_i) \cup \bigcup_{n_i} n_{pSnk}(n_i)$ are inserted to N_M, according to the following rules:

$$n_{cSrc}(n_i) = (M_{DM}.id(M_i.x_i)\_cSrc, M_i.id(M_i.x_i)\_cSrc),$$

$$n_{pSrc}(n_i) = (M_{DM}.id(M_i.x_i)\_pSrc, M_i.id(M_i.x_i)\_pSrc),$$

$$n_{cSnk}(n_i) = (M_{DM}.id(M_i.y_i)\_cSnk, M_i.id(M_i.y_i)\_cSnk),$$

$$n_{pSnk}(n_i) = (M_{DM}.id(M_i.y_i)\_pSnk, M_i.id(M_i.y_i)\_pSnk).$$

Finally, the introspection component M_{DM} is annotated with structural guarantees $C : ((A : true), (G : \langle struc\_port \rangle = \langle struc\_value \rangle))$, reflecting the information of the original component's interconnections with $struc\_value \in \nu(struc\_port)$ and:

$$struc\_port \in \bigcup_{x_i \in \chi_{M_i}^{in}} M_{DM}.id(M_i.x_i)\_cSrc \;\cup\; \bigcup_{x_i \in \chi_{M_i}^{in}} M_{DM}.id(M_i.x_i)\_pSrc$$

$$\cup \bigcup_{y_i \in \chi_{M_i}^{out}} M_{DM}.id(M_i.y_i)\_cSnk \;\cup\; \bigcup_{y_i \in \chi_{M_i}^{out}} M_{DM}.id(M_i.y_i)\_pSnk$$

Differently, for the subcomponents $M_i \in M_M^*$ the corresponding structural introspection ports allow to constrain the components' interconnections by structural assumptions $C : ((A : \langle struc\_port \rangle = \langle struc\_value^* \rangle), (G : true))$, with $struc\_value^* := \{\langle struc\_value \rangle | \langle struc\_port \rangle\}$, $struc\_value \in \nu(struc\_port)$ and:

$$struc\_port \in \quad \bigcup_{x_i \in \chi_{M_i}^{in}} M_i.id(M_i.x_i)\_cSrc \quad \cup \bigcup_{x_i \in \chi_{M_i}^{in}} M_i.id(M_i.x_i)\_pSrc$$

$$\cup \quad \bigcup_{y_i \in \chi_{M_i}^{out}} M_i.id(M_i.y_i)\_cSnk \quad \cup \bigcup_{y_i \in \chi_{M_i}^{out}} M_i.id(M_i.y_i)\_pSnk$$

That way, the structural information of a decomposition are treated as properties, which are provided from the compositional environment which embedds the instantiated components, consequently allowing for a contract based assume-guarantee reasoning in this structural view. Following from this, structural assumptions can be specified top-down, becoming part of the functional and extra-functional contracts and thus an additional validity constraints during the compatibility and refinement checking within multiple viewpoints.

6   Proof of Concept

For a first proof of concept, we evaluated our approach of structural contracts for the motivating example, outlined in Sect. 2. To this end, we implemented the component interfaces of M and its subcomponents M_0, M_1 and M_2 and provided them with contracts according to the functional and extra-functional properties given in Table 1. Based on this implementation we showed that structural contracts are able to reveal the false negative verification of the erroneous logical structure depicted in Fig. 2. Furthermore, we showed that for a correct structural decomposition our structural extension does not influence compatibility and refinement checking of the other functional and extra-functional properties. For the implementation and evaluation we used *OTHELLO (Object Temporal with Hybrid Expressions Linear-Time LOgic)* [8] for the specification of contracts and *OCRA (OTHELLO Contracts Refinement Analysis)* [7] to describe the components as *OSS (OCRA System Specification)* [7] and to check their compatibility and their refinement. To reproduce our study, our example is online available at [10].

7   Conclusion

Based on an artificial example we motivate the need for structural contracts and show how structural contracts increase the reliability of composed extra-functional multi-domain models. By the evaluation of the example we show that structural contracts can reveal failures in the logical composition structure, which otherwise remain hidden, enabling false negatives during extra-functional verification.

In the future work, we want to investigate the abstraction and refinement of our structural contracts and evaluate how structural contracts can be propagated throughout the design and abstraction hierarchies. Furthermore, we plan to examine if and which additional port annotations will become necessary enable this hierarchies and to allow for the seamless and composable integration of designer-defined extra-functional semantics based on structural contracts.

References

1. de Alfaro, L., Henzinger, T.: Interface-based design. In: Broy, M., Grünbauer, J., Harel, D., Hoare, T. (eds.) Engineering Theories of Software Intensive Systems, NATO Science Series, vol. 195. Springer, Netherlands (2005). https://doi.org/10.1007/1-4020-3532-2_3
2. de Alfaro, L., Henzinger, T.A.: Interface theories for component-based design. In: Henzinger, T.A., Kirsch, C.M. (eds.) EMSOFT 2001. LNCS, vol. 2211, pp. 148–165. Springer, Heidelberg (2001). https://doi.org/10.1007/3-540-45449-7_11
3. Benveniste, A., Caillaud, B., Nickovic, D., Passerone, R., Raclet, J.B., Reinkemeier, P., Sangiovanni-Vincentelli, A., Damm, W., Henzinger, T., Larsen, K.: Contracts for systems design. Technical Report RR-8147, Research Centre Rennes - Bretagne Atlantique, Rennes Cedex (2012)
4. Bliudze, S., Sifakis, J.: A notion of glue expressiveness for component-based systems. In: van Breugel, F., Chechik, M. (eds.) CONCUR 2008. LNCS, vol. 5201, pp. 508–522. Springer, Heidelberg (2008). https://doi.org/10.1007/978-3-540-85361-9_39
5. Bliudze, S., Sifakis, J.: Synthesizing glue operators from glue constraints for the construction of component-based systems. In: Apel, S., Jackson, E. (eds.) SC 2011. LNCS, vol. 6708, pp. 51–67. Springer, Heidelberg (2011). https://doi.org/10.1007/978-3-642-22045-6_4
6. Cardelli, L.: Type systems. ACM Comput. Surv. **28**(1), 263–264 (1996)
7. Cimatti, A., Dorigatti, M., Tonetta, S.: OCRA: a tool for checking the refinement of temporal contracts. In: 28th IEEE/ACM International Conference on Automated Software Engineering (ASE) (2013)
8. Cimatti, A., Roveri, M., Susi, A., Tonetta, S.: Validation of requirements for hybrid systems: a formal approach. ACM Trans. Softw. Eng. Methodol. (TOSEM) **21**(4), 22 (2012)
9. Lee, E.A., Sangiovanni-Vincentelli, A.L.: Component-based design for the future. In: Design, Automation & Test in Europe (DATE) (2011)
10. Nitsche, G.: Structural contracts - conceptual example in OCRA. https://vhome.offis.de/gnitsche/paper/iess2015/example/
11. Sangiovanni-Vincentelli, A., Damm, W., Passerone, R.: Taming Dr. frankenstein: contract-based design for cyber-physical systems. Eur. J. Control **18**(3), 217–238 (2012)
12. Zhao, Y., Xiong, Y., Lee, E.A., Liu, X., Zhong, L.C.: The design and application of structured types in Ptolemy ii. Int. J. Intell. Syst. **25**(2), 118–136 (2010)

Combining an Iterative State-Based Timing Analysis with a Refinement Checking Technique

Tayfun Gezgin, Björn Koopmann, and Achim Rettberg[✉]

Carl von Ossietzky University Oldenburg,
Ammerländer Heerstr. 114, 26121 Oldenburg, Germany
achim.rettberg@iess.org

Abstract. The analysis of real-time properties is crucial in safety critical areas like in automotive applications. Systems have to work in a timely manner to offer correct services. Most of the applications in this domain are distributed over several computation units, inter-connected by bus systems. In previous works we have introduced a state-based analysis approach to validate end-to-end deadlines for distributed systems. The approach is based on the computation of the state spaces of all resources, such as processors and buses, in an iterative fashion. For this, abstraction and composition operations were defined to adequately handle task and resource dependencies. During the design process of a system changes occur typically on both the specification and implementation level, such that already performed analyses of the system have to be repeated. In this work, we extend our timing analysis with a refinement checking approach, detail when it is appropriate to be used, and compare the analysis times with the computation times to perform the refinement check.

Keywords: Real-time systems · Scheduling analysis · Re-validation
Timing analysis · State-based timing analysis

1 Introduction

In recent years the co-operations and inter-connections between individual, geographically distributed systems heavily increased. Also in safety critical areas the significance of these topics increased. As an example, much effort has been invested in the development of Car-to-Car communications with the aim to increase the safety in traffic and optimize traffic flows. Another example is the dynamic partitioning of the airspace with respect to time investigated in the SESAR (Single European Sky ATM Research) program. The recent partitioning of the airspace is performed in a static manner with respect to time, i.e. the trajectories are not changed during the whole landing approach and the takeoff.

© IFIP International Federation for Information Processing 2017
Published by Springer International Publishing AG 2017. All Rights Reserved
M. Götz et al. (Eds.): IESS 2015, IFIP AICT 523, pp. 88–99, 2017.
https://doi.org/10.1007/978-3-319-90023-0_8

The shift to a dynamic partitioning, which is called 4D-trajectories, involves a much more intensive co-operation between the tower and each airplane.

For the correct functionality of safety-critical functions of such systems, timing constraints are one crucial aspect. The final product has to satisfy those constraints, as the violation of a requirement could result in high costs or even threats to human life. Nissan for example had to recall the vehicles of its premium segment cars due to some delays in the emergency program of their new steer-by-wire system. Such a problem could have been avoided, if an early analysis on timing constraints would have been performed. Unfortunately, many changes occur during the design process, such that already performed analyses have to be repeated. Our approach targets these problems.

In [1] we worked out a state-based approach for the analysis of timing properties. In analogy to model checking methods, we consider the full state space, where all task interleavings are preserved. In order to alleviate the problem of state space explosion due to state unfolding, the state space of an architecture is constructed in an iterative manner. Abstraction methods are applied to keep the interfaces between components as small as possible, while composition operations are used to combine a set of triggering sources of a component.

On top of this we worked out an impact analysis approach to minimize re-validation efforts of timing properties needed when the considered system is modified [2]. Adaptations of the architecture of an already existing and analyzed system could be for example the addition of new tasks that are allocated to the existing system. To minimize the effort of a re-validation, it is desirable to reuse the previous results of the analysis that did not change. With this, only the parts are re-validated, which were affected by the architectural changes.

This work is a consecutive extension of our previous work [2]. We illustrate the implementation of the impact analysis. We describe in which cases a refinement check can be applied to reduce the re-verification times when changes occur. We evaluate our approach by a set of test systems demonstrating the computation times needed to perform a full timing analysis and the times needed to perform the impact analysis consisting of the loading and storing of state spaces, and the refinement check between state spaces. Further, we discuss the benefit of applying abstractions of resource interfaces for the refinement relation.

Related Work

Timing analysis on distributed systems is a very large research area. Thus, we cover only the most relevant works for our approach. The classical approach is a holistic one, as it was worked out in e. g. [3,4]. Local analysis is performed evaluating fixed-point equations. These approaches are very fast and able to handle large systems. Unfortunately, the analytical approaches deliver pessimistic results if inter-ECU task dependencies exist. In [5] activation patterns for tasks are described by upper and lower arrival curves realizing a *compositional* analysis method. Based on this work a compositional scheduling analysis tool, called SymTA/S, was created by SymtaVision [6]. The concept has been developed by Richter et al. The main idea behind SymTa/S is to transform event streams whenever needed and to exploit classical scheduling algorithms for local analysis. Another related approach is the modular performance analysis (MPA) [7] which is based on a formalism with many similarities to event streams named Real-Time Calculus. Arrival functions are used to model the computation that is requested by a process, and service functions are used to model the amount of computation that can be delivered by a resource. In [8], the MPA approach has been combined with timed automata while offering methods that allow to transform the model of one formalism to another. *CARTS* is another tool for compositional real-time scheduling analysis [9]. Schedulability is checked for tasks whose resource usage is bounded by periodic resource models developed by Lee et al. Composition is done on the resource model level resulting again in periodic resource models by using abstractions.

Another approach is based on model-checking: In [10] non-preemptive schedulers are modeled in terms of timed automata. The advantage of this approach is that one gets exact solutions with respect to the modeled scheduling problem. Since the state space of the analyzed system is preserved, checking complex properties like safety is possible. Unfortunately, state-based approaches do not scale well. The authors of [11] also use timed automata to model preemptive scheduling and verify timing properties by using UPPAAL. As a front-end they employ sequence diagrams, from which timed automata are derived. In [12] these automaton models were reused and the results were compared to other techniques such as MPA or SymTA/S. In [13] timed automata are extended by clocks which may be subtracted by a natural number to handle preemption in a more natural way. The authors derive a sub-class of this formalism, where the reachability is preserved.

Outline

First, we illustrate the considered problem domain. In Sect. 3 we will detail our general analysis approach in a condensed form. In Sect. 4 we introduce our implemented impact analysis methodology. Section 5 evaluates our concept and compares plain verification times and refinement checking times. Finally, we conclude the work and give an outlook for future work.

2   Problem Domain

We are interested in safety-critical real-time systems which are typically used in the automotive domain. Typically, the design of the overall system is performed by the original equipment manufacturer (OEM). The OEM designs the software components in form of logical architectures by using, e.g., Autosar software components (SWC), inter-connected by a high level virtual function bus (VFB) like illustrated in the left part of Fig. 1. The components and parts of this system are then realized by the suppliers. In order to get adequate realizations from each supplier, the OEM has to specify the extra-functional properties and interfaces unambiguously. This is realized by the usage of so called contracts [14].

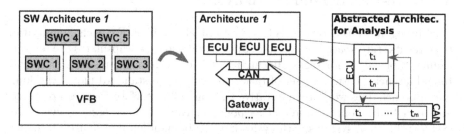

Fig. 1. General concept of modeling and analysis.

Contracts are pairs consisting of an assumption (A) and a guarantee (G). The assumption specifies how the context of the component, i. e. the environment from the point of view of the component, should behave. Only if the assumption holds, then the component will behave as guaranteed. To specify the assumptions and guarantees various formalisms like pattern-based languages could be used. Contracts follow the principle of separation of concerns, i.e., a contract does not just specify a guarantee about the behavior of a component, but also an assumption about the behavior of the environment in which the component will be integrated.

If all suppliers deliver the implementations of the SWCs, the OEM has to verify whether all SWCs *fit together*, i.e., he has to perform the consistency check in a black box manner, and whether some higher level requirements ranging over several SWCs are realized by the decomposition structure.

After the implementation of all SWCs the logical architecture has to be allocated to the hardware architecture, consisting of electronic control units (ECUs) which are inter-connected by bus systems. At this design stage technical details such as resource consumptions and timing latencies have to be verified. To perform such analyses, typically the architecture is abstracted in an appropriate manner. The abstraction we perform for our analysis is illustrated in the right part of Fig. 1: ECUs and bus systems are treated logically equivalent in the sense that both represent computation units on which a set of tasks are allocated. The order of executions of the tasks is determined by the corresponding scheduling policy like fixed priority scheduling. Dependent tasks are directly connected, tasks with no input edges are considered to work independent from other tasks. A task is characterized by a tuple $\tau = (bcet, wcet, pr)$, where $bcet, wcet \in \mathbb{N}_{\geq 0}$, $bcet \leq wcet$, are the best and worst case execution times with respect to the resource the task is allocated to, and $pr \in \mathbb{N}_{\geq 0}$ is the fixed priority of the task. We will refer to the elements of a task by indexing, e.g. $bcet_\tau$ for task τ. The set of all tasks is called T. Independent tasks are triggered by events of a corresponding event stream (ES). An event stream $ES = (p, j)$ is characterized by a period p and a jitter j with $p, j \in \mathbb{N}_{\geq}$. Such streams can be characterized by upper and lower occurrence curves as introduced in the real-time calculus [15]. In this work we restrict to event streams where $j_\tau < p_\tau$ for all $\tau \in T$. Like stated above we will further assume that dependent tasks are directly connected.

3   State-Based Timing Analysis

Our timing analysis approach is based on model-checking. For each computation resource its state space is computed. Such a state space encapsulates the relevant timing information for tasks allocated to the corresponding resource, and end-to-end latencies between a set of tasks. In contrast to standard model-checking, our approach does work in an iterative fashion. The interfaces between resources are tried to be kept as minimal as possible. Note that we assume cyclic free systems. Parts of systems with cycles have to be handled in a holistic fashion.

To build the state space of a computation resource, we have to determine its input behavior, which defines the activation times of all allocated tasks. State spaces are represented by symbolic transition systems (STS): the states determine a range of valuations of clock variables, and include the information, which task is currently running, is interrupted, or in the ready queue. A resource can have multiple sources for its inputs: the independent tasks are triggered by event streams, while dependent tasks are triggered when the tasks on which they depend, terminate. Thus, we get multiple input state spaces. To determine a *single* input state space for each resource, we have to combine all these inputs.

When the input is determined, the next step is to build the state space of the resource itself. For this, the input STS, the behavior of the scheduling policy, and the execution times and priorities of the allocated tasks are taken into account. The approach to compute the state space is illustrated in Fig. 3, where two tasks hp, lp are allocated to a single resource with a fixed priority scheduling policy. For each task a clock c_p which traces the periodic activation is needed. Further, we need a clock c_c to determine when a task is finished. If we are interested in the exact response times of a task instance, we need multiple clocks c_r, one for each instance of a task.

The computed state space of a resource is then used as an input for *dependent* resources, i. e. for resources on which dependent tasks are allocated. To keep the interface between the resources as small as possible, parts of the state space that are not relevant for the input behavior of the dependent resources are abstracted.

Consider the example in Fig. 2, which consists of three resources where on each resource two tasks are allocated. The tasks task5 and task6 on resource Resource3 depend on task2 on resource Resource1 and task3 on resource Resource2 respectively. Tasks task1, ...,task4 are activated by event streams, thus the inputs for both Resource1 and Resource2 are directly given and their state spaces can be computed (illustrated in the left part of the figure). Next, the input of Resource3 has to be determined, which depends on both the state space of Resource1 and Resource2. As timing information for the tasks task1 and task4 is not relevant for Resource3, the corresponding STSs can be reduced by abstracting from states encapsulating information about these tasks. After this minimization, the product of both STSs is computed (indicated by the right part of the figure).

The details of our timing analysis including the composition operation, the minimization, and the resource construction can be found in [1].

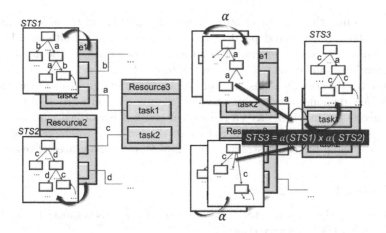

Fig. 2. Timing analysis approach; left: computation of resource state spaces; right: computation of output interfaces.

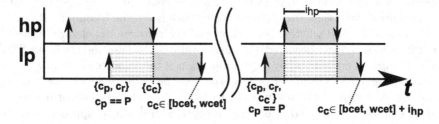

Fig. 3. Two tasks hp, lp and the interrupt scenarios. The clocks refer to the task lp. Clocks in curved brackets indicate a reset, P is the period of lp.

4 Impact Analysis Methodology

During the design process changes affecting the architecture of a system occur, such as adding a new task on an existing resource, the merge of two tasks in a single one, or even the change of the complete implementation. If such changes occur, already performed analyses have to be repeated, increasing the time needed to verify the functionality and properties of the design, and thus increasing the time to market.

To minimize the effort of a re-validation, it is desirable to reuse the previous results of the analysis that did not change. With this, only the parts are re-validated, which were affected by the architectural changes. It is required to perform an impact analysis, when changing or maintaining software because it allows to judge the amount of work required to implement a change, proposes software artifacts which should be changed, and helps to identify test cases which should be re-executed to ensure that the change was implemented correctly [16].

As our timing analysis approach works in an iterative manner (and not holistically), we are able to determine whether the interface of dependent resources is affected through the concept of our refinement analysis: we are able to check if the new interface between dependent resources refines the old interface. In such a case a re-validation of dependent resources can be omitted. The definition of an appropriate refinement relation was the topic of our previous work [2].

In the next section, we illustrate our implementation approach of the impact analysis. We demonstrate in which cases a complete re-verification of a component is necessary, in which cases a refinement check is performed, and when verification steps can be omitted. Thereafter we discuss the advantages of our approach when using further abstraction techniques on the interfaces of resources.

4.1   Concept

The concept of the implementation of our impact analysis is illustrated in Fig. 8 in terms of an UML activity diagram.

Each resource has a status flag for its resource state space called *outputIs-Consistent*, initially set to *false*. The idea of this flag is to inform dependent resources whether some non-refinement changes concerning the resource state space occurred (and thus the resource state space has to be recomputed).

First, it is checked whether some inputs of the resource has changed (*check-InputStatus*). If changes occurred, the check evaluates to *false* and the input STS (*computeInputSTS*) followed by the computation of the resource state space itself (*computeResourceSTS*)is performed as usual. As the resource STS is newly computed, the flag *outputIsConsistent* is set to *false* to signalize dependent resources that this input has changed. Last, the resource STS is stored appropriately. If on the other hand the output STSs of all resources, from which the current resource depends on, did not changed, *checkInputStatus* evaluates to *true*. Then it is checked whether an already computed resource STS of this resource exists (from previous verification steps, where the resource STS was saved). If not, it has to be computed as described above. Else, it is checked whether structural changes have occurred, i.e. changes concerning the scheduling policy of the resource, the number of allocated tasks and their properties like priorities and execution times. If these properties did not changed, the resource STS will also be not affected. Thus, the existing STS can be restored (loaded from file system). The flag *outputIsConsistent* is set to *true* indicating that nothing changed on the output.

If else some changes on the resource occurred *checkInputStatus* will evaluate to *false*. In this case, we have to re-compute the resource STS, load the previously computed resource STS and do a refinement check between both STSs. If the refinement check evaluates to *true*, *outputIsConsistent* is also set to *true* indicating that the resource STS changed in a good manner. Else it is set to *false*. Note that before the re-computation of the resource STS the input STS of the resource has also to be re-computed because if properties of independent tasks change the input STS is also affected.

4.2   Combination with Abstractions

Generally an impact analysis is useful in combination with analysis techniques
that involve abstractions. This is also a typical scenario for analytic techniques
such as in [17]. These techniques are based on the assumption that every interface
behavior can be characterized by event streams. To obtain event streams for the
outputs of a resource, the actual task behavior is generally over-approximated.

Hence changes in the behavior of a particular resource might indeed have an
impact on the already computed *exact* state-space representing its output behavior, but might not have an impact on the over-approximated output behavior of
the resource. This can be exploited by our impact analysis.

We consider event streams as the maximal abstraction of the timing behavior
of a task, as these only contain information about best- and worst-case response-
times, without any information, in which cases the corresponding response times
occurs. For example a task could have a large response time when it is interrupted
by an high priority task which is allocated on the same resource, and an small
response time, when no interrupts occur.

Though our analysis approach is an exact analysis in general, it can be combined with abstraction techniques in order to reduce the state space of the
interface transition systems. Such abstractions were the topic of our previous
works [18].

An abstraction indeed might affect the schedulability of a depending resource,
and hence may cause false negative results. On the other hand, suitable abstraction techniques may pave the way to omit re-validations.

5   Evaluation

In this chapter we will evaluate our methodology by the usage of the three test
systems illustrated in Fig. 4. Tasks with no input edge are considered as to be
independent, i.e. triggered by event streams. The scheduling policies of each
ECU is fixed priority with interruption, and the policy of the CAN bus is also
fixed priority but (of course) without interruption. The parameters of the tasks
are detailed in the table of Fig. 5, where p is the period of a task, $ecec.$ is the

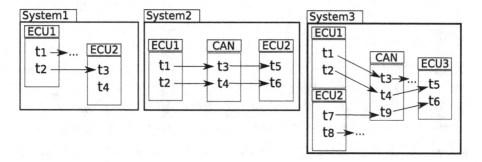

Fig. 4. Test systems.

	System 1			System 2			System 3		
	p	exec.	pr	p	exec.	pr	p	exec.	pr
t1	60	35	1	55	[4,10]	1	50	[4,10]	1
t2	5	2	2	50	[3,7]	2	50	[3,7]	2
t3	-	4	2	-	[2,6]	2	-	[2,6]	2
t4	60	12	1	-	[4,5]	1	-	[4,5]	1
t5				-	[3,5]	2	-	[3,5]	2
t6					[2,3]	1	-	[2,3]	1
t7							50	[3,5]	1
t8							50	[3,5]	2
t9							-	[4,5]	3

Fig. 5. Task parameters.

		ECU1	ECU2	CAN	ECU3
System 1	Analysis	0,16	6,33		
	Refinement	0,00016	0,0138		
	Load	0,06	1,29		
	Save	0,04	1,4		
	Sum	0,10016	2,7038		
System 2	Analysis	0,09	6,75	0,58	
	Refinement	0,0001	0,015	0,013	
	Load	0,04	0,92	0,17	
	Save	0,03	1,07	0,17	
	Sum	0,0701	2,005	0,353	
System 3	Analysis	0,01	0,03	15,31	77,52
	Refinement	0,0001	0,0001	0,12	0,31
	Load	0,0001	0,009	3,61	10,81
	Save	0,0001	0,0001	3,78	11,4
	Sum	0,0003	0,0092	7,51	22,52

Fig. 6. Measured average computation times.

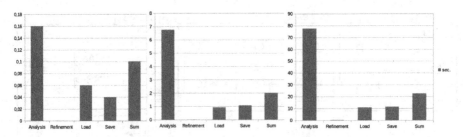

Fig. 7. Computation times for (a) $ECU1$ in $System1$ (left), (b) $ECU2$ on $System2$ (center), and (c) $ECU3$ on $System3$.

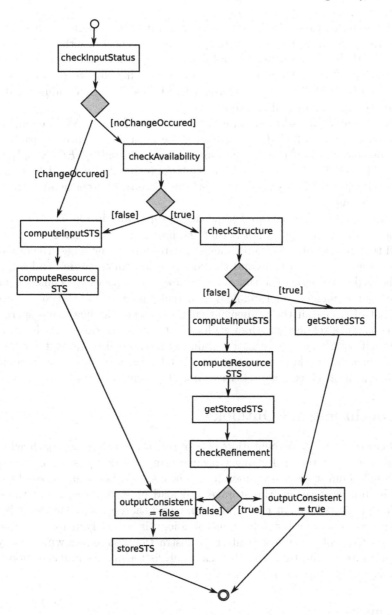

Fig. 8. Methodology of the impact analysis (timing analysis combined with refinement check).

execution time which may be a single value or an interval, if $bcet \neq wcet$, and pr is the priority of a task.

In our evaluation we compare the time needed for an analysis of each resource and the times needed to store and load a corresponding state space, and check the refinement of the state spaces of the resources. The idea is to demonstrate that the analyses times of the resources is always much larger than the times needed to store and to load the state spaces, and to check whether – if a change occurred – the old state space is a refinement of the new one.

Note that all times were measured on the same machine to preserve comparability. Each check has been performed five times. The times illustrated here are the average times of all measurements.

The measured times are illustrated in the table of Fig. 6. As an example: To analyze the timings of *ECU*2 of *System*2 we need 6.75 s. In contrast to this, the refinement check of the of state spaces (new and old) of *ECU*2 only takes 0.015 s. The cell *Sum* is the sum of the cells *Refinement, Load* and *Store* and is used to compare the times needed to perform these three steps against the plain verification time.

As an example we illustrated some cases graphically in Fig. 7.

The result of our evaluation is that the larger the state space of a resource is (and therefore the verification time of that resource), the larger the difference between the verification time and the computation times needed to load, save, and check the refinement of the old and new state spaces is. Thus, for larger systems our refinement methodology is a real gain for our analysis approach. Note that of course, if the refinement check fails, i.e. the new state space of a resource is not a refinement, than we have extra analysis times which we would not have if we always perform the plain verification directly. But fortunately these refinement checking times are not that large. Actually the complexity of the refinement check is $n(n-1)$ where n is the number of states.

6 Conclusion and Outlook

We illustrated the implementation of our impact analysis approach which is applied when architectural changes occur during the design state of a system. We evaluated our approach by measuring the computation times needed to perform the full verification, the storage and load of state spaces, and the computation of the refinement check, and compared these times. The result is that for larger systems our refinement methodology is a real gain for our analysis approach. Currently, we investigate new abstraction techniques which will yield more accurate results than the classical analysis techniques and will boost the scalability of our approach.

References

1. Gezgin, T., Stierand, I., Henkler, S., Rettberg, A.: State-based scheduling analysis for distributed real-time systems. Des. Autom. Embed. Syst. **18**, 1–18 (2013)
2. Gezgin, T., Henkler, S., Stierand, I., Rettberg, A.: Impact analysis for timing requirements on real-time systems. In: 2014 IEEE 20th International Conference on Embedded and Real-Time Computing Systems and Applications (RTCSA), pp. 1–10, August 2014
3. Tindell, K., Clark, J.: Holistic schedulability analysis for distributed hard real-time systems. Microprocess. Microprogram. **40**, 117–134 (1994)

4. Gutierrez, J., Gutierrez Garcia, J., Gonzalez Harbour, M.: On the schedulability analysis for distributed hard real-time systems. In: Proceedings of the Euromicro Workshop on Real-Time Systems, pp. 136–143 (1997)
5. Thiele, L., Chakraborty, S., Gries, M., Maxiaguine, A., Greutert, J.: Embedded software in network processors—models and algorithms. In: Henzinger, T.A., Kirsch, C.M. (eds.) EMSOFT 2001. LNCS, vol. 2211, pp. 416–434. Springer, Heidelberg (2001). https://doi.org/10.1007/3-540-45449-7_29
6. Henia, R., Hamann, A., Jersak, M., Racu, R., Richter, K., Ernst, R.: System level performance analysis - the symTA/S approach. IEEE Proc. Comput. Digit. Tech. **152**, 148–166 (2005)
7. Wandeler, E.: Modular performance analysis and interface-based design for embedded real-time systems. Ph.D. thesis. Swiss Federal Institute of Technology Zurich (2006)
8. Lampka, K., Perathoner, S., Thiele, L.: Analytic real-time analysis and timed automata: a hybrid method for analyzing embedded real-time systems. In: EMSOFT 2009: Proceedings of the Seventh ACM International Conference on Embedded Software, pp. 107–116 (2009)
9. Phan, L.T.X., Lee, J., Easwaran, A., Ramaswamy, V., Chen, S., Lee, I., Sokolsky, O.: CARTS: a tool for compositional analysis of real-time systems. SIGBED Rev. **8**(1), 62–63 (2011)
10. David, A., Illum, J., Larsen, K.G., Skou, A.: Model-based framework for schedulability analysis using uppaal 4.1. In: Nicolescu, G., Mosterman, P. (eds.) Model-Based Design for Embedded Systems, pp. 93–119 (2009)
11. Hendriks, M., Verhoef, M.: Timed automata based analysis of embedded system architectures. In: 20th International Parallel and Distributed Processing Symposium, IPDPS 2006, April 2006
12. Perathoner, S., Wandeler, E., Thiele, L., Hamann, A., Schliecker, S., Henia, R., Racu, R., Ernst, R., Harbour, M.: Influence of different system abstractions on the performance analysis of distributed real-time systems. In: Proceedings of the 7th ACM & IEEE International Conference on Embedded Software, EMSOFT, pp. 193–202 (2007)
13. Fersman, E., Pettersson, P., Yi, W.: Timed automata with asynchronous processes: schedulability and decidability. In: Katoen, J.-P., Stevens, P. (eds.) TACAS 2002. LNCS, vol. 2280, pp. 67–82. Springer, Heidelberg (2002). https://doi.org/10.1007/3-540-46002-0_6
14. Benveniste, A., Caillaud, B., Ferrari, A., Mangeruca, L., Passerone, R., Sofronis, C.: Multiple viewpoint contract-based specification and design. In: de Boer, F.S., Bonsangue, M.M., Graf, S., de Roever, W.-P. (eds.) FMCO 2007. LNCS, vol. 5382, pp. 200–225. Springer, Heidelberg (2008). https://doi.org/10.1007/978-3-540-92188-2_9
15. Thiele, L., Chakraborty, S., Naedele, M.: Real-time calculus for scheduling hard real-time systems. In: IEEE International Symposium on Circuits and Systems (ISCAS), vol. 4, pp. 101–104 (2000)
16. Lehnert, S.: A review of software change impact analysis. Ilmenau University of Technology, Technical report (2011)
17. Richter, K., Racu, R., Ernst, R.: Scheduling analysis integration for heterogeneous multiprocessor SoC. In: Proceedings of RTSS (2003)
18. Gezgin, T., Henkler, S., Stierand, I., Rettberg, A.: Evaluation of a state-based real-time scheduling analysis technique. In: 2014 12th IEEE International Conference on Industrial Informatics (INDIN), pp. 158–163, July 2014

Multi/Many-Core System Design

Hierarchical Multicore-Scheduling for Virtualization of Dependent Real-Time Systems

Jan Jatzkowski[1]([⊠]), Marcio Kreutz[2], and Achim Rettberg[3]

[1] C-LAB, University of Paderborn, 33102 Paderborn, Germany
jan.jatzkowski@c-lab.de
[2] Department of Informatics and Applied Mathematics, UFRN, Natal, Brazil
kreutz@dimap.ufrn.br
[3] Carl von Ossietzky University Oldenburg, 26129 Oldenburg, Germany
achim.rettberg@iess.org

Abstract. Hypervisor-based virtualization is a promising technology to concurrently run various embedded real-time applications on a single multicore hardware. It provides spatial as well as temporal separation of different applications allocated to one hardware platform. In this paper, we propose a concept for hierarchical scheduling of dependent real-time software on multicore systems using hypervisor-based virualization. For this purpose, we decompose offline schedules of singlecore systems based on their release times, deadlines, and precedence constraints. Resulting schedule fragments are allocated to time partitions such that task deadlines as well as precedence constraints are met while local scheduling order of tasks is preserved. This concept, e.g., enables consolidation of various dependent singlecore applications on a multicore platform using full virtualization. Finally, we demonstrate functionality of our concept by an automotive use case from literature.

Keywords: Embedded systems · Dependent real-time systems
Real-time virtualization · Multicore scheduling · Hierarchical scheduling

1 Introduction

Nowadays, there is a raising interest in multicore technology for embedded real-time systems. Using multicore hardware promises not only more computational power but also reduced system size, weight, and power consumptions. However, many embedded applications require sequential interaction between different components. Increasing system performance is not reached by parallelization of dedicated software but rather by running various applications on one multicore platform concurrently [12]. Virtualization provides means to separate various applications. Multicore architectures and virtualization are therefore known as symbiotic technologies [9].

M. Götz et al. (Eds.): IESS 2015, IFIP AICT 523, pp. 103–115, 2017.
https://doi.org/10.1007/978-3-319-90023-0_9

1.1 Hypervisor-Based Virtualization

In this paper we focus on type-1 hypervisor-based virtualization, i.e. an additional software layer – the hypervisor – is placed between hardware and operating system (OS) respectively application software. As type-1 hypervisor run baremetal, they must provide, e.g., device drivers either by their own (monolithic) or by means of some special guest system (console-guest). Hypervisor provide virtual machines (VM) that represent duplicates of the real hardware. These VMs allow to run various systems spatial and temporal separated on a single hardware platform. Literature distinguishes full and para-virtualization [9]. While guest systems running at full virtualization are not aware of the hypervisor, para-virtualized systems are adapted to run in VMs. Consequently, para-virtualization allows information exchange between guest system and hypervisor, but full virtualization does not.

1.2 Problem Statement

Temporal isolation is an important property of hypervisor-based virtualization for embedded real-time systems. Current real-time hypervisor ensure temporal isolation of various VMs by some cyclic scheduling on hypervisor-level (cf. Sect. 2.2). These approaches provide each VM a guaranteed share of processing time during a predefined period, but dependencies between VMs remain an open issue.

Dependencies between tasks hosted by the same VM must be solved by its local scheduler. But dependencies between VMs must be solved by hypervisor scheduler. Using para-virtualization, local schedulers could notify the hypervisor when tasks are finished. This may enable solutions based on servers to schedule VMs with precedence constraints. In contrast, full virtualization implies that local and hypervisor scheduler cannot actively exchange information. Hence, a-priori knowledge of local schedules and VM-dependencies are required to get an appropriate global scheduling.

1.3 Contribution

In this paper, we focus on hierarchical real-time scheduling of dependent VMs to enable full virtualization of singlecore systems deployed to multicore hardware. Here, dependencies are given by precedence constraints. The challenge is to share execution time of $p > 1$ cores to $m > p$ VMs such that deadlines as well as precedence constraints are met. Each VM encapsulates a periodic real-time system driven by its separate local singlecore schedule. Time sharing shall be realized by a fixed cyclic scheduling that guarantees holding task deadlines and precedence constraints. We consider task sets with acyclic dependencies, because cyclic task dependencies imply non-deterministic behavior. Nevertheless, resulting VM dependency graph may contain cycles. To meet deadlines as well as precedence constraints of the overall system, hypervisor scheduler has to preempt execution of VMs. For this purpose, first we decompose local schedules and then allocate time partitions of various length to those parts of VM schedules. The result of our approach is an offline multicore schedule for VMs that provides not only sufficient execution time for each VM but also considers precedence constraints.

2 Related Work

In this paper, we address hierarchical scheduling of periodic tasks with precedence constraints on a multicore platform. We therefore divide related work into approaches related to multicore scheduling and hierarchical scheduling.

2.1 Multicore Scheduling

Multicore scheduling approaches are classified as partitioned or global [1]. Davis and Burns [5] state that (i) most published research addresses independent tasks and (ii) main advantage of partitioned multicore scheduling is reuse of results from singlecore scheduling theory after allocation of tasks to cores has been achieved. Considering periodic task sets with precedence constraints, partitioned scheduling allows to apply, e.g., adapted Earliest Deadline First (EDF*) presented by Chetto et al. [2] or Deadline Monotonic (DM) based scheduling proposed by Forget et al. [6]. Both approaches adapt deadlines to solve dependencies between tasks allocated to a singlecore and thus enable deadline-based scheduling as for independent task sets. But dependencies between tasks allocated to different cores are not considered. For global multicore scheduling, e.g., some scheduling policies from singlecore scheduling were adapted. For independent tasks, global EDF schedules p tasks with earliest absolute deadline at each time, where p is number of cores. Lee [11] extended global EDF to Earliest Deadline Zero Laxity (EDZL) that was proven to dominate global EDF [1]. Cho et al. [3] presented Largest Local Remaining Execution time First (LLREF). It is an optimal offline real-time scheduling approach for independent periodic tasks with implicit deadlines $(d = T)$ and it performs non-work-conserving scheduling, i.e. cores can be idle even in case of ready tasks. Rönngren and Shirazi [15] proposed static scheduling of periodic tasks with precedence constraints for multiprocessor systems connected by a time division multiple access (TDMA) bus network. They adapt task deadlines – similar to [2,6] – and apply a heuristic that schedules tasks w.r.t. earliest starting time, laxity, etc. In contrast to these approaches, our work aims at global offline scheduling that does not adapt local schedules, i.e. task parameters as well as local execution order keep untouched.

2.2 Hierarchical Scheduling

Most approaches for hierarchical scheduling at virtualization focus on independent sub-systems, while our work allows dependencies between those systems. In [7], Grösbrink and Almeida present hierarchical scheduling for hypervisor-based real-time virtualization of mixed-criticality systems. They address independent periodic VMs and apply partitioned hierarchical scheduling, i.e. VMs are allocated as periodic servers to cores and each core schedules its servers according to Rate Monotonic (RM). Masmano et al. [13] present the monolithic hypervisor XtratuM that provides para-virtualization. It schedules VMs – called partitions – globally by a static cyclic schedule and locally by a preemptive fixed priority-based policy [4]. Xi et al. [16] present the console-guest hypervisor RT-Xen. It enables scheduling VMs as periodic or deferrable servers by EDF or DM priority schemes. Masrur et al. [14] proposed the priority-based scheduling plus simple EDF (PSEDF) to apply XEN hypervisor for mixed-criticality systems in automotive domain. But in contrast to our work, none of these approaches allows precedence constraints between VMs.

3   System Model

This paper focuses on hierarchical scheduling of periodic dependent real-time systems on a multicore platform. Usually, periodic embedded real-time systems get input from some sensors and compute output to control some acutators. But resources are limited to get input respectively set output via direct I/O access or network interfaces. To take this into account, we consider a periodic task model that allows asynchronous release of tasks:

$$\Gamma = \{\tau_i = (C_i, T_i, D_i, O_i) \mid 1 \leq i \leq n\}. \tag{1}$$

Each task $\tau_i \in \Gamma$ is characterized by its worst case execution time (WCET) C_i, period T_i, constrained deadline $D_i \leq T_i$, and offset O_i. By means of constrained deadlines and offsets, we are able to cover systems where the multicore platform is connected to a time-triggered network. We denote j^{th} instance of task τ_i by τ_{ij} and its absolute deadline by d_{ij}. Task dependencies are given by precedence constraints $\tau_i \prec \tau_j$ meaning that τ_i must finish before τ_j can start execution. This corresponds to implicit communication between tasks, i.e. tasks require input just when they start and provide output when finished. To keep software behavior deterministic, we assume acylic task graphs. Consequently, task dependencies can be described by directed acyclic graphs (DAG). We define the set of source respectively sink nodes as

$$source = \{\tau_i \in \Gamma \mid \nexists \tau_j \in \Gamma : \tau_j \prec \tau_i\}, \tag{2}$$

$$sink = \{\tau_i \in \Gamma \mid \nexists \tau_j \in \Gamma : \tau_i \prec \tau_j\}. \tag{3}$$

While tasks $\tau_i \in source$ make progress as soon as they are scheduled, tasks with predecessors ($\tau \in \Gamma \backslash source$) can only progress when required input has been delivered. Using hypervisor-based virtualization, task set Γ is mapped to a set of virtual machines (VM)

$$\Upsilon = \{v_k = (\gamma_k, \sigma_k) \mid 1 \leq j \leq m\} \tag{4}$$

where VM v_k is given by a task set $\gamma_k \subset \Gamma$ and a scheduling σ_k. In general, σ_k can be an online or offline scheduling. In this paper, however, we assume offline singlecore scheduler running within VMs, i.e. σ_k represents a fix order how tasks $\tau_i \in \gamma_k$ are scheduled. We denote worst case start time of task instance τ_{ij} scheduled by σ_k with $\sigma_k^s(\tau_{ij})$ and its worst case finishing time with $\sigma_k^f(\tau_{ij})$.

The hypervisor scheduler is a fix cyclic schedule, i.e. VMs are scheduled by means of time partitions to keep temporal isolation. Each time partition represents a time interval $I_h = [a_h, a_h + l_h[$ defined by its start time a_h and length (duration) l_h. A VM v_k mapped to a time partition I_h will be scheduled at time a_h for l_h time units. During this time, VM v_k can progress according to its schedule σ_k. The hypervisor schedule finally provides for each core a set of time partitions where each partition I_h is associated to a dedicated VM v_k. We note this association by $I_h^{v_k}$.

4   Hierarchical Scheduling with Precedence Constraints

Hierarchical scheduling comprises scheduling of schedules and thus introduces different levels of scheduling. We consider hierarchical scheduling for hypervisor-based virtualization that implies two levels: Global scheduling of VMs by hypervisor and local scheduling of tasks within each VM. We restrict local schedulers to offline singlecore schedules, i.e. execution order of tasks is fix within each VM. This restriction simplifies handling a-priori knowledge of local schedules that we require to cover full virtualization.

The main idea of our approach is to combine knowledge of local schedulers' task execution order with a-priori knowledge of tasks' WCETs and dependencies to compute worst case time partitions (WCTP) for VMs. That is, we calculate worst case VM execution time required to guarantee that a dedicated task τ has finished (cf. Sect. 4.2). In Sect. 4.3, we schedule these time partitions, which represent activation slots of the corresponding VMs, on a multicore system. In case of success, assigning execution time to VMs according to the resulting schedule ensures that task dependencies as well as tasks' deadlines are met.

4.1   Necessary Condition for Schedulability

To our best knowledge, literature provides no schedulability test that is neccessary as well as sufficient for periodic tasks with precedence constraints on multicore systems. For multicore scheduling, there are also no approaches known that convert precedence constraints to real-time constraints – as proposed by Chetto et al. [2] for singlecore scheduling. This makes transferring results of multicore scheduling theory from independent to dependent task sets challenging. However, some results from multicore scheduling theory of independent tasks can be transferred to task sets with precedence contraints at least as necessary conditions. For instance, a trivial fact from scheduling theory is that a task set Γ with computation demand higher than computation supply provided by some hardware with p cores is not schedulable. Consequently, for multicore hardware with p identical cores, utilization of feasible task set Γ cannot be higher than available number of cores, i.e.

$$\sum_{i=1}^{n} \frac{C_i}{T_i} \leq p \tag{5}$$

Although Eq. 5 is just a necessary condition, it allows to exclude at least some non-feasible task sets.

4.2 Decomposition of Local Schedules

Here, we consider local schedules that result from offline singlecore scheduling. Precedence constraints of tasks which are mapped to the same VM are solved by the corresponding local scheduler:

$$\forall \tau_i, \tau_j \in \upsilon_k: \ \tau_i \prec \tau_j \ \implies \ \sigma_k^f(\tau_{il}) \leq \sigma_k^s(\tau_{jl}) \ \forall l \in \mathbb{N} \tag{6}$$

Hence, two challenges remain to be solved by hypervisor during VM scheduling: it has to schedule VMs such that (i) deadlines of tasks running within VMs are met and (ii) dependencies between tasks hosted by different VMs are taken into account. For this purpose, we decompose local schedules of VMs based on

1. deadlines of tasks that are sink nodes of dependency graphs ($\tau \in sink$)
2. release times of tasks that are source nodes of dependency graphs
   ($\tau \in source$)
3. dependencies between tasks that are hosted by different VMs

A first step towards enabling hypervisor to keep deadlines of tasks is done by splitting local schedules at worst case finishing time of sink nodes $\tau \in sink$. This eases handling of different periods within task set Γ. Since execution order of tasks is static within a local schedule σ, fulfilling an absolute deadline d requires to run each local schedule until all task instances with absolute deadline d are finished. Therefore, we split local schedule σ at worst case finishing time of a sink node that is scheduled by σ last amongst all other sink nodes of equal absolute deadline:

$$\max \left\{ \sigma^f(\tau_{ij}) \mid \tau_i \in sink, \ d_{ij} \right\} \quad j \in \mathbb{N} \tag{7}$$

Note, that each resulting fragment of a local schedule is associated with the earliest absolute deadline d of all its tasks.

Hypervisor must also consider release time of task instances because VMs with offline schedules cannot progress as long as the currently scheduled task is not ready. To avoid that hypervisor schedules VMs that cannot progress because of unreleased tasks, we apply another decomposition step onto local schedules based on release times. We split local schedule σ at the beginning of a source node that is scheduled first amongst all other source nodes of equal release time by σ:

$$\min \left\{ \sigma^s(\tau_{ij}) \mid \tau_i \in source, \ r_{ij} \right\} \quad j \in \mathbb{N} \tag{8}$$

Our last decomposition step is based on precedence constraints of tasks hosted by different VMs. As tasks with precedence constraints are just released when all predecessors have finished execution, we split local schedules based on inter-VM dependencies as follows: if a task τ allocated to VM v_k has predecessors hosted by another VM v_l, $l \neq k$, we just split schedule σ_k at beginning of τ.

The result of the described decomposition is a totally ordered set Φ_k of scheduling fragments φ_h for each VM v_k. The order within Φ_k is such that composing all scheduling fragments $\varphi_h \in \Phi_k$ w.r.t. this order results in the original local singlecore schedule σ_k. Finally, we compute worst case time partitions (WCTP) based on these scheduling fragments and WCETs. For each local schedule fragment φ_h, we sum up WCET of task instances covered by this fragment and define a time partition I_h of this length. As this time partition is associated with the VM that hosts these task instances, we note:

$$l_h^{v_k} = \sum_{\tau_{ij} \in \varphi_h} C_i \quad \forall \varphi_h \in \Phi_k. \tag{9}$$

4.3 Multicore Scheduling of Time Partitions

Our approach for hierarchical multicore scheduling is based on time partitions I_h that were introduced in Sect. 3. While length of time partitions is set according to the WCTP resulting from decomposition of local schedules (cf. Eq. 9), starting time a_h of time partitions as well as a core must be determined by hypervisor scheduler. So, the challenge addressed by our multicore scheduling approach is to allocate time partitions $I_h^{v_k}$ to cores $\mathcal{C}_j$ and set their starting time $a_h^{v_k}$ such that all precedence constraints are met and tasks finish before their deadlines even in worst case.

We have to make scheduling decisions each time that a scheduling fragment is released or finished. As we decomposed local schedules based on precedence constraints, finishing one scheduling fragment usually implies that one or more other scheduling fragments were released during this execution. Therefore, we also make scheduling decisions when worst case finishing of a task $\tau_i \in \gamma_l$ with successor task τ_j hosted by another VM is passed. However, we just need to consider worst case finishing of the task $\tau_i \in \gamma_l$ that is scheduled by v_l last amongst all other predecessors of τ. Keeping order of local schedules guarantees that all other predecessors hosted by VM v_l are then finished, too.

As multicore decisions are not only based on deadlines but have to consider dependencies as well, we define two sets of scheduling fragments that are updated at each scheduling decision:

$$\mathcal{R} \subset \bigcup_{k=1}^{m} \Phi_k, \quad \mathcal{N} \subset \bigcup_{k=1}^{m} \Phi_k \tag{10}$$

$\mathcal{R}$ covers those scheduling fragments $\varphi_h^{VM_k}$ that are ready, i.e. predecessors required to execute $\varphi_h^{VM_k}$ are finished and $\varphi_h^{VM_k}$ is due according to local schedule σ_k. In fact, $\mathcal{R}$ is similar to a ready queue known from common task scheduling. Analogous, $\mathcal{N}$ covers those scheduling fragments $\varphi_h^{VM_k}$ that are next to become ready w.r.t. order of local schedule. Both, $\mathcal{R}$ and $\mathcal{N}$, contain at most one scheduling fragment $\varphi_h^{v_k}$ of a VM v_k. Scheduling decisions are based on the following rules with decreasing priority:

1. Schedule the fragment $\varphi_h \in \mathcal{R}$ with earliest deadline (EDF)
   Note: Here, we use deadlines associated to scheduling fragments during first decomposition step (cf. Sect. 4.2)
2. Schedule the fragment that has most successor fragments $\varphi \in \mathcal{N}$

While first scheduling rule aims at keeping deadlines, second rule addresses dependencies between different VMs.

5   Application Example

We will use an application example to demonstrate how our approach presented in Sect. 4 works. Based on the problem definition given in Sect. 1.2, we apply our approach to a minimal system that consists of $p = 2$ cores and $m = 3$ VMs. The task set Γ deployed to VMs is taken from Kandasamy et al. [8]. It covers three applications from automotive domain: Adaptive cruise control (ACC), traction control (TC), and electric power steering (EPS). Figure 1 shows the corresponding direct acyclic task dependency graphs. In Table 1, we provide original task parameters of these applications given in [8]. In addition, we adapted WCETs of tasks by some reduction. This represents a scenario where singlecore applications are consolidated on a multicore hardware with increased computational power related to original singlecore hardware.

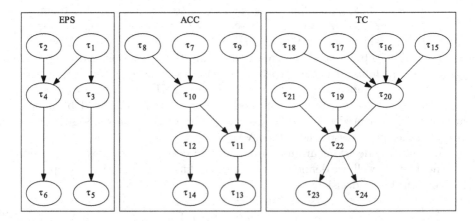

Fig. 1. Three application examples from automotive domain [8]: electric power steering (EPS), adaptive cruise control (ACC), and traction control (TC).

Table 1. Task parameters (original WCET C_i^O, adapted WCET C_i, period T_i, and relative deadline D_i) of example applications shown in Fig. 1, cf. [8].

	EPS System						ACC System							
Task τ_i	τ_1	τ_2	τ_3	τ_4	τ_5	τ_6	τ_7	τ_8	τ_9	τ_{10}	τ_{11}	τ_{12}	τ_{13}	τ_{14}
C_i^O	150	175	300	250	150	100	300	150	175	300	250	200	150	200
C_i	75	90	150	125	75	50	150	75	90	150	125	100	75	100
$T_i = D_i$	1500	1500	1500	1500	1500	1500	3000	3000	3000	3000	3000	3000	3000	3000

	TC System									
Task τ_i	τ_{15}	τ_{16}	τ_{17}	τ_{18}	τ_{19}	τ_{20}	τ_{21}	τ_{22}	τ_{23}	τ_{24}
C_i^O	200	200	200	200	150	300	175	400	150	200
C_i	100	100	100	100	75	150	90	200	75	100
$T_i = D_i$	3000	3000	3000	3000	3000	3000	3000	3000	3000	3000

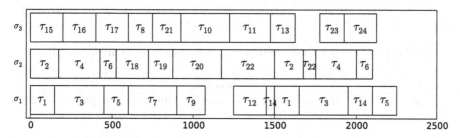

Fig. 2. Local schedules resulting from deployment of example applications to three separate singlecore schedules σ_i, $1 \leq i \leq 3$.

Task set Γ is deployed to VMs according to an approach presented by Klobedanz et al. ([10], "Algorithm 1: Initial Mapping"). This deployment originally addresses singlecore ECU-networks and thus fits to the indicated scenario of consolidating singlecore systems on a multicore platform. Figure 2 shows the resulting local offline schedules based on original WCETs. These local schedules define execution order of tasks within VMs.

5.1 Decomposition of Local Schedules

Now, we use schedule σ_2 to demonstrate decomposition of local schedules. VM v_2 hosts tasks of two example applications: EPS and TC. Tasks of EPS have deadline $D = 1500$ while deadline of TC-tasks is $D = 3000$. Our first decomposition step – splitting based on deadlines – therefore splits schedule σ_2 after finishing of $\tau_{6,1}$ and associates first fragment with absolute deadline $d = 1500$ and second fragment with $d = 3000$.

Next decomposition step – splitting based on release times – is driven by second release of EPS system at host time $t = 1500$. According to our description in Sect. 4.2, we split σ_2 before beginning of $\tau_{2,2}$. Thus, second fragment resulting from first step is splitted again. Note, that both fragments resulting from this step keep associated with absolute deadline $d = 3000$.

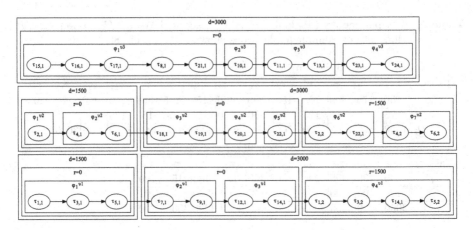

Fig. 3. Scheduling fragments resulting from decomposition of local schedules σ_i, $1 \leq i \leq 3$.

Table 2. Worst case time partition length for local scheduling fragments.

	φ_1^{v1}	φ_2^{v1}	φ_3^{v1}	φ_4^{v1}	φ_1^{v2}	φ_2^{v2}	φ_3^{v2}	φ_4^{v2}	φ_5^{v2}	φ_6^{v2}	φ_7^{v2}	φ_1^{v3}	φ_2^{v3}	φ_3^{v3}	φ_4^{v3}
$l_h^{v_k}$	300	240	125	375	90	175	175	150	160	130	175	465	150	200	175

Last decomposition step – splitting based on precedence constraints – requires to consider dependencies to other VMs. In particular, we split σ_2 at the beginning of tasks that require input from other VMs. In case of σ_2, this results in splits at the beginning of $\tau_{4,1}$, $\tau_{20,1}$, and $\tau_{22,1}$.

Applying these decomposition steps to the other local schedules of our application scenario results in the scheduling fragments depicted in Fig. 3. Rectangles clustering tasks correspond to the results of our decomposition steps: outmost rectangles result from deadline-based decomposition, middle rectangles from splitting based on release times, and innermost rectangles result from splitting based on dependencies.

Next, we compute length of these scheduling fragments using Eq. 9. Due to adaptation of tasks' WCETs, handling of preemptions – e.g., task $\tau_{14,1}$ in schedule $VMschedule_1$ – is challenging. Here, we just split WCET to execution parts of $\tau_{14,1}$ in the same proportion as it was in case of original WCET. Results are summerized in Table 2.

5.2   Multicore Scheduling by Time Partitions

Having local schedules decomposed into fragments, we now can allocate time partitions to dedicated cores of a multicore platform. In this example, we consider $m = 3$ VMs given by example applications introduced in this Section and $p = 2$ cores. Table 3 shows for each point in time – when the hypervisor can make scheduling decisions – why scheduling point occurs, what the current host time of hypervisor system is, which scheduling fragments are within sets $\mathcal{R}$ and $\mathcal{N}$,

Table 3. Offline multicore scheduling of time partitions (scheduling fragments).

Reason for scheduling	Host time	$\mathcal{R}$	$\mathcal{N}$	Core $\mathcal{C}_1$	Core $\mathcal{C}_2$
	0	$\varphi_1^{v_1},\varphi_1^{v_2},\varphi_1^{v_3}$	$\varphi_2^{v_1},\varphi_2^{v_2},\varphi_2^{v_3}$	$\varphi_1^{v_1}$	$\varphi_1^{v_2}$
$\sigma_1^f(\tau_{1,1})$	75	$\varphi_1^{v_1},\varphi_1^{v_2},\varphi_1^{v_3}$	$\varphi_2^{v_1},\varphi_2^{v_2},\varphi_2^{v_3}$	$\varphi_1^{v_1}$	$\varphi_1^{v_2}$
$\varphi_1^{v_2}$	90	$\varphi_1^{v_1},\varphi_2^{v_2},\varphi_1^{v_3}$	$\varphi_2^{v_1},\varphi_3^{v_2},\varphi_2^{v_3}$	$\varphi_1^{v_1}$	$\varphi_2^{v_2}$
$\varphi_2^{v_2}$	265	$\varphi_1^{v_1},\varphi_3^{v_2},\varphi_1^{v_3}$	$\varphi_2^{v_1},\varphi_4^{v_2},\varphi_2^{v_3}$	$\varphi_1^{v_1}$	$\varphi_1^{v_3}$
$\varphi_1^{v_1}$	300	$\varphi_2^{v_1},\varphi_3^{v_2},\varphi_1^{v_3}$	$\varphi_3^{v_1},\varphi_4^{v_2},\varphi_2^{v_3}$	$\varphi_2^{v_1}$	$\varphi_1^{v_3}$
$\sigma_1^f(\tau_{7,1})$	450	$\varphi_2^{v_1},\varphi_3^{v_2},\varphi_1^{v_3}$	$\varphi_3^{v_1},\varphi_4^{v_2},\varphi_2^{v_3}$	$\varphi_2^{v_1}$	$\varphi_1^{v_3}$
$\varphi_2^{v_1}$	540	$\varphi_3^{v_2},\varphi_1^{v_3}$	$\varphi_3^{v_1},\varphi_4^{v_2},\varphi_2^{v_3}$	$\varphi_3^{v_2}$	$\varphi_1^{v_3}$
$\sigma_3^f(\tau_{17,1})$	565	$\varphi_3^{v_2},\varphi_1^{v_3}$	$\varphi_4^{v_1},\varphi_4^{v_2},\varphi_2^{v_3}$	$\varphi_3^{v_2}$	$\varphi_1^{v_3}$
$\varphi_3^{v_2}$	715	$\varphi_4^{v_2},\varphi_1^{v_3}$	$\varphi_3^{v_1},\varphi_5^{v_2},\varphi_2^{v_3}$	$\varphi_4^{v_2}$	$\varphi_1^{v_3}$
$\varphi_1^{v_3}$	730	$\varphi_4^{v_2},\varphi_2^{v_3}$	$\varphi_3^{v_1},\varphi_5^{v_2},\varphi_3^{v_3}$	$\varphi_4^{v_2}$	$\varphi_2^{v_3}$
$\varphi_4^{v_2}$	865	$\varphi_5^{v_2},\varphi_2^{v_3}$	$\varphi_3^{v_1},\varphi_3^{v_3}$	$\varphi_5^{v_2}$	$\varphi_2^{v_3}$
$\varphi_2^{v_3}$	880	$\varphi_3^{v_1},\varphi_5^{v_2},\varphi_3^{v_3}$	$\varphi_4^{v_3}$	$\varphi_5^{v_2}$	$\varphi_3^{v_3}$
$\varphi_5^{v_2}$	1025	$\varphi_3^{v_1},\varphi_3^{v_3}$	$\varphi_4^{v_3}$	$\varphi_3^{v_1}$	$\varphi_3^{v_3}$
$\varphi_3^{v_3}$	1080	$\varphi_3^{v_1},\varphi_4^{v_3}$		$\varphi_3^{v_1}$	$\varphi_4^{v_3}$
$\varphi_3^{v_1}$	1150	$\varphi_4^{v_3}$			$\varphi_4^{v_3}$
$\varphi_4^{v_3}$	1255				
$\sigma_1^s(\tau_{1,2})$	1500	$\varphi_4^{v_1},\varphi_6^{v_2}$	$\varphi_7^{v_2}$	$\varphi_4^{v_1}$	$\varphi_6^{v_2}$
$\sigma_1^f(\tau_{1,2})$	1575	$\varphi_4^{v_1},\varphi_6^{v_2}$	$\varphi_7^{v_2}$	$\varphi_4^{v_1}$	$\varphi_6^{v_2}$
$\varphi_6^{v_2}$	1630	$\varphi_4^{v_1},\varphi_7^{v_2}$		$\varphi_4^{v_1}$	$\varphi_7^{v_2}$
$\varphi_7^{v_2}$	1805	$\varphi_4^{v_1}$		$\varphi_4^{v_1}$	
$\varphi_4^{v_1}$	1875				

and which scheduling fragments are scheduled next on cores $\mathcal{C}_1$ and $\mathcal{C}_2$. For instance, applying rules defined in Sect. 4.3, hypervisor scheduling makes first decision based on deadlines of scheduling fragments. That is, $\varphi_1^{v_1}$ and $\varphi_1^{v_2}$ get higher priority than $\varphi_1^{v_3}$.

Another interesting circumstance for making scheduling decision is at line 7 where "reason for scheduling" is $\varphi_2^{v_1}$. This is the first time, $\mathcal{R}$ does not contain scheduling fragments of all VMs because $\varphi_3^{v_1} \in \mathcal{N}$ requires input from $\varphi_2^{v_3}$ that in worst case has not finished yet. Therefore, $\varphi_3^{v_1} \in \mathcal{N}$ is not passed to $\mathcal{R}$ and thus is not considered by hypervisor. Finally, mapping of scheduling fragments to cores is used to define time partitions I_h resulting, e.g., for core $\mathcal{C}_1$ in

$$I_1^{v_1} = [0, 540[\tag{11}$$

6 Conclusion

In this paper, we presented an approach for hierarchical scheduling of periodic dependent singelcore real-time systems on a multicore hardware. We introduced a system model that covers tasks with precedence constraints as well as VMs that host subsets of these tasks. To schedule the set of VMs on a multicore hardware with full hypervisor-based virtualization, we first proposed a concept to decompose local singlecore schedules into fragments based on deadlines, release times and inter-VM dependencies. Afterwards, we presented our approach for offline scheduling of these fragments on a multicore platform. Finally, we applied our approach to an automotive use case from literature to demonstrate functionality of the proposed concept. Future work aims at taking overhead induced by virualization as well as communication costs between VMs into account.

Acknowledgment. This work was partly funded by German Ministry of Education and Research (BMBF) through project "it's OWL - Intelligente Technische Systeme OstWestfalenLippe" (02PQ1021) and ITEA2 project AMALTHEA4public (01IS14029J).

References

1. Baruah, S., Bertogna, M., Buttazzo, G.: Multiprocessor Scheduling for Real-Time Systems. ES. Springer, Cham (2015). https://doi.org/10.1007/978-3-319-08696-5
2. Chetto, H., Silly, M., Bouchentouf, T.: Dynamic scheduling of real-time tasks under precedence constraints. Real-Time Syst. **2**(3), 181–194 (1990)
3. Cho, H., Ravindran, B., Jensen, E.: An optimal real-time scheduling algorithm for multiprocessors. In: 27th IEEE International Real-Time Systems Symposium, pp. 101–110 (2006)
4. Crespo, A., Ripoll, I., Masmano, M.: Partitioned embedded architecture based on hypervisor: the xtratum approach. In: European Dependable Computing Conference (EDCC), pp. 67–72 (2010)
5. Davis, R.I., Burns, A.: A survey of hard real-time scheduling for multiprocessor systems. ACM Comput. Surv. **43**(4), 35:1–35:44 (2011)
6. Forget, J., Boniol, F., Grolleau, E., Lesens, D., Pagetti, C.: Scheduling dependent periodic tasks without synchronization mechanisms. In: 16th IEEE Real-Time and Embedded Technology and Applications Symposium (RTAS), pp. 301–310 (2010)
7. Groesbrink, S., Almeida, L.: A criticality-aware mapping of real-time virtual machines to multi-core processors. In: IEEE Emerging Technology and Factory Automation (ETFA), pp. 1–9 (2014)
8. Kandasamy, N., Hayes, J.P., Murray, B.T.: Dependable communication synthesis for distributed embedded systems. In: Anderson, S., Felici, M., Littlewood, B. (eds.) SAFECOMP 2003. LNCS, vol. 2788, pp. 275–288. Springer, Heidelberg (2003). https://doi.org/10.1007/978-3-540-39878-3_22
9. Kleidermacher, D.: System virtualization in multicore systems. In: Moyer, B. (ed.) Real World Multicore Embedded Systems - A Practical Approach, pp. 227–267. Elsevier, Amsterdam (2013)
10. Klobedanz, K., Jatzkowski, J., Rettberg, A., Mueller, W.: Fault-tolerant deployment of real-time software in AUTOSAR ECU networks. In: Schirner, G., Götz, M., Rettberg, A., Zanella, M.C., Rammig, F.J. (eds.) IESS 2013. IAICT, vol. 403, pp. 238–249. Springer, Heidelberg (2013). https://doi.org/10.1007/978-3-642-38853-8_22

11. Lee, S.K.: On-line multiprocessor scheduling algorithms for real-time tasks. In: Proceedings of TENCON 1994. IEEE Region 10's Ninth Annual International Conference. Theme: Frontiers of Computer Technology, pp. 607–611 (1994)
12. Main, C.: Virtualization on multicore for industrial real-time operating systems [from mind to market]. IEEE Ind. Electron. Mag. **4**(3), 4–6 (2010)
13. Masmano, M., Ripoll, I., Crespo, A.: Xtratum: a hypervisor for safety critical embedded systems. In: Proceedings of 11th Real-Time Linux Workshop, pp. 263–272 (2009)
14. Masrur, A., Drossler, S., Pfeuffer, T., Chakraborty, S.: VM-based real-time services for automotive control applications. In: IEEE 16th International Conference on Embedded and Real-Time Computing Systems and Applications (RTCSA), pp. 218–223 (2010)
15. Rönngren, S., Shirazi, B.: Static multiprocessor scheduling of periodic real-time tasks with precedence constraints and communication costs. In: Proceedings of 28th Hawaii International Conference on System Sciences, vol. 2, pp. 143–152 (1995)
16. Xi, S., Xu, M., Lu, C., Phan, L., Gill, C., Sokolsky, O., Lee, I.: Real-time multicore virtual machine scheduling in Xen. In: International Conference on Embedded Software (EMSOFT), pp. 1–10 (2014)

Analysis of Process Traces for Mapping Dynamic KPN Applications to MPSoCs

Andrés Goens$^{(\boxtimes)}$ and Jeronimo Castrillon

Chair for Compiler Construction, Center for Advancing Electronics Dresden (cfaed),
TU Dresden, Dresden, Germany
{andres.goens,jeronimo.castrillon}@tu-dresden.de

Abstract. Current approaches for mapping Kahn Process Networks (KPN) and Dynamic Data Flow (DDF) applications rely on assumptions on the program behavior specific to an execution. Thus, a near-optimal mapping, computed for a given input data set, may become sub-optimal at run-time. This happens when a different data set induces a significantly different behavior. We address this problem by leveraging inherent mathematical structures of the dataflow models and the hardware architectures. On the side of the dataflow models, we rely on the monoid structure of histories and traces. This structure help us formalize the behavior of multiple executions of a given dynamic application. By defining metrics we have a formal framework for comparing the executions. On the side of the hardware, we take advantage of symmetries in the architecture to reduce the search space for the mapping problem. We evaluate our implementation on execution variations of a randomly-generated KPN application and on a low-variation JPEG encoder benchmark. Using the described methods we show that trace differences are not sufficient for characterizing performance losses. Additionally, using platform symmetries we manage to reduce the design space in the experiments by two orders of magnitude.

1 Introduction

Architecture trends show a growing number of processors and heterogeneity in embedded systems. The problem of leveraging the growing complexity of modern multi-processor systems-on-chip (MPSoCs) is as relevant as ever. In many application domains it is well-established to use programming abstractions such as Kahn Process Networks (KPN) [10] or actor-based data flow models like Synchronous Data Flow (SDF) [12] and dynamic data flow (DDF) [3] for describing applications. These abstractions allow synthesis tools to reason on a high-level about physical resource allocation within the chip. They model the application by using a directed graph, where so-called actors or processes, represented by the nodes in the graph, communicate with each other via channels, which are in turn represented by edges. Much work has been done regarding the problem of mapping KPN and data flow applications to complex hardware architectures

© IFIP International Federation for Information Processing 2017
Published by Springer International Publishing AG 2017. All Rights Reserved
M. Götz et al. (Eds.): IESS 2015, IFIP AICT 523, pp. 116–127, 2017.
https://doi.org/10.1007/978-3-319-90023-0_10

for optimal throughput, resource usage or energy-efficiency [16]. The heuristics used for this, however, rely on a well-defined program behavior. In the case of SDF applications, for example, the very nature of the model allows synthesis tools to reason about mapping by using a topology matrix and finding repetition vectors in its kernel, which fully describe the communication behavior between actors [12]. Finding near-optimal solutions in more general models, which do not have constraints on the program behavior as strong as those of SDF, is a much more complex task. There are several current approaches to static mapping [7,7,14,18]. All these approaches are sensitive to the selection of the input stimuli that induce the observed trace. To deal with multiple different executions, authors suggest to compute a mapping for every situation and then pick the best configuration. For example, for buffer sizing, one approach is to select the largest size across all configurations [2]. An alternative to deal with variations is to use the so-called real-time calculus [19], in which events are modeled by arrival curves that describe upper and lower bounds on the event rates.

In this paper we seek to improve the current state of trace-based mapping flows to better support multiple traces for one application. We do this in two ways: by using trace theory, defining metrics in order to compare application traces and by using group theory to describe and utilize symmetries in the architecture. Trace theory has been a well-established model for concurrency for decades since its first formal formulation in 1977 by Mazurkiewicz [13]. Metrics for traces have been defined in very different contexts [8], or for similar applications very specific metrics have been considered [11]. To the best of our knowledge, however, trace metrics have never been used in the general context of analyzing KPN processes.

2   Process Traces and Histories

In this section we present our proposed trace analysis methods for the application side. To this end we introduce the formal concepts of traces and histories, explain their relationship and define a metric on the space of traces and of histories. We then describe experimental results obtained by applying these methods to randomly-generated KPN traces and on a JPEG encoder.

2.1   Traces and Histories

Traces and *histories* are both generalizations of strings. They are well-known as models for concurrently executing processes. Informally, we model concurrently executing processes as a string over an alphabet Σ, where the words of the alphabet represent events of the system. In a regular string all occurring characters (or events) have a well-defined sequential ordering. When two contiguous characters, however, represent independent events in the system, then we do not distinguish their order in the trace: we consider two traces as equal when we can convert one to the other by just rearranging independent characters.

More formally, let $\Sigma_1, \ldots, \Sigma_n$ be n alphabets, and consider the alphabet $\Sigma = \Sigma_1 \cup \ldots \cup \Sigma_n$, the union of those alphabets. This union is not necessarily disjoint. We define a *dependence subset* D of Σ^2 by $D = \Sigma_1^2 \cup \ldots \cup \Sigma_n^2$. From this we define the set $I = \Sigma^2 \setminus D$. It can be used to define an equivalence relation $\sim$ on the set of strings Σ^*. We say that $ab \sim ba$, if and only if $(a, b) \in I$. This induces an equivalence relation $\sim$ on Σ^* by extending it to all strings (the reflexive, transitive symmetric closure). We define the *set of traces* as the factor set of equivalence classes $\Sigma^* / \sim$. Since strings with concatenation have the algebraic structure of a monoid, and concatenation and the epimorphism to the equivalence class $\sim$ commute, $\Sigma^* / \sim$ is also a monoid with concatenation. It is therefore usually called the *trace monoid* [9].

Histories are similar. Instead of an arbitrary concatenation of the various independent strings, we consider a history to be a tuple of strings, one in each of the alphabets Σ_i. The individual alphabets represent the possible events for individual processes. These alphabets can have some common characters between them, in which case $\Sigma_i \cap \Sigma_j \neq \varnothing$ holds. These common characters represent synchronization events: they happen in two or more processes at the same time.

We can think of a history as a log of an application which represents all events in a parallel execution with different tasks or processes. The projection onto the alphabet of a single process represents the individual history of that process, independent of the others. With respect to component-wise concatenation, the set of histories over the alphabet $\Sigma = \Sigma_1 \cup \ldots \cup \Sigma_n$ is also a monoid, which is why it is often called the *history monoid* [9].

These two structures, the trace and the history monoid, are isomorphic. We either list events sequentially in a trace, where we don't distinguish the order of independent events, or we define the sequential history of each process independently. A formal proof of this fact can be found in [9].

2.2   Metrics

A metric acts as a way of measuring distance between objects. If we consider traces and histories as descriptions of the behavior of individual executions of a software built of concurrent processes, a metric acts as a way of comparing said execution behaviors.

There exists a plethora of metrics on strings, which are used from coding theory to DNA analysis and approximate string matching. Notable examples include the Hamming distance which only counts the number of equal letters, or the edit distance, which counts the minimal number of deletions, insertions and substitutions needed to go from one string to another. We can generalize these metrics to histories (and thus, traces) with the following theorem:

Theorem 1. *Let $\Sigma = \Sigma_1 \cup \ldots \cup \Sigma_n$ be an alphabet and d be a metric on the strings Σ^* over Σ. Then d induces a metric $\bar{d}$ on the set of histories H over $(\Sigma_1, \ldots, \Sigma_n)$ with projections $\pi_1, \ldots, \pi_n$ by*

$$\bar{d}(x = (x_1, \ldots, x_n), y = (y_1, \ldots, y_n)) = \sum_{i=1}^{n} d(x_i, y_i) = \sum_{i=1}^{n} d(\pi_i(x), \pi_i(y)) \quad (1)$$

Proof. Let $x, y, z \in H$ be histories.

1. Let $\bar{d}(x, y) = 0$. Then $d(\pi_i(x), \pi_i(y)) = 0$ for all $i = 1, \ldots, n$. Since d is a metric, it means that $\pi_i(x) = \pi_i(y)$ for all i. This implies that $x = y$ since it holds for all projections.
2. By definition (Eq. 1) it is immediately obvious that, since d is a metric

$$\bar{d}(x, y) = \sum_{i=1}^{n} d(\pi_i(x), \pi_i(y)) = \sum_{i=1}^{n} d(\pi_i(y), \pi_i(x)) = \bar{d}(y, x)$$

3. Finally, the triangle equation also follows in a similar fashion:

$$\bar{d}(x, y) = \sum_{i=1}^{n} \underbrace{d(\pi_i(x), \pi_i(y))}_{\leqslant d(\pi_i(x), \pi_i(z)) + d(\pi_i(z), \pi_i(y))} \leqslant \sum_{i=1}^{n} d(\pi_i(x), \pi_i(z)) + d(\pi_i(z), \pi_i(y))$$

$$= \sum_{i=1}^{n} d(\pi_i(x), \pi_i(z)) + \sum_{i=1}^{n} d(\pi_i(z), \pi_i(y)) = \bar{d}(x, z) + \bar{d}(z, y)$$

Similar to this construction, and inspired by the l_p norms, we can define other metrics on histories (and traces).

Let $p \in \mathbb{R}_{\geqslant 1}$ be a real number, greater than or equal to one. Further let $\Sigma = \Sigma_1 \cup \ldots \cup \Sigma_n$ be a history alphabet and let $d_i' : \Sigma_i^* \to \mathbb{R}_{\geqslant 0}$ be a metric on $\Sigma_i, i = 1, \ldots, n$. Let $H \subseteq \Sigma_1^* \times \ldots \times \Sigma_n^*$ be the set of histories on Σ, with the corresponding projections $\pi_i : H \to \Sigma_i, i = 1, \ldots, n$. We call the mapping

$$d_p : H \times H \to \mathbb{R}_{\geqslant 0}, (x, y) \mapsto \sqrt[p]{\sum_{i=1}^{n} d_i'(\pi_i(x), \pi_i(y))^p}$$

the p-metric on the histories. Similarly, we can define a ∞ metric d_∞ as $d_\infty(x, y) = max_{i=1,\ldots,} d(\pi_i(x), \pi_i(y))$. The proof that these induce metrics is very similar to that of Theorem 1.

2.3 Trace Analysis

To have controlled differences in our traces, we use random KPN traces. We generate them with a modification of the open-source software tool sdf^3 [17]. Concretely, we generate a random SDF application, and subsequently modify it to have a less static behavior. We do this by generating a set of possible, different input/output behaviors and randomly varying between them at run-time. For realistic behavior, we do this only on some KPN processes, while others keep their static (SDF) behavior. This method is inspired by the random KPN generation described in [5]. Once the application has been generated, different traces are created. This is achieved by fixing the possible behaviors and only randomizing the frequencies of occurrence.

For evaluating mappings we use a discrete-event-simulator similar to the one described in [6]. As the target architecture we use a virtual platform, also similar to the one described in [6]. It has two identical RISC (ARM) processors and four identical vector DSPs. A diagram of this test architecture can be seen in Fig. 1.

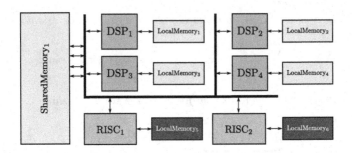

Fig. 1. A diagram of the test architecture used

For evaluating the methods proposed in this section we used a fixed, randomly generated process network which had four different processes and four FIFO channels. We generated 1000 different random process traces of diverse lengths and behaviors. For each of these 1000 traces we calculated the optimal mapping by using the discrete event simulator and exhaustively evaluating all $6^4 = 1296$ different possible (process-to-processor) mappings. For buffer sizing we used a simple strategy assigning the same size to the buffers on all traces for an accurate comparison. This approach is inefficient and time-consuming, but only by using truly optimal mappings can we achieve a valid analysis. Without the optimality of the mapping there is no guarantee that it is good for a trace, even if it was specifically calculated for it.

Random traces provide only limited insight into this problem. To validate our approach we also considered a JPEG encoder with an existing implementation as a KPN. The JPEG encoder needs to perform run-length encoding, which exhibits dynamic behavior for the KPN channels. We executed the JPEG encoder on a benchmark consisting of 200 images adapted from the BSDS500 Benchmark [1].

The exponential scaling of the exhaustive mapping evaluation is also the reason why a network with only four processes was chosen for the random traces. For larger applications where the problem size makes exhaustive evaluation prohibitively long, as is the case for the JPEG encoder, good meta-heuristics like evolutionary algorithms can be considered as a replacement. While this does not guarantee the same accuracy for the comparison, using the results of a good meta-heuristic should produce a solid basis for comparison nevertheless. For the JPEG encoder we use simple heuristics from the literature (e.g., load balancing).

2.4   Results

We chose a reference trace for comparing. Then, for each of the 1000 random traces we compared the optimal run-time obtained using the optimal mapping with the run-time obtained using the reference mapping (in general only optimal for the reference trace). From the quotient of both we obtained a slowdown factor $\geqslant 1$. Similarly, we calculated the distance between each trace and the reference one. Using this we analyze the correlation between trace distance and the slowdown from using the sub-optimal mapping. The results can be seen in Fig. 2. This figure uses three different induced metrics from two string metrics for a total of six metrics. They have been normalized to one within the data-set for comparison. The axes on Fig. 2b were adjusted not to show the trivial points at $(0, 1)$ (for the reference trace). This is for the sole purpose of a better visual scaling of the plot.

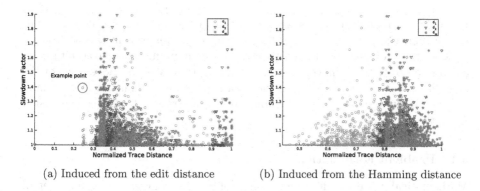

(a) Induced from the edit distance   (b) Induced from the Hamming distance

Fig. 2. Application slowdown as a function of different trace distances

As an example, consider the point marked in Fig. 2a. This point has the coordinates $(0.24, 1.42)$. It means that the distance between the trace corresponding to the point, and the reference trace was 24% of the maximal distance in the plot (concretely, $d_1 = 101$ with a maximal distance of 424). The 1.42 slowdown factor means that the execution time of the trace with the reference mapping was 42% slower than with its own optimal mapping.

Altogether, Fig. 2 shows a low correlation between the trace distance and how good the mapping of one trace is for the other one. Concretely, the correlation coefficients are -0.014, -0.077, -0.095, 0.119, 0.010, and -0.059, for the d_1, d_2 and d_∞ norms induced by the edit and Hamming distances, in that order.

JPEG Encoder

Figure 4 shows a histogram of different trace metrics for the 200 JPEG encoder executions. The traces were normalized with the distance from the reference trace to the empty trace, to give an idea of how much variation was between the traces. The JPEG encoder has variation in traces due to the run-length encoder, which is a small function that sends a different amount of tokens depending on the compressed data. However, the majority of the computation time is due to the discrete cosine transform, which has a static behavior. Even though the run-length encoder represents just a small fraction of the computation, we found performance and trace behavior deviations. By using the mapping tailored for a different trace, a slowdown of up to 1.77% was observed. More importantly though, we see that different inputs yield different behaviors, represented by different traces. We also see that these differences have a negative impact on performance, albeit a small one in this case. In the future we plan to investigate further applications where the dynamic data flow part of the application amounts to a more significant percentage of the execution.

3   Permutations of Mappings

From the trace analysis above we see that distance analysis itself does not suffice to infer the performance of different mappings. Instead, in this section we consider the problem from the perspective of the mappings and the architecture, as opposed to that of the traces and the application. We take advantage of the fact that heterogeneous platforms have some degree of symmetry. We formally define and explore this symmetry, and present a strategy to reduce the design space that leverages it.

3.1   Problem Formulation

Mathematically, we can formulate our problem as follows: Let P be a set of physical resources (e.g. processing elements, on-chip memories) and let L be a set representing logical elements (e.g., processes, FIFO channels). We define a valid mapping $m : L \to P$ as a mapping in the mathematical sense (a function), such that it respects the KPN structure. Formally, let G be a subgroup of the symmetric group of the physical resources S_P. The canonical action of the group G on P induces an action on the set of mappings $m : L \to P$: for $g \in G$ and $m : L \to P$ a mapping, i.e. $(g \cdot m)(l) := g \cdot m(l)$ for all $l \in L$. We require of a symmetry group that the run-time for all traces is an invariant of the group action. In particular, this means that the action of G on the set of mappings restricts to an action on the set of valid mappings. This implies, for example, that we only consider symmetries of the architecture that map processors to processors and communication resources to equivalent communication resources. We define equivalence classes for mappings: we say two mappings m, m' are equivalent if there exists a symmetry of the architecture $g \in G$ such that $g \cdot m = m'$, i.e., if m and m' are in the same orbit under the action induced by G on the set of valid mappings.

For example, let $P = \{\mathrm{RISC}_1, \mathrm{RISC}_2, \mathrm{DSP}_1, \ldots, \mathrm{DSP}_4\}$ be the processor set of the architecture from the experimental setup in last section (see Fig. 1), and let $L = \{p_1, \ldots, p_4\}$ be the process set of the four-process KPN used in the example from last section. For simplicity, we consider an elementary, symmetric communication model in this example where communication resources and processors are coupled. Then the group G that can swap both RISC processors and allows any permutation of the four DSP processors is the symmetry group of this architecture. It is isomorphic to $S_2 \times S_4$, i.e., the direct product of the symmetric groups on two and four elements respectively. As an example, consider the mappings

$$m_1 : p_1 \mapsto \mathrm{RISC}_1, p_2, p_3 \mapsto \mathrm{DSP}_2, p_4 \mapsto DSP_3$$
$$m_2 : p_1 \mapsto \mathrm{RISC}_1, p_2, p_3 \mapsto \mathrm{DSP}_1, p_4 \mapsto DSP_4$$
$$m_3 : p_1 \mapsto \mathrm{RISC}_1, p_2, p_4 \mapsto \mathrm{DSP}_2, p_3 \mapsto DSP_3.$$

Then, m_1 and m_2 are equivalent, however neither of them is equivalent to m_3.

The motivation for this definition of equivalence is that if two processors are equal, then it usually should make no difference if one or the other is chosen for the mapping. This can also be used for taking communication into account, for example when there is additional symmetry from multiple memories or differences in local memories break the processor symmetry.

Groups with this structure are by far the most common symmetry group for heterogeneous architectures. A heterogeneous architecture which has n_1 equivalent processing elements of type 1, n_2 equivalent processing elements of type 2, and so forth, will have a symmetry group isomorphic to $S_{n_1} \times S_{n_2} \times \cdots$. However, the symmetry group of a subset of equivalent processing elements need not be a full symmetric group. For example, consider a simple homogeneous four-core architecture with a Network-on-Chip (NoC), such that the communication latency between adjacent processors is considerably lower than to non-adjacent ones. Then the adjacency of the processors should be kept with any symmetry transformation, which means the symmetry group is a dihedral group of a regular polygon with 4 sides, instead of the full symmetric group on 4 points. This group is called D_4, though some references call it D_8 because it has 8 elements. Figure 3 shows a schematic of this symmetry and an example of an allowed symmetry, one of the two generators, and a permutation that is not a symmetry of the architecture. It depicts the symmetry transformations with the green or red arrows, and an example of the action on a mapping of four processes, represented by the green or red circles.

3.2   Algorithmic Considerations

To identify equivalent mappings we need to find out if two elements are in the same orbit. Specifically, if m, m' are mappings, we need to test if $m' \in Gm$. This can in general be done with $\mathcal{O}(|Gm||S|)$ group element applications, where $|S|$ is a generating set of the group G, see Theorem 2.1.1 of [15]. Since we do not plan to deal with very complex symmetry groups, however, we used a different approach. Our approach is tailored for groups that have the form $\times_{i=1}^{k} S_{n_i}$, for $n_1, \ldots, n_k \in \mathbb{N}$. It takes advantage of the fact that group membership testing is a simple task in groups of this family. We devised a strategy that given mappings

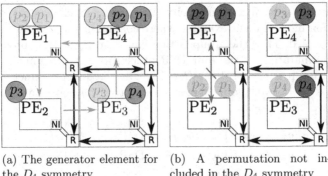

(a) The generator element for the D_4 symmetry

(b) A permutation not included in the D_4 symmetry

Fig. 3. Schematic representation on of the symmetry of a 4-core NoC architecture

m, m' generates a tentative mapping $\sigma : \{1, \ldots, |P|\} \to \{1, \ldots, |P|\}$ such that if there exists a $\tau \in S_{|P|}$ such that $\tau \cdot m = m'$, then σ is a permutation and it holds that $\sigma \cdot m = m'$. We achieve this by iterating over all elements e in the definition domain of mapping m and updating σ to be correct for that element (i.e. $(\sigma m)(e) = m'(e)$), without guaranteeing that it remains a permutation. Using this tentative mapping strategy, we can find out if two mappings are in the same orbit, and if so, obtain a permutation that maps one to the other.

Algorithm 1. Orbit membership testing for direct products of symmetric groups

---

INPUT: $m, m', n = |P|$
OUTPUT:
if $Gm = m'$ **then**
    an element $g \in G$: $gm = m'$,
else false
end if
ALGORITHM:
$\sigma = \text{tentativeMapping}(m, m', n)$;
$\text{permutation} = \text{isPermutation}(\sigma)$;
$\text{ingroup} = \text{isInGroup}(\sigma, G)$;
$\text{maps} = \text{mappingsEqual}(\sigma \cdot m, m)$;
if permutation **and** ingroup **and** maps **then**
    return σ
else
    return false
end if

Algorithm 1 is more efficient than the standard algorithm. It uses a constant, single group application instead of $\mathcal{O}(|Gm||S|)$. However, it relies on the fact that if the proposed element σ is not in G, then there exists no element $g \in G$

mapping m to m', which is by no means obvious if G is not of the form $\times_{i=1}^{k} S_{n_i}$. For the general case, the standard black-box group algorithms should be used (see [15]).

The permutation approach has limited scalability. Using Burnside's Lemma [4], it is straightforward to prove that the factor by which the size of the search space is reduced is bounded by the cardinality of the symmetry group. In particular, the asymptotic scaling behavior of the size of the search space is the same, it still is in $\mathcal{O}(|P|^{|L|})$. However, we see in the experiments in the next section that not all equivalence classes of mappings are equally common. Further investigation could concentrate on identifying the most important equivalence classes and their corresponding traces.

3.3   Experimental Results

For evaluating this approach, we used the same basic setup as in Sect. 2. Using Algorithm 1 we identified equivalence classes in the optimal-run-time mappings of the same set of 1000 random process from Sect. 2. We selected one trace and identified all traces which yielded mappings equivalent to it. In general, for a system with 6 processors total where there are two groups of 4 and 2 equivalent processors respectively, there exist exactly 83 possible mappings of four processes. This fact can be verified using Burnside's Lemma. Out of the 1000 traces a total 23 were equivalent to the first one. They all had a slowdown factor of exactly 1, as would be expected of equivalent mappings. This is, however, only a fraction of the 161 mappings with a slowdown factor of 1 compared to the first trace.

Furthermore, of all 83 possible mappings, considering symmetry, only 30 were present in the traces. Figure 5 shows a bar plot of the percentage of traces belonging to each group, for the 30 groups up to symmetry which had a trace with an optimal mapping in this group. They are ordered from most common to least common, and the remaining 53 unrepresented groups are not depicted.

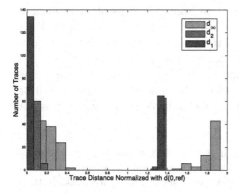
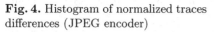
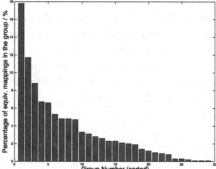

Fig. 4. Histogram of normalized traces differences (JPEG encoder)

Fig. 5. Frequency of the equivalence classes of optimal mappings

This results show that while there are quite a few possible equivalence classes of mappings, 83 in this case, only very few are actually good mappings. The two most common equivalence classes are optimal for almost 30% of the traces, while the five most common ones actually account for more than half the traces.

The JPEG encoder was not considered for this since it would be too computationally intensive to calculate optimal mappings, and it would have yielded limited insight for the lack of optimality variations between traces.

4   Conclusion

In this paper we have considered the differences in execution behaviors of KPN and dynamic data flow applications as process traces or histories. We defined a metric space structure on traces and used it to measure the relationship between the trace distance, and how good the optimal mapping of one trace works for the other. For this, we also developed a framework for comparing them, which included exhaustive search on small examples to find true optimal mappings, for a solid comparison base.

The results from the JPEG encoder showed behavioral variations for different inputs in a real application. Additionally, the results from our analysis on random traces suggest no correlation between the trace distance and the goodness of the mappings of one to the other. This is a very revealing result. Its implications are twofold. First, it means that the difference between two traces does not suffice to t if we can use the same mapping for both. In particular this means we should devise more elaborate strategies for trace grouping, probably application-specific ones. The second, less obvious implication, is that very small differences in traces can have a very big impact on performance. Further work will focus on real applications with more dynamic behavior than the JPEG encoder that was used.

Apart form the behavior in the form of the traces, we also considered the problem from the perspective of the mappings. We defined a strategy to leverage symmetries in the architecture and evaluated it with the experiments used for the traces. We managed to reduce the search space from 1296 possible mappings to 83 possible equivalence classes of mappings, and found that very few equivalence classes of mappings account for the optimal throughput in the majority of traces.

Another direction for future work is to define strategies for identifying traces at run-time and using trace-specific information about the optimal mapping for dynamically improving adaptive execution. The analysis framework can be used to consider the problem of buffer sizing for multiple traces, which was not addressed in this work.

Acknowledgments. This work is supported in part by the German Research Foundation (DFG) within the Cluster of Excellence "Center for Advancing Electronics Dresden" (cfaed). We would like to thank Silexica (www.silexica.com) for making their embedded multicore software development tool suite available to us as basis for our work.

References

1. Arbelaez, P., Maire, M., Fowlkes, C., Malik, J.: Contour detection and hierarchical image segmentation. IEEE Trans. Pattern Anal. Mach. Intell. **33**(5), 898–916 (2011)
2. Brunet, S.C.: Analysis and optimization of dynamic dataflow programs. Ph.D. thesis, Ecole Polytechnique Federale de Lausanne (EPLFL) (2015)
3. Buck, J.T., Lee, E.A.: Scheduling dynamic dataflow graphs with bounded memory using the token flow model. In: 1993 IEEE International Conference on Acoustics, Speech, and Signal Processing, ICASSP 1993, vol. 1, pp. 429–432. IEEE (1993)
4. Burnside, W.: Theory of Groups of Finite Order (1911)
5. Castrillon, J., Leupers, R.: Programming Heterogeneous MPSoCs: Tool Flows to Close the Software Productivity Gap. Springer, Cham (2014). https://doi.org/10.1007/978-3-319-00675-8
6. Castrillon, J., Leupers, R., Ascheid, G.: Maps: mapping concurrent dataflow applications to heterogeneous MPSoCs. IEEE Trans. Ind. Inf. **9**(1), 527–545 (2011)
7. Castrillon, J., Tretter, A., Leupers, R., Ascheid, G.: Communication-aware mapping of KPN applications onto heterogeneous MPSoCs. In: Proceedings of the 49th Annual Conference on Design Automation, DAC 2012 (2012)
8. de Bakker, J., Zucker, J.I.: Denotational semantics of concurrency. In: Proceedings of the Fourteenth Annual ACM Symposium on Theory of Computing, pp. 153–158. ACM (1982)
9. Diekert, V., Rozenberg, G., Rozenburg, G.: The Book of Traces, vol. 15. World Scientific, Singapore (1995)
10. Gilles, K.: The semantics of a simple language for parallel programming. In: Proceedings of the IFIP Congress Information Processing 1974, vol. 74, pp. 471–475 (1974)
11. Kengne, C.K., Ibrahim, N., Rousset, M.-C., Tchuente, M.: Distance-based trace diagnosis for multimedia applications: help me ted! In: 2013 IEEE Seventh International Conference on Semantic Computing (ICSC), pp. 306–309. IEEE (2013)
12. Lee, E.A., Messerschmitt, D.G.: Synchronous data flow. Proc. IEEE **75**(9), 1235–1245 (1987)
13. Mazurkiewicz, A.: Concurrent program schemes and their interpretations. DAIMI Rep. Ser. **6**(78), 1–51 (1977)
14. Pimentel, A.D., Erbas, C., Polstra, S.: A systematic approach to exploring embedded system architectures at multiple abstraction levels. IEEE Trans. Comput. **55**(2), 99–112 (2006)
15. Seress, Á.: Permutation Group Algorithms, vol. 152. Cambridge University Press, Cambridge (2003)
16. Singh, A.K., Shafique, M., Kumar, A., Henkel, J.: Mapping on multi/many-core systems: survey of current and emerging trends. In: Proceedings of the 50th Annual Design Automation Conference, p. 1. ACM (2013)
17. Stuijk, S., Geilen, M., Basten, T.: SDF³: SDF for free. In: Proceedings of 6th International Conference on Application of Concurrency to System Design, ACSD 2006, pp. 276–278. IEEE Computer Society Press, Los Alamitos, June 2006
18. Thiele, L., Bacivarov, I., Haid, W., Huang, K.: Mapping applications to tiled multiprocessor embedded systems. In: Seventh International Conference on Application of Concurrency to System Design, ACSD 2007, pp. 29–40. IEEE (2007)
19. Thiele, L., Chakraborty, S., Naedele, M.: Real-time calculus for scheduling hard real-time systems. In: Proceedings of The 2000 IEEE International Symposium on Circuits and Systems, ISCAS 2000, Geneva, vol. 4, pp. 101–104 (2000)

Modeling and Analysis of SLDL-Captured NoC Abstractions

Ran Hao, Nasibeh Teimouri[(✉)], Kasra Moazzemi, and Gunar Schirner

Department of Electrical and Computer Engineering,
Northeastern University, Boston, MA 02115, USA
{hao.R,moazzemi.k}@husky.neu.edu, {nteimouri,schirner}@ece.neu.edu

Abstract. With increasing number of IP cores, parallel communication architectures including NoCs have emerged for many-core systems. To efficiently architect NoCs, early analysis of crucial run-time metrics such as throughput, latency and saturation time is required. This requires abstract modeling of NoCs. Modeling abstraction, and consequently the modeling granularity impacts the accuracy and speed of simulation. While a fine-grained model will slowly lead more accurate information, a coarser model simulates faster and yields less accurate predictions. This paper first identifies possible levels of abstraction for NoC models and correlating captured features with the accuracy/speed trade-off. Second, this paper proposes two NoC models at different abstraction levels: a finer grained Bus-Functional Model (BFM), and a coarser Transaction-Level Model (TLM). The BFM updates the system status after any events happening during data unit transmission, while the TLM updates the system status at the end of data unit transmission.

Our evaluation results show moving to higher abstraction (from BFM to TLM) gains 10x to 50x speedup at the cost of 10%–20% accuracy loss on average. Our analysis approach and results guide system architects in exploring NoC architectural alternatives and help identifying suitable abstract levels.

1 Introduction

Chip Multiprocessing (CMP) as one essential solution for parallel processing and high performance computing has evolved to exploit parallelism in the form of integrating multiple processor cores on a single chip which is known as System on Chip (SoC). To power and performance efficiently connect the cores, reusable interconnect architectures are required that provide scalable bandwidth and parallelism.

These requirements cannot be met by traditional interconnect architectures like single shared bus or even hierarchy of buses due to their poor scalability as they allow only one (or a few number of) sender-to-receiver communication(s) at a time [1]. Promising alternatives are Networks on Chip (NoCs). NoCs avoid the need for dedicated wires for each individual communication, and connect IP cores

© IFIP International Federation for Information Processing 2017
Published by Springer International Publishing AG 2017. All Rights Reserved
M. Götz et al. (Eds.): IESS 2015, IFIP AICT 523, pp. 128–141, 2017.
https://doi.org/10.1007/978-3-319-90023-0_11

through an on-chip network. Several advantages compared to dedicated wires include delivering high-bandwidth, low-latency and low-power communication over a flexible and modular medium [2,3].

Different NoC design parameters (e.g. topology, communication mechanism, routing method and switching mode) impact a multi-dimensional trade-off space between latency, throughput, communication load, energy consumption, and silicon area. Therefore, early evaluation of NoC is in high demand [4]. Recent approaches on NoC emulation aim for accuracy. However, they could be too slow, especially when considering the tight time-to-market [5].

System level modeling can relieve time to market pressures and the expense of NoC simulation/emulation tools with providing faster architecture exploration, performance evaluation, and functional validation [6]. Abstract modeling of an NoC poses the question of abstraction levels (the amount of detail to be retained in the model). Ultimately, this poses a trade-off between simulation speed and accuracy [7] as visualized in Fig. 1.

A highly abstract NoC model abstracts away much of the underlying communication details, and in result yields a very fast but inaccurate simulation. Conversely, an accurate model would capture more of the communication principles, resulting in a slower but more accurate simulation. Although [8] discusses about different abstraction levels, their precise definition and modeling abstraction rules are not clearly presented. Defining abstraction levels helps designers to select communication features to model given a desired speed/accuracy.

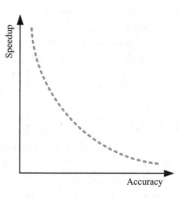

Fig. 1. Speed accuracy trade-off

This paper first identifies different NoC abstraction levels according to the visibility of implementation details and communication granularity. A most abstract model treats the whole NoC as one black box, only revealing input and output traffic. Conversely, the most detail level exposes how individual flits are handled at the micro-architecture level. This paper defines accuracy impact factors at each level, highlights contention points over shared resources within an NoC and identifies the required arbitration points.

Next, the paper proposes an abstract NoC model using Transaction Level Modeling (TLM). It realizes the structure of Hermes router model [4] with 5 bidirectional (both input/output) ports to the four neighboring IP cores and one port to the local IP core. The model implements XY routing and wormhole switching. The proposed TLM captures all the router features and arbitration events over its shared resources at cycle-level. It updates the system status at each cycle independent of how many arbitration events are notified during that cycle.

To evaluate the performance and accuracy of the proposed TLM versus an accurate model, this paper also introduces a more detailed model, a Bus

Functional Model (BFM). The BFM follows the bus functional modeling principals [6] aiming to be as accurate as an RTL implementation. The BFM captures much more structural and micro-architectural detail and it updates the system status upon any arbitration event. This improves accuracy at the cost of simulation speed. Our TLM is 10 times faster than the BFM at the cost of 10% to 20% error.

The rest of this paper is organized as follows: Sect. 2 discusses related work in NoC modeling and analysis. Section 3 defines different abstraction levels for NoC modeling. Section 4 first presents the structure of modeled router, then proposes our TLM and BFM NoC abstract models. Following that, Sect. 5 validates the proposed BFM as accurate against an RTL implementation of NoC and then evaluates the proposed TLM versus BFM. Finally Sect. 6 concludes the paper.

2   Related Work

Exploring the design trade-offs of NoC metrics including bandwidth, power, performance and silicon area can be done at different levels of accuracy and details based on the design requirements. For instance, SW development needs fast simulation. Conversely, performance estimation demands a finer set of details and higher accuracy for proper validation [9]. In general, work on evaluating NoC can be categorized in 3 groups: emulation/simulation frameworks, static analysis, and abstract modeling.

Emulation/Simulation Framework: Many NoC simulators and emulators have been developed; the emulation platform proposed by Dally et al. as a flexible emulation environment implemented on FPGA based on a complete mixed HW-SW NoC emulation framework, Xmulator [10] as an event-driven simulator and Booksim [11] as a cycle-driven simulator are a few instances of tools in this category. All instances impose high implementation cost, maintenance difficulty and long emulation/simulation time.

Some works [12,13] aim to reduce the emulation/simulation time by changing the kernel scheduler, simulation/evaluation semantics by adding local clocks/schedulers. Nevertheless, their improvements are case-specific, for instance [12] gains more as the size of NoC gets larger.

Static Analysis: Static analysis like [14,15] rapidly yields timing parameters such as router service time and packet arrival time. These methods have low accuracy as they abstract away dynamic behaviors influencing NoC performance and bandwidth.

Abstract Modeling: Abstract modeling might be placed in between two above categories. It abstracts away some implementation detail (such as bit-level communication details) and takes into account only the events occurring per transmission of coarser data granularity. The goal is to accelerate the NoC evaluation while maintaining some accuracy. The architectural model in [9] is one example. It models the HERMES [4] router architecture as a bus and all cores/routers connected to it as individual modules. With keeping track of all routers' active flows

in different FIFOs and prioritizing their requests based on the pre-defined priorities, all the competitions over the shared resources are captured. The drawback
of this work compared to the proposed TLM is its evaluation for worst-cases;
when all possible contentions over the shared resources happen. Similarly, [16]
proposes an accurate abstract model for on-chip interconnects. It uses bus protocol specifications to identify a reduced set of timing points. Finding the set of
optimal timing points is the drawback of this work compared to the proposed
TLM.

3 NoC Abstraction Models

Conceptually, many abstraction levels are possible that may range from an
extremely coarse grain model the treats the whole NoC as one black box, to a
very fine-grained model that exposes micro architectural implementation details
of all the NoC elements. Abstracting NoC can occur with different levels of
details; from low covering details such as observing the whole NoC as a communication box to considering all micro-architectural implementation details of all
NoC elements. When comparing abstraction levels, the following aspects should
be considered:

Granularity of Data defines the smallest unit of data transferred through the
   NoC.
Visibility defines the level of implementation details of NoC communication
   observable in the model.
Arbitration Points lists the shared resources for which contention is dynamically resolved.
Timing Accuracy outlines the resulting estimation accuracy; meaning that at
   which level of accuracy, an NoC model can estimate the timing behavior of a
   real NoC.

Given the characteristics above, we propose five abstraction levels. Table 1
summarizes the models, and Fig. 2 illustrates the 3 most abstract models.

Network-Level Model: models the whole NoC as a black box and only exposes
   the local ports. This model abstracts away everything inside NoC including
   traffic paths and contentions over the shared resources. The model estimates
   network latency based on statistical information like average/worst case network latency per pre-defined size of traffic and the amount of traffic transferred through the network.
Router-Level Model: realizes NoC as a set of routers connected to each other
   via physical channels. In this model, routers are modeled as black boxes which
   receive packets as input and sends output packets over a physical link to the
   next router. This model estimates the NoC performance/latency based on
   the number and size of packets as well as the length of path taken by each
   packet. It dynamically resolves contention on physical links.

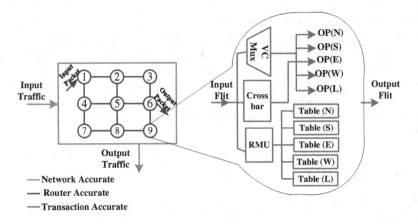

Fig. 2. NoC modelling granularities

Transaction-Level Model: more details over the router-level model by modeling router internal modules, including input/output ports, cross-bar, routing
management, virtual channel (VC) allocation and flow control management.
In this model, at the end of any transaction, the contentions (and arbitration
events to resolve them) which change the system status are collected and the
system status is updated. Based on [17], a transaction is defined as injecting
the header flit (first part of a packet) by initiator and receiving the last flit
of the packet by the receiver.

Pin-Level Model: implements all the internal wires/pins per router modules
and updates the system status after any individual contention (and arbitration to resolve that) happening per transmission of each bit of the transaction.

Micro-Architectural-Level Model: implements the Pin-Accurate model and
all of it's router operations at gate level for final validation. This model is
practically an RTL model, very close to the final implementation, most accurate but also the slowest.

From the network-level model to micro-architectural level model, communication and implementation details are added to the model, increasing accuracy
at the cost of simulation speed. Table 1 summarizes the abstraction levels.

Table 1. NoC abstraction overview

Model	Visibiltiy	Granularity	Arbitration Point	Time Unit
Network-Accurate	-	Traffic	-	Loosely Time Estimated
Router-Accurate	Channel	Packet	Routers	Approximate Time Estimated
Transaction-Accurate	Channel	Flit	Router Modules	Cycle Estimated
Pin-Accurate	Wire	Bit	Router Modules	Cycle
Micro-Arch	Wire	Bit	Router Modules	Cycle

4   Proposed NoC Models

4.1   Router Architecture

Our router models are based on the HERMES router architecture [4] with slight changes.

Figure 3 outlines the router's internal structure with 4 important functional units: Input/Output Ports, Routing Management Unit (RMU), Flow Control Unit (FCU) and crossbar unit. RMU includes Routing Logic Unit (RLU) and central table to record the status of virtual channels (VCs) of the output ports. FCU for promulgating free ports to the neighboring output ports. Crossbar unit forwards the packets to the next router determined by the RMU.

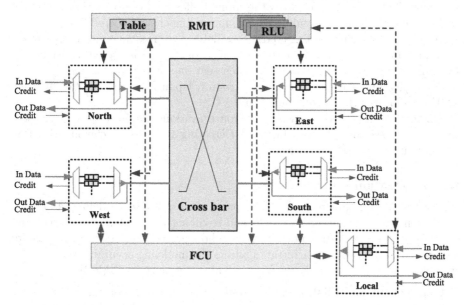

Fig. 3. The router architecture in the proposed NoC abstract models

Each router is connected to 4 neighboring routers through the 4 input/output ports. One local port connects the router to the local IP core. Each input port has a configurable (8bits in Hermes, 32bits in our model) size of VC-buffers to record the received data/control flits. A flit is the smallest part of a packet. There is no buffer in the output ports as the buffer in the next router's input port is used. For this, a credit-based flow control mechanism is employed to notify the sending side about the available space on the receiving side. This way, flit is only sent if there is space on the receiving side. The RLU (part of RMU) computes which output port to sent a packet to. The VC allocation unit selects which VC to use for a given output port. One of our changes over the Hermes architecture is supporting individual RLUs for each input port in order to avoid congestion inside the router. Similar to Hermes, the routing method is XY; approaching the destination always first horizontally, then vertically or vice versa. Routing decision is made per header flit which contains destination information and packet length. Flits are switched using the wormhole method.

4.2 Packet Transmission

Example a received flit is stored in the VC buffers of that input port. In case of a header flit, it's destination is forwarded to the RMU to determine the output port. After selecting the output port, the RLU consults RMU table to find an available VC on the output port.

After selecting output port and VC, the input port refers to FCU to check if there is enough room for receiving this flit in the next router. In our credit-based flow control, each VC has a credit and when the VC is used by a flit, its credit is decreased. When the flit leaves the input buffer of the destination router, a credit is sent back to the sending router, increasing the VC's credit count.

Assuming sufficient sending credit is available, the crossbar sends the flit from the input port to the output port (and subsequently sends a credit upstream). The remaining flits of this packet are then sent one by one consulting the FCU about receive buffer credits to the next router. Upon receiving the tail flit, the RMU de-allocates the output buffer and VC.

During packet transmission within a router, various shared resources are used for which accesses need to be arbitrated. Detecting and resolving/arbitrating the contentions impacts the accuracy.

4.3 Arbitration Points

One of the most important aspects impacting accuracy in modeling is detecting contentions over shared resources and resolving them. Shared resources are FCU, crossbar, and output ports. The way how access requests to these shared resources are collected and arbitrated affects the modeling accuracy. We identify one contention type for each resource (see also summary in Table 2):

1. **Connection Establishment:** if a router receives two header flits that target the same output port, their requests contend for the RMU. An arbiter is required to select one of requests. The selected request gets access to the RMU (central table of RMU), then starts connection and sends data.
2. **Request Flow Control Grant:** simultaneous flow control requests at the same FCU for different VCs create contention over FCU access. Concurrent requests are feasible, as they have already received the credit to send data. In order to guarantee that at one point of time, only one traverse is allowed to a specific output port, an arbiter is necessary to give flow control grant signal to one of the requests. We define this arbitration point as arbitration for same output accesses.
3. **Crossbar Access:** when more than one VCs at the same input port gets the flow control grant simultaneously, there is contention on the crossbar. In our design, to avoid this contention, we define an arbiter for crossbar access from the same input port. This arbiter grants crossbar access to only one of the requests.

Table 2. Contention events and arbitration points

Arbitration point	location	Resource	Arbitration (BFM)	Arbitration (TLM)
Connection Establishment	RMU	RMU table	FIFO	random
Request Flow Control Grant	FCU	output port	FIFO	random
Crossbar Access	IP	crossbar	Round-robin	random

4.4   NoC Abstract Models: TLM and BFM

This paper captures two abstract models of NoC; Transaction-Accurate Model (TLM) and Pin-Accurate Model (BFM) in the System-level Design Language (SLDL), SpecC [18]. Both models take into account the arbitration points explained in Sect. 4.3 as well as the characteristics of Table 1. However, they differ in the way that requests to the shared resources are collected and arbitrated. The BFM gathers resource access requests based on sampling and driving of every single wire at each cycle. Conversely, the TLM gathers the access information at transaction. Consequently, the BFM updates the system status at any cycle, while the TLM updates at transaction boundaries. As the granularity of updating the system status affects the accuracy, TLM is less accurate than BFM.

Both models implement the same arbitration policies. However, as the TLM makes a decision at a coarser granularity, it is more susceptible to the order in which access requests appear. Within the same time quantum, the TLM cannot distinguish between concurrent requests. As the execution order is not specified by the underlying discrete event simulation semantics, the effective arbitration policy for simultaneous (same quantum) becomes random.

Moreover, the BFM is driven by an explicit clock, while the TLM virtually times routers by using the instruction $waitfor$. In some sense the TLM can be considered time driven, while BFM is event-driven. Both models also differ in the number of threads (sc_module in SystemC, or behavior in SpecC) used for simulation. The BFM employs active threads for each router module. Conversely, the TLM is mainly channel based (ie. is call driven) and only uses one behavior (or sc_module) for each VC. For instance, assuming 4 VCs per physical link, the BFM has 41 simultaneous threads and the TLM only 20. With the lower number of active threads, the TLM can perform faster (avoiding context switches). Table 3 compares BFM and TLM.

Table 3. Comparing TLM and BFM

	BFM	TLM
Communication Implementation	Behavior	Channel
Arbitration Policy	FIFO & Round-robin	Random
Timing	Event driven (explicit clock)	Time driven ($waitfor$)

5   Experimental Results

This section explores the proposed BFM and validates its accuracy and functionality with respect to the RTL implementation. It then compares the TLM versus the BFM based on speed and accuracy.

For evaluation of the models, we mainly use hot spot traffic [19]; some nodes in the network receive most of the traffic.

5.1   BFM Validation

System performance and throughput are two important metrics for analyzing NoC architectures. Average packet latency is a representative of system performance, and link utilization is a representative of throughput. Packet latency is the packet life-time defined as the difference between its start time label and its end time label.

Link utilization/load is the ratio of link busy time over the whole simulation time. Link busy time is defined as the total time when the link is busy carrying traffic.

In this part and for validation of the proposed BFM, we adopted 40%-hot spot traffic and defined packet size as 10 flits. 40%-hot spot traffic means that 40% of the nodes are the destinations of total traffic injected to the network. Each injector (hot node) injects 100 packets to the network. Figure 4 shows the simulation results including link load, average packet latency and simulation time for hotspot traffic injected into the 8*8 mesh. The results are correlated with the results of VC extended HERMES router structure on FPGA [20].

Figure 4a shows link load for different numbers of VCs as the injection rate increases. At small injection rate, the link load increases linearly for all VCs. However, the link load starts to level off from a specific injection rate, around 10%, 15%, 20% and 30% respectively for 1 VC, 2 VCs, 4 VCs and 8 VCs. Based on [20], this point is called saturation point. The saturation degree of network for multiple VCs in our model is higher than what is reported in [20]. The reason lies in the different implementations of the network interfaces. In our work, we define multiple VCs for local connections as well, which means at the destination node, traffic from different ports can sink into the local PE without being blocked. With the improved mechanism, the network throughput for VCs of 8 can reach 100% under hotspot traffic.

Figure 4b shows the average latency as injection rate increases. Up to the saturation point, the average latency is constant for all VCs. With increasing the number of VCs, the average latency drops in a half when VCs goes from 1 to 2. Similar situation for 2 VCs to 4 VCs. However, the average packet latency for VCs of 4 and 8 are similar. The reason is that using 4 VCs has already eliminated most of packet blocking.

Figure 4c shows the overall finish/transmission time as the injection rate increases. This time is when all the packets reach their destinations. Since more VCs leads to more traffic overlap on the fly, 8 VCs yields the shortest overall transmission time.

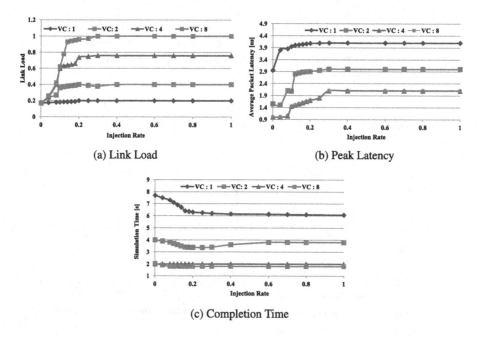

(a) Link Load   (b) Peak Latency

(c) Completion Time

Fig. 4. BFM performance validation (8×8 mesh, 40%-hot spot)

5.2   TLM Evaluation

This section evaluates the TLM compared to the BFM with respect to speedup and accuracy.

SpeedUp: depending on the amount of implementation details and number of context switches, the simulation time varies. For comparing the models, simulation speedup is reported. Simulation speedup of the model with higher level of abstraction (H) compared to the model with lower level of abstraction (L) is defined as 1.

$$Speedup_{H2L} = Simu. \, Time_L / Simu. \, Time_H \qquad (1)$$

As the simulation time strongly depends on the number of context switches, the simulation speed is closely correlated with the network size and traffic intensity. Both network size and traffic intensity affect the number of behaviors and context switches. Network size is the number of nodes in the network. Network intensity is defined as the number of transactions (number of packets) from sender nodes to the receiver nodes. With larger network or intense traffic simulation time increases.

To evaluate the effects of network size and traffic intensity, 40%-hot spot traffic is simulated with 4 VCs per physical link and 100% injection rate. Figure 5a shows the simulation time for increasing network (mesh) size from $2 * 2$ to $8 * 8$. The TLM is 10x to 16x faster than the BFM. With larger networks, TLM achieves higher speedup as a result of abstracting away higher ratio of communication details. Figure 5b illustrates the simulation time for network intensity. With increasing the transaction size (from 1 packet to 100 packets), TLM achieves an increasing speedup (from 14x to 50x) again as res ult of the more abstract simulation.

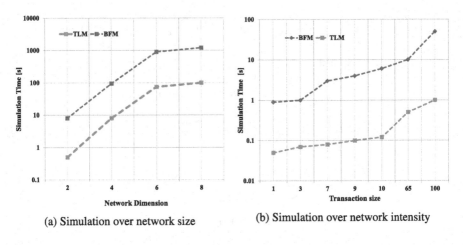

(a) Simulation over network size

(b) Simulation over network intensity

Fig. 5. Comparing simulation time of BFM and TLM (8 * 8 mesh, 40%-hot spot)

To measure the accuracy loss, we define accuracy error for each packet. As Eq. (2) defines, this accuracy error has correlation with the difference between packet latency in the TLM and BFM. Packet latency is the difference between start time label and end time label of the packet.

$$Error = |PacketLatency_L/PacketLatency_H|/PacketLatency_L \qquad (2)$$

As the TLM differs from the BFM in the effective arbitration policy (due to collection of requests and arbitration among them), measuring the accuracy loss in the TLM requires simulation scenarios with different amount of contentions (requests) over the shared resources. The amount of contentions over the shared resources is determined by the amount of traffic injected to the network. The more the injection rate, the higher the number of simultaneous requests for the same resources and higher contention and accuracy loss as a result. To demonstrate this, 40%-hot spot traffic is adopted into the TLM and BFM models of 6 * 6 NoC with 4 VCs per physical links and 100% injection rate. We simulate 100 transactions through the NoC and measure the transmission delay of packets in both models BFM and TLM. To aggregate the results, we report the average error, as well as the cumulative error for 50-percentile and 96-percentile as Fig. 6a. The 50-percentile (96-percentile) cumulative error indicates the maximal error experienced by 50% (96%) of transactions. As Fig. 6a represents, increasing the injection rate, increases the cumulative error probability. Increasing the injection rate from 0.1 to 0.2 increases the average error from 10% to 20%. At 0.1

injection rate 96% of packets observe less than 40% error, while 50% see less then 10% error. Increasing the injection rate to 0.6, makes 50% of packets experience up to 30% error.

Increasing the injection of rate increases the contention over shared resources. One indicator is the congestion rate over physical links. Figure 6b shows the cumulative error probability over increasing congestion. All three metrics are strongly related to congestion. And increase until congestion hits 50%. Then, 50% show at most 38% error, while the maximum error measured for 96% of packets reaches 100%. Conversely, at lower congestion rate, e.g. 5%, 96% of packets experience less than 20% error.

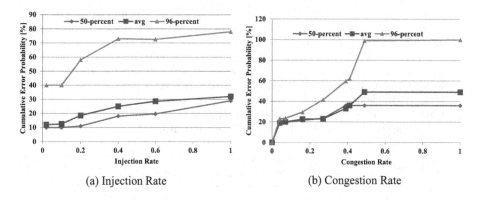

(a) Injection Rate   (b) Congestion Rate

Fig. 6. Cumulative probability of accuracy error

6   Conclusion

Modeling of NoCs is important for early exploration of NoC design alternatives. In this context, fast and accurate simulation is important. However, when abstracting NoC models, a trade-off between simulation speed and accuracy exists. This paper has identified NoC abstraction levels, differing in data granularity, visibility of internal structures and modeling of contention points. This paper has introduced two NoC models, an detailed Bus-Functional Model (BFM) which models and arbitrates at each clock cycle and a more abstract Transaction Level Model (TLM) that operates on coarser transactions. Both models have been captured in the SpecC SLDL. We have validated our BFM to sufficiently match the RTL implementation. The TLM simulates 10x to 50x faster than BFM at a cost of 10%–20% accuracy. Both speedup and accuracy loss increase with network size and traffic.

References

1. Sgroi, M., Sheets, M., Mihal, A., Keutzer, K., Malik, S., Rabaey, J., Sangiovanni-Vencentelli, A.: Addressing the system-on-a-chip interconnect woes through communication-based design. In: Design Automation Conference (DAC), pp. 667–672. ACM (2001)
2. Owens, J., Dally, W., Ho, R., Jayasimha, D.N., Keckler, S., Peh, L.-S.: Research challenges for on-chip interconnection networks. Micro IEEE **27**(5), 96–108 (2007)
3. Dally, W., Towles, B.: Route packets, not wires: on-chip interconnection networks. In: Design Automation Conference (DAC), pp. 684–689 (2001)
4. Moraes, F., Calazans, N., Mello, A., Möller, L., Ost, L.: HERMES: an infrastructure for low area overhead packet-switching networks on chip. Integr. VLSI J. **38**(1), 69–93 (2004)
5. Foroutan, S., Thonnart, Y., Hersemeule, R., Jerraya, A.: An analytical method for evaluating Network-on-Chip performance. In: Design, Automation Test in Europe (DATE), pp. 1629–1632 (2010)
6. Schirner, G., Dömer, R.: Abstract communication modeling: a case study using the CAN automotive bus. In: Rettberg, A., Zanella, M.C., Rammig, F.J. (eds.) From Specification to Embedded Systems Application. IFIPAICT, vol. 184, pp. 189–200. Springer, Heidelberg (2005). https://doi.org/10.1007/11523277_19
7. Schirner, G., Dömer, R.: Quantitative analysis of transaction level models for the AMBA bus. In: Design, Automation and Test in Europe (DATE), vol. 1, pp. 1–6 (2006)
8. Lu, K., Muller-Gritschneder, D., Schlichtmann, U.: Accurately timed transaction level models for virtual prototyping at high abstraction level. In: Design, Automation Test in Europe Conference Exhibition (DATE), pp. 135–140 (2012)
9. Indrusiak, L., dos Santos, O.: Fast and accurate transaction-level model of a wormhole network-on-chip with priority preemptive virtual channel arbitration. In: Design, Automation Test in Europe Conference (DATE), pp. 1–6 (2011)
10. Nayebi, A., Meraji, S., Shamaei, A., Sarbazi-Azad, H.: XMulator: a listener-based integrated simulation platform for interconnection networks. In: International Modeling Simulation (AMS), pp. 128–132 (2007)
11. Jiang, N., Becker, D., Michelogiannakis, G., Balfour, J., Towles, B., Shaw, D., Kim, J., Dally, W.: A detailed and flexible cycle-accurate network-on-chip simulator. In: IEEE International Symposium on Performance Analysis of Systems and Software (ISPASS), pp. 86–96 (2013)
12. Hosseinabady, M., Nunez-Yanez, J.: SystemC architectural transaction level modelling for large NoCs. In: Forum on Specification Design Languages (FDL), pp. 1–6 (2010)
13. Viaud, E., Potop-Butucaru, D., Greiner, A.: An efficient TLM/T modeling and simulation environment based on conservative parallel discrete event principles. In: Design, Automation and Test in Europe (DATE), pp. 1–6 (2006)
14. Suboh, S., Bakhouya, M., Gaber, J., El-Ghazawi, T.: Analytical modeling and evaluation of network-on-chip architectures. In: High Performance Computing and Simulation (HPCS), pp. 615–622 (2010)
15. Ogras, U., Bogdan, P., Marculescu, R.: An analytical approach for network-on-chip performance analysis. IEEE Trans. Comput.-Aided Des. Integr. Circuits Syst. **29**(12), 2001–2013 (2010)
16. van Moll, H., Corporaal, H., Reyes, V., Boonen, M.: Fast and accurate protocol specific bus modeling using TLM 2.0. In: Design, Automation Test in Europe (DATE), pp. 316–319 (2009)

17. Ghenassia, F.: Transaction-Level Modeling with SystemC: TLM Concepts and Applications for Embedded Systems. Springer, New York (2006). https://doi.org/10.1007/b137175
18. Gerstlauer, A., Dömer, R., Peng, J., Gajski, D.D.: System Design: A Practical Guide with SpecC. Springer, Heidelberg (2001). https://doi.org/10.1007/978-1-4615-1481-7
19. Fulgham, M.L., Snyder, L.: Performance of chaos and oblivious routers under non-uniform traffic. Technical report (1993)
20. Mello, A., Tedesco, L., Calazans, N., Moraes, F.: Virtual channels in networks on chip: implementation and evaluation on hermes NoC. In: Integrated Circuits and System Design, pp. 178–183. ACM (2005)

Memory System Design

Taming the Memory Demand Complexity of Adaptive Vision Algorithms

Majid Sabbagh$^{(\boxtimes)}$, Hamed Tabkhi, and Gunar Schirner

Department of Electrical and Computer Engineering,
Northeastern University, Boston, MA, USA
{msabbagh,tabkhi,schirner}@ece.neu.edu

Abstract. With the demand for utilizing Adaptive Vision Algorithms (AVAs) in embedded devices, serious challenges have been introduced to vision architects. AVAs may produce huge model data traffic while continuously training the internal model of the stream. This traffic dwarfs the streaming data traffic (e.g. image frames), and consequently dominates bandwidth and power requirements posing great challenges to a low-power embedded implementation. In result, current approaches either ignore targeting AVAs, or are limited to low resolutions due to not handling the traffics separately. This paper proposes a systematic approach to tackle the architectural complexity of AVAs. The main focus of this paper is to manage the huge model data updating traffic of AVAs by proposing a shift from compressing streaming data to compressing the model data. The compression of model data results in significant reduction of memory accesses leading to a pronounced gain in power and performance. This paper also explores the effect of different class of compression algorithms (lossy and lossless) on both bandwidth reduction and result quality of AVAs. For the purpose of exploration this paper focuses on example of Mixture-of-Gaussians (MoG) background subtraction. The results demonstrate that a customized lossless algorithm can maintain the quality while reducing the bandwidth demand facilitating efficient embedded realization of AVAs. In our experiments we achieved the total bandwidth saving of about 69% by applying the Most Significant Bits Selection and BZIP as the first and second level model data compression schemes respectively, with only about 15% quality loss according to the Multi-Scale Structural Similarity (MS-SSIM) metric. The bandwidth saving would be increased to 75% by using a custom compressor.

1 Introduction

The demand for vision capabilities in embedded devices is rising more than ever. Embedded devices, ranging from tiny medical implants to smart cars and distributed smart cameras, need advanced vision capabilities and visual scenes analysis. Among different types of vision algorithms, the need is toward the algorithms that can dynamically adapt to the varying scene conditions. AVAs are considered as the dominating class of algorithms for advanced visual analysis.

© IFIP International Federation for Information Processing 2017
Published by Springer International Publishing AG 2017. All Rights Reserved
M. Götz et al. (Eds.): IESS 2015, IFIP AICT 523, pp. 145–158, 2017.
https://doi.org/10.1007/978-3-319-90023-0_12

They are based on the machine-learning principles and are able to capture the runtime changes in the scene (e.g. MoG background subtraction and Support Vector Machine (SVM)).

While AVAs have been realized for fairly long time in algorithm-development environment (e.g. Matlab), their embedded low power realization is still very challenging. Embedded devices are bounded in computation/communication resources with limited energy/power budget. In contrast, AVAs demand for a significant computation and communication capabilities which results in a power consumption far beyond the embedded system budgets. Realization of computation through custom design and High-Level Synthesis is well-formulated. On the other hand, communication appears as the primary bottleneck hindering implementation of AVAs on embedded devices.

The main limitation of AVAs is significant communication traffic imposed by algorithm itself. Due to inherent learning properties of AVAs, they maintain and continuously update model data of the scene. The model data is algorithm-intrinsic and its existence is independent of algorithm implementation. The size of model data is often very large exceeding the capacity of today's on-chip memories, forcing the designers to utilize off-chip memory. In result, accessing and updating the model data results in huge off-chip bandwidth demand and its associated power consumption. For instance, the bandwidth demand for updating the MoG background subtraction algorithm at Full-HD resolution is about 8 GB/s, based on the analysis of the standard OpenCV algorithm. This contributes to about 90% of total power consumption [1]. Therefore, to open efficient realization of AVAs on embedded devices, the first step is to manage huge communication demands associated with the model data.

Existing approaches often ignore embedded realization of AVAs and focus on the non-adaptive ones, or only implement AVAs at very low resolutions (300 * 400) [2–4]. However, current trend is toward utilizing AVAs to deliver advanced vision capabilities at Full-HD resolution (1920 * 1080). Overall, optimizing the model data has received less attention despite being crucial for real-time low-power implementations of AVAs. The need is toward systematic approaches that can provide a guideline on how to efficiently manage model data communication traffic.

This paper introduces a system level approach for taming the memory demand complexity of Adaptive Vision Algorithms. The main goal of this research is to open a path toward efficient management of model data traffic. By focusing on model data, we explore the opportunity of shifting the current trend in compressing the streaming data (i.e. applying different video/image encoding methods), toward compressing the model data to reduce the bandwidth and power. Following a system-level approach, this paper also explores the effect of different classes of compression algorithms, lossy and lossless, on both bandwidth reduction and resulting quality. Based on the observations, this paper offers design choices and trade-offs for finding the best compression methods.

For the purpose of exploration, this paper focuses on the example of MoG background subtraction [5]. Our results on the example of MoG demonstrate

50% reduction in communication bandwidth by applying a lossy linear compression (Most Significant Bits selection) with minimal quality loss. A higher bandwidth saving 69% can be achieved by BZIP general-purpose lossless compression with no quality loss. Further bandwidth saving is also achieved by a customized compression scheme (e.g. 75% in [6]).

This paper is organized as following: Sect. 2 overviews relevant prior work. Section 3 briefly provides background and additional motivation. Following that, Sect. 4 describes our systematic approach for bandwidth quality trade-off on different class of compression algorithms. Section 5 concludes the paper and touches on future work.

2   Related Work

The embedded realization of vision algorithms is still at early stages. Most of the previous work on embedded vision have been bounded to basic vision filters, e.g., Canny edge detection, with regular computation and much less communication demand [7,8]. Only few researchers have targeted adaptive vision algorithms (e.g., MoG, KLT, optical flow) on embedded devices. What all previous approaches share in common is lack of insight about source and nature of the traffic. Therefore, they mainly propose a common communication interface for transferring all types of data. Thus, they either ignore the algorithm-intrinsic traffic, or assume that it is hidden in the communication hierarchy. In the result, their proposed solutions works at low resolutions (300 * 400) which is far below Full-HD resolution (1920 * 1080) [2–4,9]. However, in [1] authors propose Data Separation concept for Adaptive Algorithms, in which the streaming data is handled differently compare to the model data. That helped them to realize the MoG algorithm for background subtraction in Full-HD resolution at 30 frames per second. We based our studies on [1] for applying different compression schemes on model data and analyzing its effect on the system performance and output quality.

A recent work [6] hints about the significant communication volume of MoG background subtraction algorithm. It also provides a promising lossless compression method which can reduce the bandwidth demand for updating MoG parameters down to 50%. Although their compression method sounds to be very efficient and promising, their approach lacks a holistic approach which studies different compression schemes and can generalize the concept of compression on model data for AVAs.

The general observation is that optimizing the model data has received much less attention despite being crucial for real-time low-power implementation of AVAs. In contrast to previous approaches, this paper focuses on optimizing and managing huge communication demand for updating and accessing model data in AVAs.

3   Background

This section briefly provides background information on traffic separation in the context of AVAs, and for MoG background subtraction algorithm as an example of AVAs.

3.1   Data Separation

Data separation, proposed by [1], distinguishes two types of data: streaming data and model data. Figure 1 highlights these two types of traffic in the context of AVAs. The streaming data (pixels) is the input/output data to the algorithm, while the model data is the intrinsic part of algorithm for realizing targeted processing. In AVAs, typically the model data is much bigger than streaming data. The size of model data exceeds the capacity of today's on-chip memories, forcing the designers to utilize the off-chip memory. Furthermore, since the model data should keep up with the streaming data, the bandwidth demand for reading and writing the model data from/to the memory would be a real limitation. Data Separation provides the opportunity for targeted optimization on both streaming data and model data.

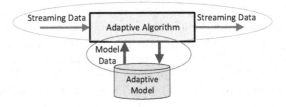

Fig. 1. Streaming data vs model data

The traffic separation also streamlines the construction of complete vision flow out of multiple AVAs executing different parts of applications over the streaming data. Each AVA has its own model data which hits the memory hierarchy while streaming data is passed across the kernels. This further motivates us to have a systematic solution toward ever increasing communication complexity of AVAs. The Data Separation insight helps us to explore and tailor the compression opportunities on model data.

3.2   MoG Background Subtraction

MoG background subtraction is a very good representative of AVAs [5]. In this paper, we also use this algorithm to present our results. MoG is used in vision computing for identifying moving objects from the background scene. Figure 2 includes the MoG coarse-grain mathematical formulation. MoG uses multiple Gaussian distributions, also called Gaussian components, to model a pixel's

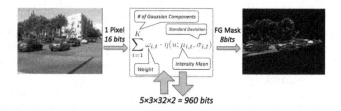

5×3×32×2 = 960 bits

Fig. 2. Memory access per pixel in MoG algorithm

background. Each Gaussian component has its own set of Gaussian components: weight ω_i, an intensity mean μ_i and a standard deviation σ_i. In Full-HD resolution, for storing all Gaussian parameters about 74 MB of storage is required which may exceed the on-chip memory capacity available in embedded platforms. As a new pixel arrives, all Gaussian parameters are updated to track BG changes of the pixel at frame basis. On the other hand, the bandwidth demand for updating the Gaussian parameters, assuming 32 bit per Gaussian parameter with 3 Gaussian components per pixel, is about 8 GB/s (for processing at Full-HD resolution 60 fps), which is 30 times more than streaming bandwidth, which is 265 MB/s for transferring 16-bit input pixel and 1-bit output foreground mask.

4 Systematic Model Data Compression

4.1 System-Level Roadmap

Real-time embedded realization of AVAs forces the system architects toward systematic approaches. Figure 3 highlights our design flow for tackling the complexities of AVAs. It starts from analysis of algorithms to identify orthogonal axises of optimization with separated axises for computation and communication. There is a computation/communication trade-off at which point the computation and communication axises meet. The trade-off occurs when compressing the model data adds to the computation demand while reduces the bandwidth demand.

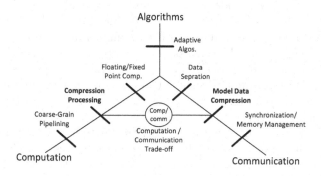

Fig. 3. System-level design flow

In this study, we mainly focus on communication axis because of significant communication demand in AVAs for periodically accessing and updating the model data. Complexities in computation axis, include but not limited to, multi-dimensional processing, complex operations, floating point computation which can be explored separately and are not part of this study.

Using the data Separation insight, we propose a shift from current trend in compressing streaming data toward compressing model data. As shown in Fig. 4, compression/decompression units could be placed in the access interface of model data, providing the opportunity of significantly reducing the model update bandwidth.

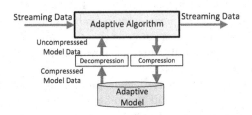

Fig. 4. Compression/decompression on model data access

There are two major categories in compression methods, lossy and lossless. In lossy compression, there is a trade-off between the achievable bandwidth saving and output quality while in the lossless compression schemes there would be no quality loss probably with the cost of higher computation demand. Overall, the primary metrics needed to be considered for choosing a suitable compression algorithm are: (1) achievable bandwidth saving, (2) quality effect (lossy/lossless), and (3) computation demand for compressing/de-compressing model data.

4.2   Experimental Setup

For the purpose of study, we focus on MoG background subtraction algorithm explained in Sect. 3.2. We modeled MoG in SpecC System Level Design Language (SLDL) [10]. The high-level diagram of the experimental model is shown in Fig. 5. The stream of input pixels will be fed from stimulus block to the MoG which at the same time receives the corresponding parameters, i.e. model data, from the Read Param block. Read Param block receives the decompressed parameters from the decompression unit. Decompression unit reads the compressed model data from a file, decompress it, and sends the individual parameters out when the corresponding pixel arrives at input of MoG. Then, after finishing the processing, MoG block outputs foreground masks as the output stream and updated parameters as model data. Model data will be written back to a file after being compressed by the compression unit. In the following section, we will study the effect of applying different compression methods on MoG's model data.

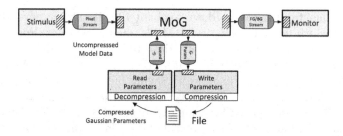

Fig. 5. High-level diagram of evaluation model for MoG

During the exploration, we assess the quality against the ground-truth (MoG with no compressed Gaussian parameters). We use MS-SSIM metric. MS-SSIM focuses on the structural similarity between two frames which is more similar to human perception [11]. MS-SSIM quantifies the quality as a value between 0 to 1 where a higher value means closer similarity and thus lower quality loss compared to ground-truth.

4.3   Evaluation of Compression Schemes

MSBSel. The simplest compression method is to statically select the most significant bits of parameters. We call this method Most Significant Bits Selection (MSBSel). Although MSBSel is a lossy compression, it has almost no computation overhead especially considering a hardware implementation. We call the model with MSBSel compression method the reference model in later explanations.

This compression scheme introduces the Quality-Bandwidth trade-off as illustrated in Fig. 6. Based on Fig. 6, the quality and bandwidth have a non-linear relationship and it is possible to reduce bandwidth without quality loss (in the

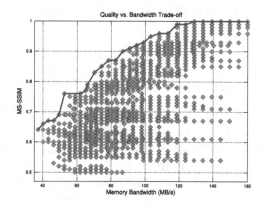

Fig. 6. Quality-bandwidth trade-off in MSBSel compression scheme

bandwidth range from 160 MB/s down to about 120 MB/s). Moreover, by reducing the bandwidth down to 50%, i.e. 80 MB/s, quality will not drop more than 15% according to MS-SSIM quality metric. Although this is due to the nature of MoG algorithm, but same trend could be observed for other AVAs. Selecting fewer bits leads to higher bandwidth saving but also higher degradation in quality. A high dynamic range or precision is essential for accurate background subtraction. This raises a need for complex/advanced compression algorithms to further reduce the bandwidth requirements for updating model data.

JPEG-2000. To further explore the compression effect on MoG parameters, JPEG-2000 compression applied as the second-level compression after MSBSel to evaluate if it can reduce the bandwidth without affecting the quality significantly. JPEG is a well-known image compression method developed by Joint Photographic Experts Group [12]. JPEG-2000 is the newer version of JPEG, which also supports 16-bit gray-scale images.

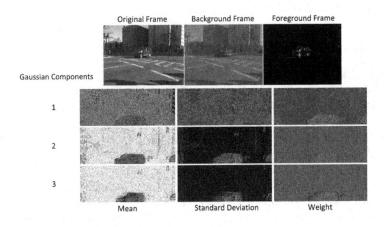

Fig. 7. Visual structure of Gaussian parameters.

Since JPEG has been customized for compressing images, we only limit the JPEG compression for parameter *Mean*. Parameter *Mean* keeps background mean values for pixels and it has a visual structure similar to an image. Figure 7 illustrates the visual structure of all Gaussian parameters. On top from left to right, the original, background and foreground frames are shown. Below the frames, Fig. 7 also presents the images of all Gaussian parameters for three Gaussian components: *Mean*, *Standard Deviation* and *Weight*, from left to right.

Figure 8a shows the effect of JPEG-2000 compression on *Mean* parameter over the bandwidth demand for updating parameter *Mean*. Figure 8b plots the total bandwidth saving (over all parameters), by compressing only parameter *Mean*. For this experiment, a sequence of 650 frames with resolution of 320 × 240 has been chosen as the input test set. Both figures show the effect of different

JPEG compression ratios (2:1–10:1). The JPEG-2000 is significantly reducing the bandwidth demand for updating the *Mean* parameter. For the best compression ratio of 0.1 (10:1), the bandwidth saving for updating parameter *Mean* is about 85%, indicating that the size of compressed *Mean* image is on average 15% of its original size. Also, as shown in Fig. 8b, overall bandwidth saving is about 29%. The overall bandwidth saving is limited as JPEG-2000 is not applicable on other MoG parameters (Standard Deviation and Weight).

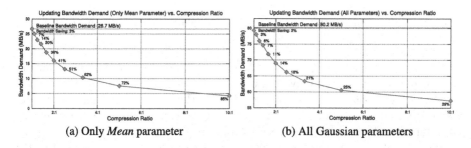

(a) Only *Mean* parameter   (b) All Gaussian parameters

Fig. 8. Bandwidth demand vs. compression ratio for JPEG-2000 compression

The bandwidth saving corresponding to the compression ratio was less than the expected value. For example, the expected bandwidth saving of 10:1 compression ratio, is 90%. However, in practice it is about 85%. The effect of noise on degrading the performance of compression methods is already studied in literature. For example, a study in [13] shows that noise reduces the inter-pixel correlation which compression ratio increased. Some approaches, such as [14,15], filters the effect of noise from the source image. However, all based on assumption that feature of filtering solutions is that they consider noise in images as unwanted data. In contrast, the visual distortion that is observable in MoG parameters are actually the values produced by the algorithm and are required in next iteration for computation. Therefore, eliminating the distortion which is seen in MoG parameters in fact reduce the quality of MoG.

To study the effect of JPEG bandwidth saving on the MoG quality (the foreground masks), we compared the output of MOG with JPEG compression against the reference model. The outputs are compared using the MS-SSIM quality metric in a simple scene, with few object movements and variations, and a complex scene, with lots of object movements and crossings. Figure 9 plots the quality across total bandwidth saving when applying JPEG compression for parameter *Mean*. The maximum achievable output quality is about 0.46 out of 1, in the simple frame sequence. This is even worse in complex frame sequence which the maximum output quality is 0.22 with bandwidth saving of only 2% on average. With increasing compression rate to further reduce the bandwidth, the quality degradation would be more pronounced reaching to a point which basically MoG is not functional anymore.

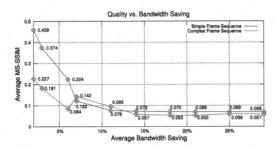

Fig. 9. Quality-bandwidth trade-off when for simple and complex frame sequences

Overall, we conclude that JPEG-2000 have severe degradation effect on the final output quality of MoG. We can trace back this issue to the adaptive behavior of the MoG algorithm, meaning that since the MoG parameters are recursively accessed and updated, even a small error can accumulate, resulting in degradation of background subtraction robustness and eventually output quality loss. All of these observations motivate us to explore other possibilities for compression of model data, therefore we will look into the opportunity of using lossless compression schemes.

Lossless Compression. The principal feature of lossless compression algorithms is that they do not affect the quality of data being compressed. Therefore, rather than quality loss, the designer may change the focus to other characteristics of compression algorithms, such as the achievable compression ratio and computation demand. In our study, five different lossless compression methods have been explored: QZIP, LZ4, BZIP, GZIP and ZIP. QZIP and LZ4 are two compression algorithms which are in high-speed categories, while BZIP, GZIP and ZIP are three regular compression methods. The experiments are done over 4500 parameter images that are the MoG parameters of 3 Gaussian components, each having 3 parameters (Mean, Standard Deviation and Weight) for 500 frames of original 1024×768 resolution. All of the lossless compression methods are applied as the second level compression after MSBSel. To further explore the granularity of source data which a certain algorithm will operate on, we divide the input frames to smaller blocks. A 1024×768 frame could be divided into 25.6 blocks of 40×30, 12.8 blocks of 80×60, 6.4 blocks of 160×120, 3.2 blocks of 320×240, 1.6 blocks of 640×480 and 1 block of 1024×768 resolution.

Figure 10a presents the average bandwidth saving over different block sizes for all compression algorithms. The maximum bandwidth saving could be achieved, when using the 1024×768 block size. In fact, by reducing the block size to less than 1024×768, all algorithms perform poorly in bandwidth reduction, at the best case reaching to less than 10% bandwidth saving. The best average bandwidth savings captured in lossless experiments is about 38%, corresponding to BZIP compression scheme with block size of 1024×768.

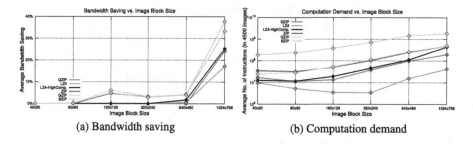

Fig. 10. Bandwidth saving and computation demand over different block sizes.

Figure 10b shows the average computation demand over different block sizes for all compression algorithms. To estimate the computation demand, we used Pin - Dynamic Binary Instrumentation Tool [16], from Intel. The block size of 1024×768, equal to full image size, leads to largest computation demand. Overall, the computation demand varies across the algorithms. In QZIP and ZIP, the lowest computation demand is achieved by using block size of 80×60, for LZ4 320×240 and for GZIP and BZIP 40×30. Figure 10a and b also present the result of LZ4 algorithm in the high-compression mode (LZ4 High-Comp.). In high-compression mode, LZ4 could provide better compression ratio with the cost of higher computation demand.

Combining Fig. 10a and b, we can derive Fig. 11 showing the trade-off between bandwidth saving and computation demand. In Fig. 11, the numbers over the stars show the average bandwidth saving, while the crosses show the range of achievable bandwidth demand corresponding to a certain computation demand. For different algorithms, the trend is that lower bandwidth demand or higher bandwidth saving, is achievable by having more computation. Among all algorithms, LZ4 in fast-mode has the lowest computation demand, which is about 100 millions instructions for compression and decompression of a frame, and at the same time the lowest bandwidth saving of 17%, while the BZIP achieves highest bandwidth saving of 38% with the highest computation demand of about 1 billion instructions. Note that, computation demand of LZ4 for compression and decompression of a frame in high-compression mode is about 10 times higher than its computation demand in fast-mode.

Custom Compression. The previous studied lossless compression methods are general algorithms developed to compress any sort of data. The results of our experiments illustrate that although there are lots of options for compressing the model data, but for AVAs such as MoG, which have special type of model data produced by statistical and non-linear processing, general purpose image or data compression methods might not provide the desirable performance for designers. There is a demand for lossless compression algorithm customized for compressing model data in context of AVA. This fact, motivates designers such

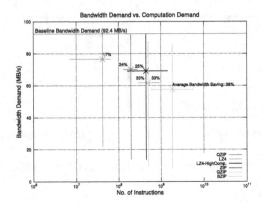

Fig. 11. Bandwidth saving/computation demand trade-off

as in [6] to devise custom model data compression schemes only for a certain type of algorithm. One preliminary example, has been already proposed by [6].

In [6], the authors propose a DPCM-based compression algorithm for compression of MoG parameters. Their algorithm, extracts and uses the inter-correlation of parameters for different Gaussian Components of MoG and intra-correlation of parameters for within the Gaussian Components, to represent every two parameters with one compressed parameter, in a lossless process, reducing the bandwidth demand down to 50%. In terms of computation demand, the FPGA implementation of their algorithm shows reasonable resource utilization of about 2282 LUTs and 1876 FFs in Virtex-5 FPGA, without any use of DSP Blocks and more importantly Block RAMs.

4.4 Results Summary

To summarize, Using the Data Separation insight, we explored the opportunity of applying different compression schemes on model data, to shift the compression trend from streaming data to model data. During the experiments we evaluated several trade-offs:

- **Lossy Compression**
  - Quality-Bandwidth Trade-off (for MSBSel only and MSBSel+JPEG-2000): For having better quality, higher bandwidth is needed
  - Bandwidth-Compression Ratio (for MSBSel+JPEG-2000): By changing the configurable compression ratio in JPEG-2000, different bandwidth demands are achievable
- **Lossless Compression**
  - Computation Demand-Block Size Trade-off (For all 5 lossless algorithms): Different block sizes lead to different computation demands, highest computation demand is when the block size is equal to the whole frame being compressed

- Bandwidth Saving-Block Size Trade-off (For all 5 lossless algorithms): Different block sizes lead to different Bandwidth Saving, biggest saving in Bandwidth achieved when largest block size is used
- Bandwidth Demand-Computation Demand Trade-off (For all 5 lossless algorithms): For having lower bandwidth demand or highest bandwidth saving, there is need for more computation
- Bandwidth Demand-Computation Demand Trade-off for LZ4 algorithm in high-compression mode and fast-mode: By using LZ4 in high-compression mode, higher bandwidth saving is achievable with the cost of higher computation demand.

Overall, by applying BZIP as the second level compression scheme over MSB-Sel, the total bandwidth saving of about 69% is achievable, while the bandwidth saving could be increased to about 75% by using a custom compressor instead of BZIP. The overall output quality loss would not be more than 15% according to the MS-SSIM metric for both of these cases. These trade-offs could help the system architects for AVAs, choose the right compression algorithm for model data based on the application requirements. Furthermore, designers might have to use or devise tailored algorithms for AVAs' model data, such as the compression method proposed in [6] for compressing the MoG parameters.

Altogether, using the Data Separation insight and by applying compression on model data, realization of AVAs could be facilitated as the overall system bandwidth demand became manageable, taming the complexity of AVAs realization. We would consider power consumption in future works as it is a very important factor in embedded systems, while in this work we focus on evaluating the compression ratio and computation demand in lossless compression schemes.

5 Conclusions

This paper proposes a systematic approach for tackling the complexity of AVAs. We focus on the main challenge which is the communication complexity due to huge bandwidth demand for updating model data in AVAs. Using the Data Separation insight and by applying compression on model data, realization of multiple vision kernels could be facilitated on a single platform. Also, throughout our study we evaluated different lossy and lossless compression algorithms, providing the system architects with various trade-offs and intuitions for choosing the right method of compression for model data.

References

1. Tabkhi, H., Sabbagh, M., Schirner, G.: Power-efficient real-time solution for adaptive vision algorithms. IET Comput. Digit. Tech. 16–26 (2015)
2. Xu, J., et al.: A case study in networks-on-chip design for embedded video. In: Design, Automation and Test in Europe (DATE), vol. 2, pp. 770–775 (2004)
3. Lv, T., et al.: A methodology for architectural design of multimedia multiprocessor SoCs. IEEE Des. Test Comput. **22**(1), 18–26 (2005)

4. Chen, G., et al.: Energy savings through compression in embedded Java environments. In: International Symposium on Hardware/Software Codesign, CODES 2002 (2002)
5. Stauffer, C., Grimson, W.E.L.: Adaptive background mixture models for real-time tracking. In: IEEE Computer Society Conference on Computer Vision and Pattern Recognition, vol. 2, pp. 246–252 (1999)
6. Ratnayake, K., Amer, A.: Embedded architecture for noise-adaptive video object detection using parameter-compressed background modeling. J. Real-Time Image Process. (2014)
7. Xilinx: Programming vision applications on Zynq using OpenCV and high-level synthesis. Xilinx technical report (2013)
8. Tang, Z., Shen, D.: Canny edge detection codec using VLib on Davinci series DSP. In: 2012 International Conference on Computer Science Service System (CSSS) (2012)
9. Swaminathan, K., Lakshminarayanan, G., Ko, S.-B.: High speed generic network interface for network on chip using ping pong buffers. In: International Symposium on Electronic System Design (ISED), pp. 72–76 (2012)
10. Gerstlauer, A., Dömer, R., Peng, J., Gajski, D.D.: System Design: A Practical Guide with SpecC. Kluwer Academic Publisher, Dordrecht (2001)
11. Wang, Z., et al.: Image quality assessment: from error visibility to structural similarity. IEEE Trans. Image Process. $13(4)$, 600–612 (2004)
12. JPEG. http://www.jpeg.org
13. Lo, S.-C., Krasner, B., Mun, S.: Noise impact on error-free image compression. IEEE Trans. Med. Imaging (1990)
14. Cosman, P., Gray, R., Olshen, R.: Evaluating quality of compressed medical images: SNR, subjective rating, and diagnostic accuracy. Proc. IEEE (1994)
15. Melnychuck, P.W., Barry, M.J., Mathieu, M.S.: Effect of noise and MTF on the compressibility of high-resolution color images (1990)
16. Pin - a dynamic binary instrumentation tool. https://software.intel.com/en-us/articles/pin-a-dynamic-binary-instrumentation-tool. Accessed 30 Aug 2015

HMC and DDR Performance Trade-offs

Paulo C. Santos$^{(\boxtimes)}$, Marco A. Z. Alves, and Luigi Carro

Informatics Institute - Federal University of Rio Grande Do Sul, Porto Alegre, Brazil
{pcssjunior,mazalves,carro}@inf.ufrgs.br

Abstract. The evolution of main memories, from SDR to the current
DDR, presents multiple technological breakthroughs, but still far from
the requirements of the processors. With the advent of Hybrid Memory Cube (HMC), a promise of high bandwidth with low energy consumption and less area may provide better efficiency than the traditional DDR modules. This is especially attractive for embedded systems. In this paper, we perform a comprehensive performance comparison between HMC and DDR memories, to understand the capabilities
and limitations of both. Simulation results running SPEC-CPU2006 and
SPEC-OMP2001 benchmarks show that applications with low memory
pressure behave similarly with HMC or DDR. We make the new observation that HMC performs better than DDR specially for applications
with a high memory pressure and low spatial data locality. However, for
applications with a streaming behavior, commonly present in the embedded system domain, our experiments show that current HMC row-buffer
specifications do not take advantage of the spatial locality present in
those applications.

Keywords: HMC · DDR · Main memory · Performance evaluation

1 Introduction

Due to increasing requirements from embedded applications, the architectures of
embedded systems are becoming similar to high performance computers in the
sense that performance techniques are being adapted to this new context. Following this trend embedded systems are commonly applying Double Data Rate
(DDR) memories. The evolution of DDR systems brought benefits in terms of
performance, while keeping power consumption levels constant. However, for the
new Hybrid Memory Cubes (HMCs), the trade-off between energy consumption
and performance is more interesting. The industry is predicting that HMC will
provide both higher performance and considerably lower energy consumption in
comparison to the current memory systems [1,20]. However, simulation platforms
and evaluation experiments are required to understand the new trade-offs.

In this paper, we aim to understand the performance difference between
the HMC and traditional DDR 3 memories. In addition, we intend to evaluate

P. C. Santos—We acknowledge the support of CNPq and CAPES.

© IFIP International Federation for Information Processing 2017
Published by Springer International Publishing AG 2017. All Rights Reserved
M. Götz et al. (Eds.): IESS 2015, IFIP AICT 523, pp. 159–171, 2017.
https://doi.org/10.1007/978-3-319-90023-0_13

what type of application exploits more efficiently each memory architecture. We also adapt a cycle-accurate simulator to model both memory systems to perform detailed experiments, which are capable of explaining the sources of performance differences between these two memory systems.

The main contributions of this paper are the following:

HMC simulator: We extended a cycle-accurate simulator to implement a detailed HMC model, considering the internal vaults, the DRAM signal latencies and the link bandwidth.

DDR and HMC comparison: Using 29 single-threaded and 7 multi-threaded benchmark applications, we performed an analysis comparing HMC to DDR 3 memories, in order to understand the limits imposed by the number of DDR 3 channels and HMC links, as well as the characteristics that allow each application to benefit most from each memory system.

Application behavior correlation: In our experiments we show, as expected, that applications with low memory pressure keep the performance at the same level when changing between HMC and DDR 3 memories. We make the new observation that applications with high memory pressure (i.e., memory pressure higher than 0.5 GB/s) with low spatial memory locality benefits more from the HMC, because of the closed-row policy and the high bank parallelism. However, applications with a high memory locality performs better with DDR 3 memories mainly because of its 8 KB row buffer.

We evaluate the HMC and DDR 3 memories modeling an Atom-inspired embedded system consisting of 8 cores with 32 KB L1 and 256 KB L2 caches. Simulations executing the SPEC-CPU2006 and SPEC-OMP2001 benchmarks show that HMC with 4 links improves the performance by up to 27% for SPEC-CPU2006 and up to 109% for SPEC-OMP2001 when compared to the DDR 3 with 4 channels, and improves up to 27% and 50% respectively when compared to the DDR 3 with 8 channels. Such improvements are observed for those applications with high memory pressure and non-contiguous data access behavior. However, for applications with high memory pressure and a contiguous data access behavior, DDR 3 with 8 channels performed up to 26% better.

2   Technological Constraints of Memory Designs

In this section, we present the architecture of DDR devices and the HMC internals. For the rest of this paper, we focus on the DDR 3 and HMC specification version 2.0. The DDR and the HMC systems are presented at a level of abstraction that is sufficient to understand the terminology and key concepts of this paper. For a detailed description, we refer the reader to [5, 6, 9].

2.1   DRAM and DDR Architectures

Traditional main memory modules are formed by multiple devices that act in a coordinated way [9]. The highest memory structure level is the module, which

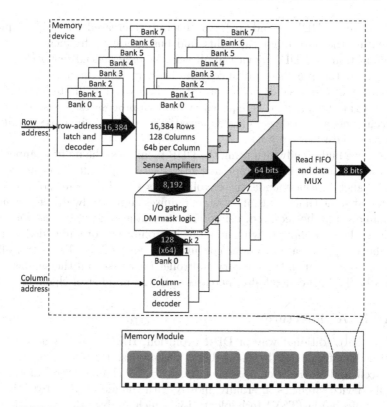

Fig. 1. DDR 3×8 functional block diagram of a single device. Adapted from [12].

consists of a set of devices. A module may have multiple ranks, each rank consisting of multiple devices, which will operate in synchrony. The devices are composed of a set of banks, and all the devices in a given rank react to an operation signal, always operating in the same bank for a given signal. These banks are composed of sub-arrays, formed by rows that are accessed per column. Figure 1 shows a basic schematic of the DDR 3×8 device.

The DRAM protocol manages these arrays using these 5 basic, simplified operations: *precharge* (prepares the arrays and sense amplifiers to read a new row), *row access strobe* (reads a specific row using the sense amplifiers into a SRAM row buffer, with 1 buffer for each bank), *column access strobe* (bursts data of a specific column of the row buffer from the DRAM devices to the bus), *column write* (receives data from the bus and overwrites the addressed column of an opened row) and *refresh* (refresh capacitor charges a row, usually done automatically by each device).

Since processors have been increasing their throughput demand, DRAM-based memories have evolved trying to meet the requirements of modern processors. DDR memories emerged as a major technological breakthrough, providing the ability of transmitting data at both clock edges. However, its evolutions as

DDR 2, DDR 3, DDR 4 and so forth generally increased the I/O frequency by increasing the data burst capability and bus operating frequency. However, the organization of a DDR device in all versions experienced few architectural modifications. Despite these advancements in memory technology, the operating frequency of the basic devices to a certain data width is limited, providing a lower throughput than what is required by modern processors. Thus, besides the burst technique, sets of devices are deployed in a module to increase parallelism and increase data throughput.

To achieve high bandwidth using the DDR memories, the multi-channel technique is widely adopted. This approach allows accessing multiple memory modules in parallel and independently, enabling data transfers from more than one row buffer at same time. Thus, if a system requires large bandwidth, for example, four channels may be required, using 256 wires in a half-duplex fashion. However, such a large number of wires in a bus is prohibitive for embedded systems, mainly because of area and power consumption constraints. To control all the devices of each channel, the memory controller must issue all the signals to the devices's bank. This control also increases with the number of channels [21].

2.2   HMC Architecture

Breaking the traditional way of DDR evolution, HMC is not concerned with increasing I/O frequency by using burst techniques. Despite using the same DRAM cell and its restrict accessing times, HMC changes the paradigm by hiding its device latencies internally, mostly with the aid of 3D integration and Through-Silicon Via (TSV) technology [13], which enables the integration of a massive bank parallelism [5,10,15].

Basically HMC memories are composed of up to 8 layers of DRAM memory and one logical layer per vault, all integrated in the same device. Figure 2 illustrates the main HMC architectural details. The three main components inside the HMC are the following:

Memory vaults: HMC memories store data on contiguous row buffers, interleaving throw the memory vaults and then to memory banks inside the vaults. HMC may have up to 32 vaults, each one can be composed by up to 16 banks, where each row in the bank has up to 256 bytes. In theory, the HMC can fetch data from 32 different banks (one per vault) in parallel and copy it to the internal read buffers. Only after the data is ready in the read buffers, the links may send it to the processor's memory controller.

Memory controller: The 3D integration technology enabled the integration of memory and logic in the same chip on different layers. Thus, an HMC has a dedicated memory controller attached to each vault, providing great data access parallelism. In this way, the processor's memory controller can be simplified to work with simple data request commands, reducing its complexity, area and energy consumption.

Serial links: Unlike DDR 3 memories, which transmit 64 bits per channel, HMC memory uses serialization, to transmit data through 16 full-duplex lanes

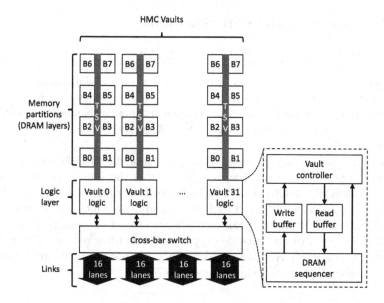

Fig. 2. HMC block diagram formed by 32 vaults with 8 banks each. Adapted from [5].

per link (each lane is a pair of differential signal lines). However, each link is not strongly attached to a specific portion of the memory, which means that any link can be used to transfer data from/to any HMC vault. The adoption of this communication technique leads to a smaller area for buses. Moreover, these links are capable of achieving higher frequencies with less interference during the transmissions [5, 19].

As mentioned, other differences between HMC and DDR memories are the row buffer size and the bank parallelism. Typically, DDR memories have row buffers of 8192 bytes per bank (split among the devices), while HMC specifies row buffers of up to 256 bytes per bank. Meanwhile, the DDR modules provides only 8 memory banks which can act in parallel, while the HMC has up to 512 DRAM banks.

Previous work mentions that these architectural differences in the HMC architecture may result in up to 70% less energy consumption than DDR3-1333, and a 15 times theoretical speedup of the system [5,10,15]. However, it is not clear if all applications can benefit from the HMC. In the remainder of this paper, we present the methodology for our experiments and the results showing the most important aspects of an application to perform better in the HMC compared to DDR memories.

3 Evaluation Methodology

This section presents the simulation details, the application kernels and the evaluation methodology, showing how we compare our mechanism to the baseline embedded system and previous work.

3.1   Modeling DDR and HMC Simulation

To evaluate DDR and HMC memories, we used an in-house cycle-accurate simulator [2,3]. Simulator of Non-Uniform Cache Architectures (SiNUCA) is a trace-driven simulator, thus it executes traces generated on a real machine with a real workload without the influence from the OS or other processes. The traces are simulated in a cycle-accurate way, where each component is modeled to execute its operations on a clock cycle basis. SiNUCA currently focuses on the x86_32 and x86_64 architectures.

SiNUCA originally offered support only for modeling DDRx memories with an open-row policy. However, few modifications in the source code were necessary to model HMC, due to SiNUCA's high parameterization. To model a HMC, the memory controllers are used as HMC controllers, which are located inside the HMC device. The channels can be configured to act as memory vaults. However, changes were made to provide support on closed-row policy and new HMC instructions. Although HMC-aware compilers are not available yet, synthetic codes can be evaluated with this version of SiNUCA.

3.2   Configuration Parameters and Workload

The simulation parameters are inspired by Intel's Atom processor with the Silvermont Out-of-Order (OoO) micro-architecture [8]. Table 1 shows the simulation

Table 1. Baseline system configuration.

OoO Execution Cores - 2 GHz; 8 cores; Front-end 2-wide; 16 B fetch block size
14 stages (3-fetch, 3-decode, 3-rename, 2-dispatch, 3-commit);
24-entry fetch buffer, 32-entry decode buffer, 32-entry ROB; 16-entry BOB;
INT: 2-alu, 1-mul. and 1-div.; FP: 1-alu, 1-mul. and 1-div. (1-3-20; 5-5-20 cycle);
1-load and 1-store functional units (1-1 cycle); MOB entries: 10-read and 10-write;
Branch Predictor - 1 branch per fetch; 4 K-entry 4-way set-associative BTB;
Two-Level PAs predictor; 16 K-entry BHT, 2-bits prediction;
L1 Data + Inst. Cache - 32 KB, 8-way, 2-cycle; 64 bytes line; LRU policy;
MSHR entries: 10-request, 8-write-back; Stride Prefetcher: 1-degree, 16-strides table;
L2 Cache - 256 KB shared for every 2 cores; 8-way, 4-cycle; 64 bytes line; LRU policy;
MSHR entries: 10-request, 6-write-back; Inclusive LLC; MOESI coherence;
Stream Prefetcher: 2-degree, 16 prefetch distance, 32-streams;
Low Power DDR3-1600 Controller and Interconnection - Bi-directional ring,
1~8-channels; 8 LP-DRAM banks, 8 KB row buffer per bank (1 KB per device), 8 burst length; Open-row first policy; CAS, RP, RCD, RAS and CWD latency (12-17-14-34-6 cycles);
HMC Module and Interconnection - Bi-directional ring, 1~4-links @ 8GHz;
32 Vaults, 16 LP-DRAM banks per Vault @ 800 MHz, 256 B row buffer per bank, 2 burst length; Closed-row policy; CAS, RP, RCD, RAS and CWD latency (12-17-14-34-6 cycles);

parameters used for our tests. The Silvermont micro-architecture only supports 2 memory channels. In order to build a possible future scenario for comparison, we also extrapolate the baseline configuration with up to 8 memory channels. We apply the same extrapolation idea to the HMC, in order to evaluate the influence of the number of links to the performance.

As the workloads for our experiments, we chose the 29 serial applications from the SPEC-CPU2006 [7] and 7 parallel applications from the SPEC-OMP2001 [18] benchmark suite. The SPEC-CPU2006 benchmark suites (integer and floating point) were executed using the *reference* input set, executing a representative slice of 200 million instructions selected by PinPoints [14]. The SPEC-OMP2001 benchmarks were executed using the *reference* input set as well, executing up to one time step from its parallel region.

4   Experimental Results

This section presents the results for SPEC-CPU2006 and SPEC-OMP2001 benchmark suites when simulating HMC and DDR memories.

4.1   SPEC-CPU2006 Results

The first result regarding the SPEC-CPU2006 benchmark suite shows the average performance when executing all the applications for each one of the systems, with DDR 3 varying the number of channels and the HMC varying the number of links. Figure 3 presents the speedup results over the DDR 3 with 1 channel.

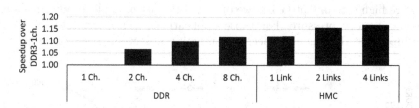

Fig. 3. Performance results for SPEC-CPU2006.

Memory Usage and Pressure: In order to understand the behavior of the different applications executing on HMC 4 links and DDR 3 8 channels, we correlate performance compared to the memory footprint and the memory pressure.

Figure 4 presents the SPEC-CPU2006 applications sorted by their performance. It shows the speedup of the HMC over the DDR 3, also showing in the secondary axis the amount of requests per second (pressure) the HMC serviced on average. On the top of the figure, the memory footprint is presented.

The plot shows some performance difference between DDR 3 and HMC only for those applications with pressure higher than 0.50 GB/s. This also correlates

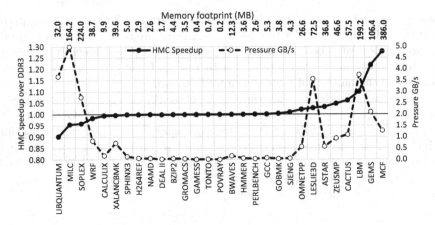

Fig. 4. HMC speedup over DDR 3 and the memory pressure (GB/s) for SPEC-CPU2006 applications.

with the memory footprint, where applications with more than 32 MB tends to have some performance difference between DDR 3 and HMC.

Both metrics show insignificant performance change for applications with low memory footprint and consequently low memory pressure. However, both metrics (memory footprint and pressure) cannot explain alone if a specific application will benefit or not from the HMC.

Memory Contiguity: Selecting only the SPEC-CPU2006 benchmarks with pressure higher than 0.50 GB/s, we obtained the list of applications with a reasonable memory pressure. For those applications, Fig. 5 correlates the HMC speedup with the memory access contiguity observed. The contiguity was

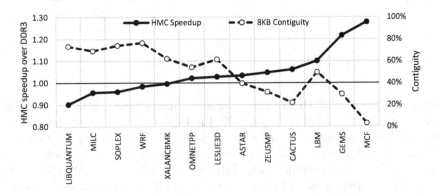

Fig. 5. HMC speedup and contiguity results for SPEC-CPU2006.

obtained for the 8 KB row buffer hit ratio of the DDR 3. Thus, the higher contiguity indicates that more contiguous accesses happened in a short period of time.

The main aspects from the DRAM architecture that influence the performance of contiguous accesses are the row buffer size, and the row buffer policy. In the case of the DDR 3, the row buffer contains 8 KB of contiguous data, while for HMC it holds only 256 B. Regarding the row buffer policy, the DDR 3 usually adopts the open-row policy, while the HMC specification describes the use of closed-row policy.

The HMC uses smaller row buffers compared to DDR 3 mainly to reduce the energy DRAM array consumption while it also increases the parallelism between the vaults. Open-row policies makes more sense with large row buffers. Considering that smaller row buffers will service less cache misses, the closed-row policy will close the row buffer as soon as the actual request is serviced. Performing the early row precharge command improves the performance for future accesses to different rows, while it can hurt performance if future accesses map to the recently closed row.

In our experiments, we implemented a smart closed-row policy, which identifies if multiple requests inside the read/write buffer map to the same row, and just close the actual row after all the requests have been serviced. However, even with such scheme, the performance is reduced when contiguous accesses happen.

4.2 SPEC-OMP2001 Results

In order to understand if scenarios with higher memory pressure would change our conclusions, we evaluated the multi-threaded applications from SPEC-OMP2001. Figure 6 presents the results when executing the applications with a different number of threads. The speedup results are normalized to the DDR 3 with 1 channel.

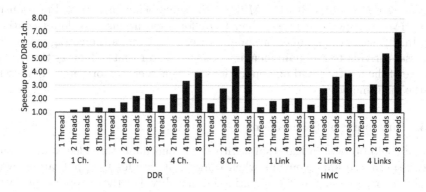

Fig. 6. Performance results for SPEC-OMP2001.

We can observe that HMC with a single link performed 50% better than DDR 3 with a single channel. Comparisons considering the maximum commercial products, HMC with 4 links and DDR 3 with 4 channels, show and average speedup of 1.75 for HMC. Comparing the best version of the DDR 3 and the HMC, we can observe that HMC performed 15% better.

Memory Contiguity: To evaluate the speedup change between the HMC and DDR memories, we took the DDR 3 with 8 channels and HMC with 4 links execution cycles in order to calculate the speedup between the HMC and its counterpart with DDR. Figure 7 presents the results with different numbers of threads, showing the HMC speedup for each application, compared to the same application with same amount of threads using DDR. In order to observe how contiguous the applications from the SPEC-OMP2001 benchmark suite are, the figure also presents in the secondary axis the contiguity ratio (8 KB row buffer hit ratio) for each application with different numbers of threads.

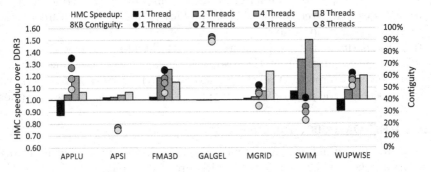

Fig. 7. HMC speedup over DDR 3 and the contiguity ratio for SPEC-OMP2001 applications.

We can observe for SPEC-OMP2001 the same behavior reported previously, that HMC can perform better than DDR for applications with lower contiguity. In this case, the number of parallel threads influences the contiguity of the accesses arriving to the main memory. Another factor that influences the performance of the multi-threading applications is the higher memory pressure present in the main memory.

4.3   Summary of Evaluations

As we could observe in the results with single and multi-threaded applications, the performance improvements when using HMC are for the applications with high memory pressure and low spatial data locality. For those applications with low memory pressure, the performance differences between HMC and DDR memories are negligible. Due to its smaller row buffers and closed-row policy, the HMC can hurt the performance of applications with contiguous data access behavior.

We can observe that when executing parallel applications, the spatial locality of the addresses arriving to the main memory reduces. It can be explained by the domain division per thread, where each thread tends to work in a different range of addresses. Moreover, with multi-threads generating requests, the memory pressure rises leading to a better exploration of the multiple HMC vaults.

In our experiments, we showed that applications with low memory pressure do not benefit from a different memory architecture. In this sense, low-end systems with very low performance processors may not benefit from HMC memories. The same can be said for streaming applications with high spatial locality, which benefit more from the DDR row buffer size. Furthermore, for systems with higher processing capabilities, the HMC can become more interesting when executing multi-threaded or multi-programmed workloads, which may create enough memory pressure with low spatial locality.

5   Related Work

The work presented in [16,17] verifies the maximum HMC memory bandwidth achievable, evaluating different high performance computing systems. The authors used the HMC-Sim simulator [11] varying HMC configurations coupled to a 16-core x86 processor. The authors only performed the experiments based on the HMC specification version 1.0 [4], which states a maximum theoretical bandwidth of 160 GB/s through 256 memory banks.

Fujitsu XIfx [20] introduces the usage of 8 HMC memories coupled to a set of SPARC64 processors. The work shows the performance achieved when HMC memory is adopted replacing DDR 3 memories. The processor coupled with HMC memories is 3.5 times faster on average, than previous DDR 3 memories with 4 channels. Due to the great reduction of the main memory bottleneck with the adoption of HMC, processor performance is dramatically expanded.

The HMC-Sim [11] is a cycle accurate simulator for HMC memories only, not modeling the cache hierarchy, interconnections and the processor. We choose to adapt the SiNUCA [3] memory model to support HMC, due to its capabilities of simulating the full system. Thus, we provide another tool capable to model HMC, while we can compare the findings with the other simulator.

Previous work explore only high performance processors, leaving it unclear whether the same behavior presents itself in the embedded system domain. In this work, we model an embedded system environment comparing the HMC 2.0 specification which supports up to 512 DRAM banks. In our evaluations we show the performance difference between HMC (with 1~4 links) and DDR 3 (with 1~8 channels), explaining the application behavior behind the performance results.

6   Conclusions and Future Work

Following the trend to move embedded systems closer to the high performance system domain, several high-end embedded systems are adapting multiple high performance mechanisms, such as DDR memories. However, the new HMC memories lack evaluations regarding their trade-offs when compared to DDR memories, especially in the embedded domain.

In this paper, we present a performance evaluation comparing HMC and DDR memories, in order to understand the possible speedup scenarios of this new memory architecture. We point the new finding that applications with streaming behavior that have high memory access locality perform better on DDR 3 memories, while sparse accesses are better serviced by the HMC. However, applications with low memory pressure keep the same performance in both systems.

As future work, we intend to extend the evaluation for the energy consumption domain. We also plan stress different processor parameters that most affect the memory pressure, such as the number of entries in the Memory Order Buffer (MOB), and cache Miss-Status Handling Registerss (MSHRs), as well as memory disambiguation techniques.

References

1. Altera: Hybrid memory cube controller IP core user guide (2015). https://www.altera.com/solutions/technology.html
2. Alves, M.A.Z.: Increasing energy efficiency of processor caches via line usage predictors. Ph.D. thesis, Universidade Federal do Rio Grande do Sul (2014)
3. Alves, M.A.Z., Diener, M., Moreira, F.B., et al.: SiNUCA: a validated microarchitecture simulator. In: High Performance Computation Conference (2015)
4. Hybrid Memory Cube Consortium: Hybrid memory cube specification rev. 1.0 (2011). http://www.hybridmemorycube.org/
5. Hybrid Memory Cube Consortium: Hybrid memory cube specification rev. 2.0 (2013). http://www.hybridmemorycube.org/
6. Davis, B.T.: Modern DRAM architectures. Ph.D. thesis, University of Michigan (2001)
7. Henning, J.L.: SPEC CPU2006 benchmark descriptions. ACM SIGARCH Comput. Archit. News **34**(4), 1–17 (2006)
8. Intel: Intel Atom Processor E3800 Product Family. Technical report (2015)
9. Jacob, B., Ng, S., Wang, D.: Memory Systems: Cache, DRAM, Disk. Morgan Kaufmann, Burlington (2008)
10. Jeddeloh, J., Keeth, B.: Hybrid memory cube new DRAM architecture increases density and performance. In: Symposium on VLSI Technology, pp. 87–88, June 2012
11. Leidel, J., Chen, Y.: HMC-sim: a simulation framework for hybrid memory cube devices. In: International Parallel Distributed Processing Symposium Workshops, pp. 1465–1474, May 2014
12. Micron: 1Gb: x4, x8, x16 DDR3 SDRAM features, 1Gb_DDR3_SDRAM - Rev. N 11/14 EN (2006)
13. Olmen, J.V., Mercha, A., Katti, G., et al.: 3D stacked IC demonstration using a through silicon via first approach. In: International Electronic Devices Meeting (2008)
14. Patil, H., Cohn, R., Charney, M., et al.: Pinpointing representative portions of large Intel Itanium programs with dynamic instrumentation. In: International Symposium on Microarchitecture, pp. 81–92, December 2004
15. Pawlowski, J.: Hybrid memory cube (HMC). In: Hot Chips 23 (2011)
16. Rosenfeld, P.: Performance exploration of the hybrid memory cube. Ph.D. thesis, University of Maryland (2014)

17. Rosenfeld, P., Cooper-Balis, E., Farrell, T., Resnick, D., Jacob, B.: Peering over the memory wall: design space and performance analysis of the hybrid memory cube. Technical report UMD-SCA-2012-10-01, University of Maryland (2012)
18. Saito, H., Gaertner, G., Jones, W., et al.: Large system performance of SPEC OMP2001 benchmarks. In: International Symposium on High Performance Computing, pp. 370–379 (2006)
19. Thanh-Hoang, T., Shambayati, A., Deutschbein, C., Hoffmann, H., Chien, A.: Performance and energy limits of a processor-integrated FFT accelerator. In: High Performance Extreme Computing Conference, pp. 1–6, September 2014
20. Yoshida, T., Hondou, M., Tabata, T., et al.: SPARC64 XIfx: Fujitsu's next generation processor for HPC. IEEE Micro **35**(2), 6–14 (2015)
21. Zhu, Z., Zhang, Z., Zhang, X.: Fine-grain priority scheduling on multi-channel memory systems. In: International Symposium on High-Performance Computer Architecture, pp. 107–116, February 2002

Managing Cache Memory Resources
in Adaptive Many-Core Systems

Gustavo Girão[1]([⊠]) and Flávio Rech Wagner[2]

[1] Digital Metropolis Institute, Federal University of Rio Grande do Norte,
Natal, Brazil
girao@imd.ufrn.br
[2] Informatics Institute, Federal University of Rio Grande do Sul, Porto Alegre, Brazil
flavio@inf.ufrgs.br

Abstract. In the last decades, the increasing amount of resources in
embedded systems has been leading them to the point where an efficient
management of these resources is mandatory, especially for the memory
subsystem. Current MPSoCs have more than one application running
concurrently. Hence, it is important to identify the memory needs of
these applications and provide them accordingly. In this work we propose the use of a cluster-based, resource-aware approach to provide this
efficient environment. The solution proposed here improves the overall
performance of these systems by aggregating memory resources in clusters and redistributing these resources among applications based on a
fairness criterion. For this memory clustering proposal, we use the information of external memory access-es as an estimate of the amount of
memory required by each application. T Experimental results show that,
depending on how the redistribution of memory resources among application occurs, the overall system can improve performance up to 18%
and the energy savings can reach up to 20%.

Keywords: Many-core · Resource management
Adaptable memory hierarchy · Network-on-chip

1 Introduction

The memory resources in many-core systems must be even more abundant than
processing elements. As a classical and perennial bottleneck of computer systems,
the memory resources must be managed with the outmost efficiency in order to
provide decent performance.

The aggregation of resources as well as their efficient distribution among concurrent applications may lead to substantial gains for the overall system. It is
a well-known fact that applications may have different needs of processing and
memory requirements. Processing requirements refer to the needs of the application to execute its code faster, for instance using TLP (Thread Level Parallelism) and ILP (Instruction Level Parallelism) techniques. As a usual solution,

© IFIP International Federation for Information Processing 2017
Published by Springer International Publishing AG 2017. All Rights Reserved
M. Götz et al. (Eds.): IESS 2015, IFIP AICT 523, pp. 172–182, 2017.
https://doi.org/10.1007/978-3-319-90023-0_14

processing demands must be addressed by assigning more processor elements (e.g. cores or specialized hardware) and/or more time slices to applications. On the other hand, certain applications manipulate considerably higher amounts of data and, therefore, the use of more memory resources (e.g. L1/L2 caches) would increase their efficiency. Figure 1 shows the memory demands of applications from the SPEC benchmark [1]. For these applications, it is possible to see that the amount of memory access instructions (read or write) can range from 30% to 70% of all instructions. It is clear that an efficient memory resource distribution system, in an environment that can run several applications like those, can be advantageous. In this work, we explore various aspects of a memory resource management approach in an NoC-based MPSoC platform used as case study. First, we introduce a mechanism that is able to assign each L2 memory bank in the system to the exclusive use of a given application (and its respective tasks). This mechanism is based on dynamically changeable association tables present in every L1 cache, which indicate the L2 cache banks assigned to the application, their memory address range, and their NoC addresses. Second, we establish a mechanism to redistribute the L2 cache banks among the applications. Experimental results show that an overall system improvement can be reached at the expense of the performance of some individual applications. The key observation is that some applications have more impact on the overall system execution than others, and, consequently, reducing the memory latency of these critical applications can lead to performance gains. Results show that the overall execution time decreases up to 18% and energy savings reach up to 20% in the best case.

The remaining of this paper is organized as follows. The next section presents the baseline architecture considered in this work and the Memory Clustering mechanism itself, including the redistribution approach and redistribution mapping. Section 3 exposes the experimental setup, while Sect. 4 presents the results. Related work is discussed in Sect. 5, and, finally, in Sect. 6 conclusions are drawn and future work is outlined.

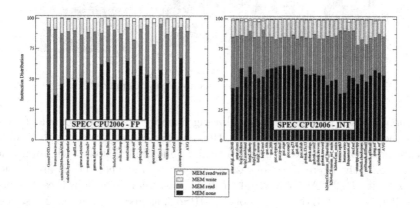

Fig. 1. Memory requirements from SPEC. [1]

2 Memory Clustering

Let us consider the baseline architecture for this mechanism as an NoC-based MPSoC whose nodes are as presented in Fig. 2. In this case, the memory subsystem is homogeneous and composed of local private L1 caches and distributed shared L2 caches. Inside each of the four nodes in the corners, there is also an external memory controller, which has a very important role in this approach. The key idea of this methodology, called Memory Clustering, is to assign the L2 memory blocks according to the needs of each application. The intuition here is that reserving more memory resources to applications that deal with more data will lead to a faster execution overall.

It is important to notice that, as the goal is to improve the *overall* performance and energy savings, the Memory Clustering approach must act on the address spaces of all applications (through the L2 caches) instead of simply redistributing the L1 cache resources, which apply only to the address space of the application currently running in the processor to which each L1 is attached.

The mechanism proposed in this work is a cluster-based resource-aware approach for the memory subsystem. In a previous work [2], this cluster-based approach for resource management has been introduced. However, only processing resources have been considered. In this paper we consider a cluster as an aggregation of physical resources (more specifically, L2 caches) delegated to an application. More than one application may be running in the system, and each one has its own set of resources. Due to the importance of the memory subsystem to the overall system performance, it is desirable to reduce memory latency for data-intensive applications.

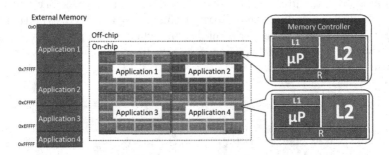

Fig. 2. Example of data space for a set of applications.

The proposed process for redistributing memory resources occurs as follows. Since the beginning of the execution, the memory controllers count the number of external memory accesses made by each application cluster (each application cluster being the aggregation of resources initially assigned to each application, as shown in Fig. 2). At some point during the system execution, these memory controllers (located in the corners of the MPSoC, as presented in Fig. 2) use these statistics to define which application has more cache misses. A synchronization step is performed when one of these memory controllers (henceforth known as master controller) receives messages from the other controllers informing the number of cache misses of the various applications. After that, this master controller uses some redistribution policy (to be detailed in the next sections) to establish how many memory resources (L2 memory banks) each application cluster should have. This number of L2 memory banks allocated to each cluster will be proportional to the percentage of cache misses from the corresponding application. This strategy is an attempt to reproduce, at runtime, the knowledge presented in Fig. 4, which shows, for a system concurrently running four applications, the amount of memory accesses extracted from an application profile at design time.

In order to redistribute memory resources, this approach takes advantage of a previously introduced directory-based cache coherence mechanism [3]. This mechanism uses a small table called ATA table on each cache in the system, which relates an address range to the memory module in the system that may have blocks that belong to such range. This means that each cache memory only perceives a certain amount of physical memory modules in the system, depending on the memory address range of its current memory blocks.

As explained before, at the beginning of the execution each application cluster has its own set of L2 caches and all L1 caches in this cluster have an ATA table that indicates which range of addresses is possibly available in each L2. Each L2 cache controller also knows which addresses should be placed in its own memory.

Let us assume a small scenario of only four L2 caches for an application. As presented in Fig. 3, each cache bank can have a certain contiguous range of addresses from the external memory address space. On the left side of the figure, there is a representation of the ATA table of L1 caches in the cluster assigned to this particular application, where each line corresponds to the range of addresses assigned to each node of the cluster.

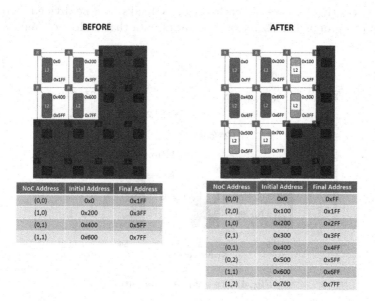

Fig. 3. ATA table and MPSoC before and after resource distribution.

After the synchronization step, as illustrated in Fig. 3, the master controller may reach to the conclusion that this cluster needs four additional memory banks. After choosing which memory banks in the system shall be aggregated to this cluster (the dashed L2 cache banks represent these recently added resources), the ATA tables must be updated. On the bottom-right side of Fig. 3, the new ATA table is illustrated. It is important to notice that the addresses from the application address space are equally divided among the L2 cache banks.

3   Redistribution Policies and Mapping

Once established how the number of L2 caches associated to each L1 cache can be modified, the next decision in the memory clustering mechanism regards the moment when resources (in this case, L2 caches) are taken/given from/to a cluster, thus creating a resizable cluster. Two main approaches are presented here: *Pre-defined Distribution* and *On-demand Distribution*.

The Pre-defined distribution is the model used as baseline for the experimental results. The idea is, based on a design time profiling of the application, to establish beforehand the number of L2 memory modules that each application should have. This distribution takes into account the amount of input data for each application. Since external memory accesses can be very costly, the goal here is to minimize this situation by giving more cache memory space for the most data-intensive applications. This is a static offline approach and is used only to establish how good the second approach is. The graph on Fig. 4 presents the amount of memory accesses for each application used in the experiments and for each scenario with different MPSoC sizes (number of nodes). The memory resources (in this case, L2 cache memory banks) can be divided among the applications proportionally to the amount of data that each one handles.

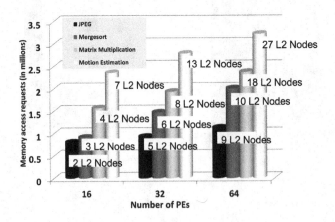

Fig. 4. Pre-defined distribution.

However, this information depends on profilling and it may not always be available. Therefore, some runtime approach should be considered. In the On-demand distribution, all clusters initially use the same amount of L2 caches.

After a certain amount of cycles, the external memory cache controllers (located on the corners of the MPSoC) exchange information, and, based on the number of external memory accesses, the master controller defines which clusters need more memory nodes. The master memory controller then redefines the ATA tables of L1 caches (potentially, all of them), thus redistributing the memory resources in the system.

The biggest question here is how we define the time instant at which the memory controllers must take action to redistribute resources. In this paper we will call this instant in the execution a *redistribution point*. Intuitively, this point must not happen too soon along the overall system execution, because the clustering mechanism needs values that characterize the memory demands for each application and are statistically significant. On the other hand, by doing it too late in the execution time, the pattern will be well defined, but it may be too late to overcome the overhead caused by the redistribution itself. Therefore, some trade-off should be considered in this approach.

By giving more L2 memory banks to some applications, there is no alternative but to take these resources away from other applications. The hope is to efficiently take the correct amount of L2 caches from applications that need them less and give them to applications that need them most. The aspect to be explored is which L2 caches shall be taken away at the moment of the redistribution.

The policy used in this case is to gather new resources that are closer to the resources originally allocated to the application. In this policy, it is reasonable for the applications to exchange resources placed on the edge of their clusters. That condition has the goal of keeping the resources close together, thus avoiding cluster fragmentation. The master memory controller starts by assigning the new resources to the cluster with more memory needs. Next, this process is repeated with the second cluster with more memory needs. This process goes on, with each cluster taking turns on the resource assignment, until the number of resources to be redistributed is reached.

4   Experimental Setup and Results

The experiments consider four applications: a matrix multiplication, a motion estimation algorithm, a Mergesort algorithm, and a JPEG encoder.

Considering the data inputs for the applications described above, Fig. 5 represents their communication workload regarding different numbers of processors. Based on this chart, it is expected that the Motion Estimation algorithm will generate a larger amount of data exchanges. This shows that the benchmarks used here are capable of generating significant amount of communication traffic. This would make an efficient memory hierarchy even more required in order to avoid unnecessary memory requests.

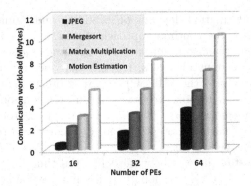

Fig. 5. Communication workload.

Experiments evaluate two characteristics: performance, measured by the total execution time of each application, and the overall dynamic energy spent, including processors, network, and memories. For the energy of the processors, a cycle-accurate power simulator [4] is used. For the network (including buffers, arbiter, crossbar, and links), the Orion library [5] is applied, and for the memory and caches the Cacti tool [6] is used.

All experiments were performed in a SystemC cycle-accurate MPSoC virtual platform that can instantiate architectural components as illustrated in Fig. 2. Due to their smaller size, this virtual platform uses MIPS processors as cores implementing MIPS I ISA. The configuration used in all experiments in this platform is presented in Table 1.

The remainder of this section presents results regarding the memory clustering experiments using the Pre-defined and On-demand Distribution policies. In this second policy the experiments were performed using four distinct redistribution points. Goal of these experiments is to find the best moment during the execution of applications to perform a memory redistribution, in a way that, after this point, the system can have an overall performance boost. The ideal time point at which the redistribution of the memory subsystem must be performed depends on each scenario, considering number of cores, number of L2 caches, execution time of all applications, etc. Since we are dealing with different MPSoC sizes, the overall execution time can vary drastically. Therefore, the

Table 1. Configuration of the virtual platform.

Number of processors	16; 32; 64
Number of L2 caches	16; 32; 64
Total number of initial tasks per application	32
L1 cache size	8192 bytes
Block size	32 bytes

redistribution points for the four experiments were defined at 10%, 25%, 50% and 75% of the overall execution time in each case, such that we can explore the impact of different values for this parameter.

Figure 6 presents the performance and energy results using the Pre-defined Distribution. One can notice that the applications with higher input data (Motion Estimation and Matrix Multiplication) have large benefits, as opposed to the JPEG and Mergesort applications. These last two applications actually present a drop in performance, down to 22%. However, there has been an increase in the overall system performance (i.e. the amount of time to execute all applications) of 34% in the best case. As for the energy results, they present a very similar pattern when compared to the performance results, reaching up to 40% of savings.

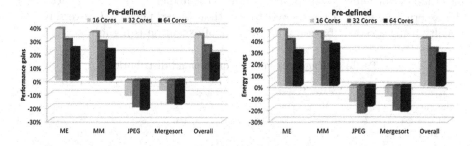

Fig. 6. Pre-defined distribution performance and energy results.

These performance and energy improvements happen because the larger applications have higher impact on the system. Obviously, due to the overhead discussed previously, these numbers are virtually impossible to achieve in practice. However, they give a good basis for understanding how good this approach can be.

Table 2 presents the results of the On-demand Distribution policy considering redistribution points of 10%, 25%, 50% and 75% of system execution time. By the results of overall performance it is possible to see that the best results occur when a redistribution point of 50% is used. This means that the execution at this point is enough to obtain a reasonable distribution of memory resources in the system. When this redistribution point occurs too early, as in the case of 10%, it almost does not affect the performance of the system. This seems to be due to the fact that this short amount of execution time is not enough to characterize memory demands of all applications correctly. Experiments with later redistribution points do not present the best results as well. There are two explanations for this behavior. First, when leaving the redistribution to occur that late in the system, the applications that needed more memory resources were not prioritized for the most part of their execution. This would have a considerable impact on the overall performance. Second, at 75% of execution time, there is not much time left to compensate the overhead caused by the memory redistribution itself.

Table 2. Performance results for on-demand distribution.

Redistrib. pts	10%			25%			50%			75%		
No. of cores	16	32	64	16	32	64	16	32	64	16	32	64
Motion Est.	3%	2%	1%	18%	12%	7%	23%	20%	16%	−5%	−3%	−2%
Matrix Multipl.	3%	2%	2%	11%	7%	5%	17%	14%	10%	−3%	−2%	−1%
JPEG	−4%	−5%	−6%	−3%	−8%	−10%	−9%	−14%	−20%	−2%	−1%	−1%
Mergesort	−2%	−3%	−5%	−3%	−6%	−7%	−2%	−5%	−8%	−3%	−2%	−1%
Overall	1.2%	0.1%	−0.6%	12%	6%	3%	18%	14%	11%	−3.5%	−2.3%	−1.4%

Table 3 presents the energy results for the On-demand Distribution. As in the case of the Pre-defined Distribution, the energy results follow a similar pattern when compared to the performance results. There are slightly higher energy savings than performance gains, probably due to the higher energy costs of accessing the external memory if com-pared to the time access penalty. Conversely, the penalty using a redistribution point at 75% of execution is higher.

Table 3. Energy results for on-demand distribution.

Redistrib. pts	10%			25%			50%			75%		
No. of cores	16	32	64	16	32	64	16	32	64	16	32	64
Motion Est.	4%	1%	1%	20%	19%	8%	25%	23%	18%	−7%	−4%	−3%
Matrix Multipl.	5%	3%	2%	12%	7%	7%	21%	19%	12%	−6%	−4%	−2%
JPEG	−5%	−6%	−7%	−3%	−8%	−9%	−9%	−15%	−22%	−3%	−2%	−3%
Mergesort	−2%	−4%	−6%	−4%	−7%	−6%	−3%	−8%	−10%	−4%	−3%	−1%
Overall	2%	0.6%	−0.2%	13%	9%	4%	22%	18%	13%	−5.6%	−3.7%	−2.3%

5   Related Work

Even though no approaches using dynamic cluster-based approaches for managing memory resources were found in the literature, some works propose resource management techniques that could be extended to the memory subsystem. In this section we present some of these works.

Qureshi and Patt [7] present a redistribution mechanism in an L1 private/L2 shared cache architecture. In this mechanism, the evicted lines from one cache (called spiller) can be allocated in another cache (called receiver) in the system through a snooping mechanism. This is an approach with the goal of extending the size for one cache (the spiller) and to make the data stay inside the chip longer. This approach considers a single address space and several threads from the same application while ours is a global approach.

Recent works propose a paradigm of multicore programming called Invasive Computing [8–10]. The proposal is to take advantage of a large many-core processor in the best possible way. The idea leverages on malleable applications where the degree of parallelism can change on the fly. At the application level, the programmer uses functions that trigger the invasion process. When an application sends an invade request, a distributed resource manager evaluates the request based on the amount of resources required and the estimated speed-up per core. This Invasive Computing works at different levels of abstraction, and, therefore, the programmer must have some notion of the methodology. In the case of the Memory Clustering approach proposed in this paper, all mechanisms are transparent to the programmer.

6 Conclusion

In this paper we introduce the con-cept of Memory Clustering. Since some applications have more memory needs than others, the key idea of this mechanism is to reserve more memory resources (in fact L2 caches) for the more time-consuming applications, taking them away from other applications that do not need them as much. Overall results presented show that, depending on the time point where the redistribution of memory resources occurs, there is room for performance and energy gains for the system as a whole.

In the future, we intend to investigate other methods to determine the right moment for the memory redistribution. In the experiments presented here, the best time points for the redistribution (25% and 50% of the overall system execution time) have been identified for specific experiments. Therefore, in a situation where there is no previous knowledge of the applications, the best redistribution point can be different from those values. In the future, we will investigate further the cache misses before and after the redistribution points, in order to better characterize causes of the initial performance loss and effects of the memory redistribution.

References

1. Jaleel, A.: Memory characterization of workloads using instrumentation-driven simulation - a pin-based memory characterization of the SPEC CPU2000 and SPEC CPU2006 benchmark suites. Intel Corporation, VSSAD. Technical report (2007)
2. Girão, G., Santini, T., Wagner, F.R.: Exploring resource mapping policies for dynamic clustering on NoC-based MPSoCs. In: Design, Automation Test in Europe Conference Exhibition (DATE), pp. 681–684. IEEE Press, New York (2013)
3. Girão, G., Santini, T., Wagner, F.R.: Cache coherency communication cost in a NoC-based MPSoC platform. In: Proceedings of the 20th Annual Conference on Integrated Circuits and Systems Design, pp. 288–293. ACM, New York (2007)
4. Chen, B., Nedelchev, I.: Power compiler: a gate-level power optimization and synthesis system. In: IEEE International Conference on Computer Design, pp. 74–79. IEEE Press, New York (1997)
5. Kahng, A.B., Bin, L., Peh, L.-S., Samadi, K.: ORION 2.0: a power-area simulator for interconnection networks. IEEE Trans. VLSI 20, 191–196 (2011)
6. Wilton, S.J.E., Jouppi, N.P.: CACTI: an enhanced cache access and cycle time model. IEEE J. Solid-State Circuits 31, 677–688 (2002)
7. Qureshi, M.K., Patt, Y.N.: Utility-based partitioning of shared caches. In: 39th Annual IEEE/ACM International Symposium on Microarchitecture, pp. 423–432. IEEE Press, New York (2006)

8. Teich, J., et al.: Invasive computing: an overview. In: Hübner, M., Becker, J. (eds.) Multiprocessor System-on-Chip Hardware Design and Tool Integration, pp. 241–268. Springer, Heidelberg (2011). https://doi.org/10.1007/978-1-4419-6460-1_11
9. Henkel, J., et al.: Invasive manycore architectures. In: 17th Asia and South Pacific Design Automation Conference, pp. 193–200. IEEE Press, New York (2012)
10. Kobbe, S., et al.: DistRM: distributed resource management for on-chip many-core systems. In: 9th International Conference on Hardware/Software Codesign and System Synthesis, pp. 119–128. IEEE Press, New York (2011)

Embedded HW/SW Design and Applications

A UML Profile to Couple the Production Code Generator TargetLink with UML Design Tools

Malte Falk[1], Stefan Walter[2], and Achim Rettberg[1,3(✉)]

[1] Carl von Ossietzky University Oldenburg, Oldenburg, Germany
malte-falk@gmx.de
[2] dSPACE GmbH, Paderborn, Germany
swalter@dspace.de
[3] Hella Electronics, Lippstadt , Germany
achim.rettberg@iess.org

Abstract. When modelling architecture of complex embedded systems proper architecture languages and tools are necessary. UML [1] has become a proven and well accepted design language to express system as well as software architecture. For definition of internal behavior of components composed and specified during software design, Simulink is commonly used, especially for automotive and aerospace applications. As common practise, code is generated directly from such behavior models. Therefore, code generators such as TargetLink [2] are used. In this paper we propose a UML profile to describe specific properties necessary to adapt UML models to the code generator TargetLink.

1 Motivation

To cope with today's growing complexity of requirements in embedded systems development adequate development methods are crucial to develop high quality systems. Today's embedded systems often consists of distributed functionalities where software components could run on the same or on a different hardware platform within the distributed system. To define such complex system structures an architectural design phase in the development process is essential. As a de-facto standard language to be used in software and system architecture modelling the Unified Modelling Language (UML) [1] and the System Modelling Language (SysML) [3] is widely used in different fields. At a certain step during development of embedded systems, one have to model and implement the behavior of the defined software components. A common tool for behaviour modelling is Simulink from The Mathworks [4]. Especially in the automotive industry but also for development of airborne software both modeling environments UML and Simulink are used extensively. After modelling the behavior of a software component, in best case the embedded code to be integrated on the electronic control unit is directly generated from the behavior model, in this paper from Simulink.

M. Götz et al. (Eds.): IESS 2015, IFIP AICT 523, pp. 185–196, 2017.
https://doi.org/10.1007/978-3-319-90023-0_15

Generating code from Simulink software specifications which is then directly used on electronic control units is de-facto standard in state of the art development processes especially in the automotive industry. The technique of autocode generation is well accepted and widely used especially in safety critical projects. One of the major tools used by the industry is TargetLink from dSPACE GmbH [2]. In this paper we propose a mapping between UML component architecture models and TargetLink models.

2   Related Work

Various research work deal with mapping of MATLAB/Simulink models to UML like [5]. In contrast to this paper, [5] discusses a possibility to illustrate the MATLAB/Simulink models and the behaviour of it in UML and replaces Simulink hereby.

Other publications discuss a possibility to describe systems with UML and redescribe it in MATLAB/Simulink. In [6] it is discussed how software architectures which are described in UML could be transformed to simulation models which are described with MATLAB/Simulink. These publications describe a similar approach compared to this paper. In contrast to other publications this paper describes a possibility to map a TargetLink model, which is based on MATLAB/Simulink, to UML. The benefit is to reuse properties such as interface description, etc. from an architecture model and annotate it to a TargetLink model, which is later used for automatic code generation.

3   TargetLink

TargetLink is a Toolbox for MATLAB/Simulink in order to generate series production code by a push of a button from a Simulink model. Beside generation of regular ANSI-C code for fixed point or floating point processors it is also possible to generate code for certain processor/compiler combinations. To enhance a Simulink model to a TargetLink model used for code generation, certain parameters need to be set, to describe how the code generated by TargetLink looks like. To maintain all parameters for all blocks within the TargetLink model the TargetLink Data Dictionary is used. The TargetLink Data Dictionary represents a data container in order to describe all elements. These elements represent information for the model design, the code generation and the implementation of a model on an electronic control unit. TargetLink elements are described by various properties and can be referenced by TargetLink models. In the following section we will introduce and discuss the relevant TargetLink elements used for UML mapping.

3.1   TargetLink Data Dictionary Elements

The TargetLink Data Dictionary is used to parameterize and describe all elements used in TargetLink models. Below all elements which are relevant to be mapped to UML are specified. A more in-depth and formal description of the various element properties can be found in [7,8].

Pool. The TargetLink Data Dictionary is divided into three areas *Config*, *Pool*, and *Subsystem*. In this paper only the *Pool*-area is considered. This area contains all data elements which are required for code generation. Examples of elements in the Pool area are scaling values of fixpoint variables the or type definition of variables.

Blocks. Blocks are the main elements in TargetLink Data Dictionary and therefore essential for the code generation. Based on the Block description, Simulink Blocks could be generated directly from the TargetLink Data Dictionary. Even though various types of Blocks are available inside the TargetLink Data Dictionary, this paper focusses only on Blocks of type *TL_Function*. Those Blocks represent the base architecture of the software component to be developed.

Signature and SignaturePort. A Signature contains Signature-Ports, whereas Signature-Ports are divided in *in-*, *out-*, and *user*-ports. Signatures are used to describe which in- and out-ports are available at the TL_Function Block. In contrast to in- and out-ports, user-ports are freely configurable for different use cases, e.g. calibration-ports.With ports it is possible to connect TL_Function Blocks with Variables, either incoming or outgoing.

Variable. Variables are used to exchange information between different TL_Function Blocks. The properties of variables define the appearance within the generated code. The actual type of Variable is defined by a *Typedef* element as described in the following paragraphs. A min, max range can be set by a reference to a *Scaling* element as described in the following paragraphs.

Typedef. The Typedef element specifies the datatype of a Variable element. In the TargetLink Data Dictionary Typedefs are referenced by Variables.

Scaling. A Scaling is used to define the value range of a Variable. This is necessary in case of fixed-point code generation. Furthermore, it is possible to define values for Least Significant Bit (LSB), Offset, and, physical unit within the Scaling properties.

Module. The characteristics of the code modules in the generated code are specified by Module elements, e.g. the memory location. Properties of these elements are TargetLink specific and do not have any implication on architecture level. Due to this fact it is not considered in scope of this paper.

FunctionClass. FunctionClass properties define how the generated code for a referenced TL_Function Block would look like. Because FunctionClasses are usually predefined, they are not considered in the further course of this paper.

VariableClass. VariableClasses are similar elements compared to Function-Classes. The difference is that VariableClasses specify Variables in the generated code. Because VariableClasses are usually predefined, they are not considered in the further course of this paper.

TargetLink Data Dictionary Model. In the context of this paper a TargetLink Data Dictionary model is a finite set of all above described elements. In Sect. 4 of this paper a mapping of TargetLink Data Dictionary model to UML is described.

3.2   Relationship Between TargetLink Elements

This section describes the relationship between the TargetLink Data Dictionary elements as specified in Sect. 3.1. This description could be later used to derive the connection between the different UML elements in an UML profile. An analysis of the dependencies could be realised by a tree structure diagram with breadth-first search.

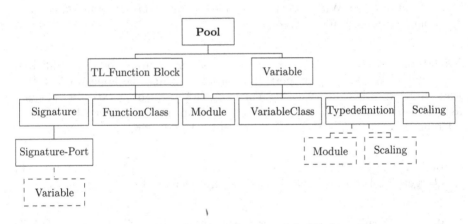

Fig. 1. Tree structure diagram of the Pool area

Figure 1 shows the Pool area with all defined elements of the TargetLink Data Dictionary. The figure clearly shows the dependencies between all elements. It is obviously depicted in Fig. 1 that Variables are independent from other TargetLink Data Dictionary elements. This means a Variable could exist without a TL_Function Block, e.g. global Variables. Figure 1 also indicates that Variables and TL_Function Blocks are split into different branches. This implies that those two elements need to be considered differently when defining the UML profile.

Another fact of the tree structure shows that a TL_Function Block is linked to Variables over a Signature and Signature-Port, whereas one Signature-Port of a Signature is linked to exactly one Variable. On the other hand a Variable could be linked to different Signature-Ports.

4   Prototype TargetLink Model in UML

Based on the previous definitions, in this section a prototype for describing TargetLink models in UML is suggested. The section is subdivided into two subsections. The first subsection explains the UML diagram type selected to be used for expressing the TargetLink model elements. In the second subsection it is described which element of the selected UML diagram type is mapped to a specific element of the TargetLink Data Dictionary.

4.1   Composite Structure Diagram

With composite structure diagrams it is possible to describe the internal structure of a class or the collaboration between different classes. It is similar to the component diagram and therefore as described in [9] on page 93 it could be combined with such diagram types. In addition, a composite structure diagram provides two different views on a system. The first view is the structural-dynamic view which focusses on the function of the system and which parts are needed for the functions. The second view is shown in Fig. 2 as a class diagram.

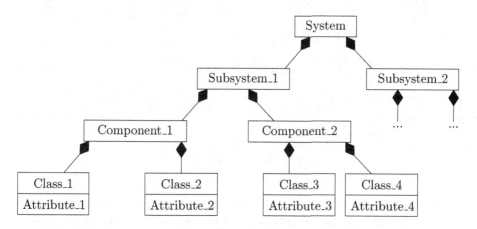

Fig. 2. Structural static view [8, p. 194]

In a first step the system is partitioned into various subsystems. In the following these different subsystems are divided into various components. Each component comprises several classes with attributes. This way to describe systems can be found on system level (Hardware) or on software level (GUI split into application, windows, etc.) [8, p. 194].

The metaclasses of the composite structure diagram are classes, parts, ports, interfaces and connectors. In the following all relevant elements are shortly described. A class is a kind of construction plan for an object. Parts are used to split a class into subsets. Parts could be extended by ports in order to implement

interaction points for communication between elements. To connect different
ports of parts connectors are used. In the following section a possible prototype
which describes how TargetLink Data Dictionary elements are mapped to UML
elements is presented [9, p. 125ff].

4.2 Prototype

The prototype differentiates between a system and variable level. The distinction
was made based on results of the previously described tree structure diagram
analysis. On system level it is possible to describe TL_Function Blocks, Signatures and Signature-Ports. Whereas on variable level Variables, Typedefs and
Scalings are described. In Figs. 3 and 4 both, the system level and variable level
is depicted.

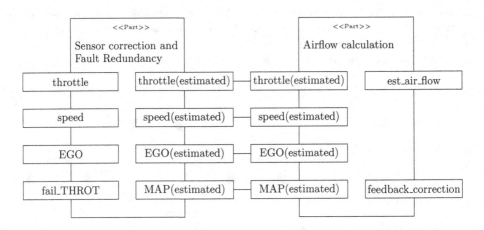

Fig. 3. System level in UML

UML Parts are used to separate a system into different subsystems whereas
one Part contains the specification of a subsystem as a piece of the entire system. A TL_Function Block is an element that encloses all other elements except
the global Variables with its Typedefs, Scalings, etc. A TargetLink model can
consist of several TL_Function Blocks. Therefore, a TL_Function Block contains
a certain aspect of the specification of a model. Thus, in Fig. 3 TL_Function
Blocks are depicted as Parts. The formal description as defined in [8, p. 23f]
summarizes TL_Function Blocks and Signatures. For this reason Parts include
the description of Signatures as well.

Signature-Ports are mapped to UML Ports in the concept described in this
paper. Parts could use UML Ports for communication with other UML Parts.
Signature-Ports enable communication between TL_Function Blocks using Variables, as shown in Fig. 1. On Variable level all variables a TL_Function Block
could contain are specified.

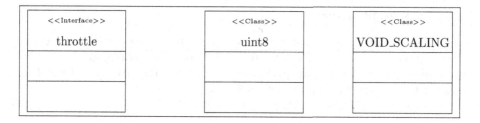

Fig. 4. Variable level in UML

As shown in Fig. 1, on Variable level it is possible to describe Variables and its dependencies. Furthermore, specification of variable types (Typedefs) and scalings are done on Variable level. Figure 4 shows an excerpt from a specification of Variable, Typedef and Scaling elements on Variable level used for communication between different TL_Function Blocks via Ports. In the TargetLink context Variables specify the interface of TL_Function Blocks. Therefore, in this concept Variable elements are mapped to UML interfaces.

Typedefs and Scalings represent a construction plan for Variables in TargetLink Data Dictionary. These elements describe the appearance of Variables in the production code. In UML classes have a similar functionality. They influence objects and provide so some kind of construction plan by attributes and operations [9, S.32]. For this reason Scaling and Typedef elements are represented by classes.

With mapping UML Parts to Signatures and TL_Function Blocks, UML Interfaces to Scalings and Typedefs, UML Class to Variables and UML Ports to Signature-Ports all profile relevant TargetLink elements are described in the UML profile. These elements are a subset of all TargetLink elements.

5   Definition of the TargetLink UML Profile

In the previous section a possibility on how to specify TargetLink Data Dictionary elements in UML was described. To enable specifying TargetLink Data Dictionary relevant elements in UML composite structure diagrams, the semantics of those diagrams need to be extended. In UML such kind of extensions are defined in UML profiles, mainly consisting of *stereotypes*, *tagged values* and *constraints*. Stereotypes expand the UML metaclasses and represent the extended elements. Tagged values expand stereotypes by properties as name-value pairs. Constraints define additional constraints for the stereotypes and enable users to check a model by the specified constraints. In the further course of this paper first the structure of different packages of the TargetLink Data Dictionary UML profile is described. In a second step the structure of the profile is illustrated. A more in-depth description of the UML profile can be found in [8].

5.1   Package Structure

This subsection describes the structure of the various packages of the TargetLink Data Dictionary UML profile. Different UML packages partition the various required elements of the UML profile. Figure 5 shows the structure of the TargetLink Data Dictionary profile with different packages.

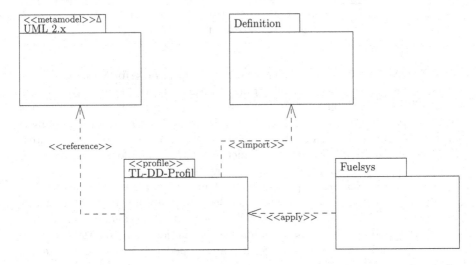

Fig. 5. Package structure

The figure shows a subdivision of the structure in four different UML packages. The package *UML 2.x* provides all metaclasses of the UML version 2.x. Because the TargetLink Data Dictionary profile expands the semantics of a composite structure diagram it is essential to use UML 2 or higher [10].

The UML 2 metaclasses used by the package *TL-DD-Profil* are provided via *<<reference>>*-connection to the package *UML 2.x*. This connection enables to expand metaclasses, such as ports or classes, with stereotypes. This kind of connection is called metamodel-reference because all metaclasses of UML 2.x which are provided with the *<<metamodel>>*-package are referenced by the profile package.

The definition of the profile itself can be found in the package *TL-DD-Profil*. The stereotype *<<profile>>* is used to declare that the package contains UML profiles. The *TL-DD-Profil* represents the key package within the package diagram. It contains all required metaclass extensions such as stereotypes, tagged values representing the TargetLink Data Dictionary properties and additional constraints. Using the *<<import>>*-connection the *TL-DD-Profil* package imports different predefined elements from the *Definition*-package.

As mentioned above, the Definition-package describes different elements to be used in the *TL-DD-Profil*. Among others, basic data types of the TargetLink

Data Dictionary are determined in this package. For example, predefined elements such as VariableClasses are defined in this package. The *Fuelsys*-package represents the actual application model which is described by applying the TargetLink UML profile.

5.2   Profile Structure

The following section explains the internal structure of the profile package TL-DD-Profil based on the previous prototype. The different metaclasses in the profile package are extended by stereotypes. The different metaclasses are provided by the <<reference>>-connection between profile package and UML 2.X package which is illustrated in Fig. 5. The different extensions of metaclasses by stereotypes are depicted in Fig. 6. This paper concentrates on the structure and the dependencies between the different stereotypes. A precise description of the UML profile is given in [8].

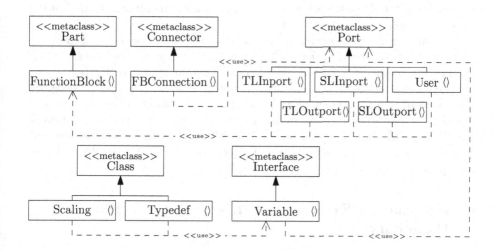

Fig. 6. Profile structure

The different <<*use*>>-connections, as depicted in Fig. 5, represent the associations between the different stereotypes. Furthermore, the connection shows which elements are in communication. For example the figure obviously shows the connection between TL_Function Blocks and different ports (e.g. TLInport, SLInport, ...).

Moreover, Fig. 5 shows which metaclass is extended by which stereotype. The prototype in Sect. 4.2 defines Scaling elements as a UML class. Therefore, the metaclass Class is extended by the stereotype Scaling. Another example is the stereotype Typedef which extends the metaclass Class as well. The Scaling element and the Typedef element will be provided by both extensions in the UML profile. Another element that is provided by the UML profile is the stereotype

Variable. In Sect. 4.2 Variable elements are defined as interchangeable elements that carries information. These elements are mapped to UML interfaces. Therefore, the UML metaclass interface is extended by the stereotype Variable. The so called variable level that is described in Sect. 4 only contains those three element types.

TL_Function Blocks, Signatures, and all kinds of Signature-Ports are applied on system level. Each TL_Function Block specifies a part of the entire system in the prototype and are therefore mapped to UML Parts. Thus, in Fig. 6 it is depicted that the metaclass Part is extended by stereotyp TL_Function Block.

Various stereotypes, representing different kind of communication ports, extend the metaclass Port. In UML, ports specify interaction points of parts and its environment. In the profile ports are used to represent the different Signature-Ports. Signature-Ports are interaction points of TL_Function Blocks used to consume and provide Variables. Signature-Ports can represent in-, out-, or user-ports. This is the reason why the metaclass Port is extended by different stereotypes. In detail the stereotypes differentiate only by its names. With the various Signature-Port stereotypes a user can directly recognize the kind of the Signature-Port.

The stereotype FBConnection extends the metaclass Connector. Signature-Ports can be connected to each other via FBConnection. These connections can not be mapped to the TargetLink Data Dictionary but in UML it shows the connection between all elements via ports. A user could easily recognize the interconnection between different TL_Function Blocks. Those connections represent the information flow within a system. A more detailed description of the UML profile can be found in [8]. The following section gives an overview on how to couple UML tools and the TargetLink Data Dictionary to exchange information.

6   Information Exchange UML - TargetLink Data Dictionary

With the UML profile defined in this paper it is possible to already add TargetLink Data Dictionary properties which will be used in a later step for production code generation to UML elements during system design. However an automatic exchange of those properties between the UML model specified during design phase and the TargetLink Data Dictionary is not yet possible. A common format to exchange information between programs and software tools is XML. Also the TargetLink Data Dictionary is able to import XML files containing a specific data structure. By importing XML files into the TargetLink Data Dictionary it is possible to either expand or overwrite available elements.

A standard for exchanging models between UML tools is the XML Metadata Interchange (XMI) which is published by the Object Management Group (OMG). The import and export of this XML based data format is supported by all major UML tools. XMI files describe complete UML diagrams in textual form. Even if XMI is a standard data format, each UML tool implements its own interpretation of this standard, which slightly differs in structure of properties and used XMI vocabulary. In other words although XMI is a standard, each XMI-file exported from a different UML tool looks different. For this reason it is difficult to design a generic compiler for the transformation between XMI and TargetLink Data Dictionary XML.

In the following section we briefly describe the steps undertaken to design a transformation between UML XMI and TargetLink Data Dictionary XML. Due to the variations in the XMI standard as mentioned in the previous section, we focussed our analysis on the two most commonly used tools in the industry, Enterprise Architect [11] and Rational Rhapsody [12]. As a first step we have implemented the previously described UML profile in both tools. Based on this profile we design a demo system that includes all in Sect. 5 defined elements. In the second step the demo model was exported to XMI, using the standard export mechanism of the UML tools. Based on the exported XMI files we have to analyse the structure and the different vocabularies of both files. On the basis of analysis results a grammar is developed which describes the relevant items of the XMI export of both UML tools.

After the gramatic was derived from the XMI export, now the TargetLink Data Dictionary XML file is analysed. For each export, the structure and the vocabulary of this file is always the same. Therefore, it is sufficient to consider all in Sect. 3.1 defined TargetLink Data Dictionary elements. Also for the TargetLink Data Dictionary export a grammar is defined, which is similar to the one developed for the XMI export. By specifying transformation rules the XMI grammar is mapped to the XML grammar of the TargetLink Data Dictionary. The transformation rules describe an unambiguous mapping between the information of the TargetLink Data Dictionary and the XMI file.

As a last step an algorithm was implemented that is able to compile the XMI grammar in the XML grammar. If the grammar is expressed in an adequate language, e.g. antlr [13], a parser generator could be used to generate this algorithm automatically. The definition of the grammar and the transformation rules is not focus of this paper. A detailed declaration of these grammars can be found in [8].

7   Conclusion and Future Work

This paper summarizes a possibility to describe TargetLink Data Dictionary elements in UML to provide a smoother transition between software architecture definition and functional component design. Therefore, a UML profile was defined which provides various TargetLink Data Dictionary elements to be used in UML diagrams. The specified UML profile extends semantics of the composite structure diagram. Using this UML profile it is possible to connect UML tools to the production code generator TargetLink. This coupling is an important step in development of complex software architectures where software design tools such as UML as well as automatic code generators such as TargetLink became a defacto standard. The smooth transition between UML tools and

TargetLink supports the consistent exchange of software components and its interfaces between different engineering teams, responsible for software architecture and software component design. Following this approach, each development team could import their subsystems from the entire software architecture description automatically into the TargetLink Data Dictionary to describe the functional behaviour with MATLAB/Simulink and generate production code with TargetLink.

With the concept described in this paper we could not solve the problem that every UML tool needs its own compiler due to the ambiguous definition of XMI structure and vocabulary. A generic methodology of transforming UML XMI files to TargetLink Data Dictionary readable XML files is subject to future work.

This paper is a rough overview about the topic. More in-depth information on different aspects e.g. details on grammar specification and complete definition of the UML profile can be found in [8].

References

1. Unified Modeling Language (UML) Resource Page. http://www.uml.org
2. dSPACE TargetLink - Automatische Seriencode-Generierung. https://www.dspace.com/de/gmb/home/products/sw/pcgs/targetli.cfm
3. OMG Systems Modeling Language. http://www.omgsysml.org
4. MathWorks. http://de.mathworks.com/
5. Sjöstedt, C.-J., Shi, J., Törngren, M., Servat, D., Chen, D., Ahlsten, V., Lönn, H.: Mapping simulink to UML in the design of embedded systems: investigating scenarios and transformations (2007)
6. Walter, S: Übersetzung von UML-Software-Spezifikation in Simulationsmodelle. Fern Universität in Hagen (2014)
7. TargetLink Help Desk for Releases 2014-A
8. Falk, M.: Definition eines Profils zur Kopplung des Seriencode-Generators TargetLink an UML-Werkzeuge. Carl von Ossietzky University Oldenburg (2015)
9. Booch, G., Rumbaugh, J., Jacobson, I.: The Unified Modeling Language User Guide. Addison-Wesley, Reading (2005). Shanklin, J.C. ISBN 0-321-26797-4
10. Rupp, C., Queins, S.: UML 2 glasklar - Praxiswissen fr die UML-Modellierung, 4th edn. Hanser Verlag, Munich (2012). ISBN 978-3-446-43057-0
11. Enterprise Architect - Model Driven UML Tools. http://www.sparxsystems.de/start/startseite/
12. Rational Rhapsody family. http://www-03.ibm.com/software/products/de/ratirhapfami
13. ANTLR. http://www.antlr.org
14. OMG Systems Modeling Language - The official OMG SysML site. http://www.omgsysml.org

Rapid, High-Level Performance Estimation for DSE Using Calibrated Weight Tables

Kasra Moazzemi, Smit Patel[✉], Shen Feng, and Gunar Schirner

Department of Electrical and Computer Engineering,
Northeastern University, Boston, MA, USA
{moazzemi.k,patel.smi}@husky.neu.edu, schirner@ece.neu.edu

Abstract. Automated Design Space Exploration (DSE) is a critical part of system-level design. It relies on performance estimation to evaluate design alternatives. However, since a plethora of design alternatives need to be compared, the run-time of performance estimation itself may pose a bottleneck. In DSE, fastest performance estimation is of essence while some accuracy may be sacrificed. Fast estimation can be realised through capturing application demand, as well as Processing Element (PE) supply (later on called weight table) in a matrix each. Then, performance estimation (retargeting) is reduced to a matrix multiplication. However, defining the weight table from a data sheet is impractical due to the multitude of (micro-) architecture aspects.

This paper introduces a novel methodology, WeiCal, for automatically generating Weight Tables in the context of C source-level estimation using application profiling and Linear Programming (LP). LP solving is based on the measured performance of training benchmarks on an actual PE. We validated WeiCal using a synthetic processor and benchmark model, and also analyse the impact of non-observable features on estimation accuracy. We evaluate the efficiency using 49 benchmarks on 2 different processors with varying configurations (multiple memory configurations and software optimizations). On a 3.1 GHz i5-3450 Intel host, 25 million estimations/second can be obtained regardless of the application size and PE complexity. The accuracy is sufficient for early DSE with a 24% average error.

1 Introduction

Recent advances in technology have expanded the design options in terms of number and type of processors as well as their configurations such as interconnects and memory hierarchy. When this flexibility of design is coupled with the increasing pressure of time to market, performance exploration of the design space becomes exponentially difficult. Current approaches try to automate the Design Space Exploration (DSE). In any DSE, two questions need to be addressed. One is how to traverse the design space and other is how to assess

© IFIP International Federation for Information Processing 2017
Published by Springer International Publishing AG 2017. All Rights Reserved
M. Götz et al. (Eds.): IESS 2015, IFIP AICT 523, pp. 197–209, 2017.
https://doi.org/10.1007/978-3-319-90023-0_16

the fitness of each design instance - all unique combinations of platforms and mappings. Millions of design options will be traversed before making a design decision. Evaluating the fitness of each design option falls on the time critical path of DSE and is at most importance here. Simulation based approaches can be highly accurate but too slow for DSE. New approaches are needed for rapid high-level performance estimation in context of DSE.

This paper revisits the retargetable profiling for rapid, early system-level design space exploration, introduced in [1] and improves upon it. The retargetable profiler [1] uses a weight table, which is a matrix of Processing Element's (PE) performance cost (cycles) of each high-level operation for all data types. One of the main challenges of retargetable profiling is that the weight tables need to be manually defined. The accuracy of weight table impacts the accuracy of final estimation. Due to manual extraction of these weight tables from the data sheet, this process is time consuming and error prone. Moreover, because of the high-level abstraction, only a few features of the processor are observable (can be quantified). For example, C statements do not reveal from where an operand needs to be fetched from within the memory hierarchy. Therefore, the cycles captured in the weight tables have to statistically include these non-observable characteristics such as memory accesses and pipeline stalls. These elements which can affect the performance but are not observed during execution make it very difficult to manually populate the weight table. In this paper, we present a methodology and a framework Weight Calibration (WeiCal) to automatically populate more realistic weight tables paving the way to efficient DSE.

The WeiCal framework consists of Calibration and Retargeting. A set of training benchmarks are profiled along-with the actual execution of those benchmarks on the target PE in calibration phase, generating a Linear Program (LP). This is fed to an LP Solver which defines the weight table of the particular PE, implicitly considering the vast number of architectural and micro architectural features. To estimate the performance of a target application, in the retargeting phase, it is profiled once to extract computational demand. Then, performance is estimated purely through a static approach by a simple matrix multiplication of the PE weight table and the application's computational demand. With this, multiple iterations of the retargeting step can rapidly estimate the performance of different target processors. The advantage of this method is that the application is simulated only once (for profiling), avoiding long repetitive simulations. In addition, due to fast computation in retargeting stage, this approach is particularly suitable for rapid comparisons in early DSE.

We validate WeiCal using a synthetic processor and benchmark model, and also analyse the limitations of this approach. We evaluate the efficiency of the proposed methodology using 49 benchmarks on 2 different processors with varying configurations (multiple memory configurations and software optimizations). On a 3.1 GHz i5-3450 Intel host, 25 million estimations/second can be obtained regardless of the application size and PE complexity. The accuracy is sufficient for early DSE with a 24% average error.

The rest of this paper is organised as follows: Sect. 2 presents an overview of work related to this approach. Section 3 introduces retargetable profiling. Section 4 presents WeiCal and Sect. 5 presents implementation. Section 6 presents a synthetic model to validate the approach. Section 7 shows experimental results and Sect. 8 concludes the paper.

2   Related Work

Many estimation methods have been proposed trying to solve different challenges in estimation such as accuracy, speed and being application specific. They generally estimate based on one of three abstraction levels: : source-level (high-level), intermediate-level and binary-level (low-level). At high-level, fewer details are taken into account. It is faster and retargetable but less accurate in terms of absolute performance numbers. On the other side, low-level estimation benefits from more target architecture knowledge increasing accuracy at cost of simulation speed. While low-level may produce cycle approximate estimations for detailed analysis, high-level estimation is more suitable for DSE due to estimation speed.

Various high-level estimation techniques have been proposed. The authors of [2] propose an approach which has limitations due to compiler optimizations. Wang and Herkersdorf [3] present an approach which takes compiler optimizations into account. However, both these approaches rely on simulation for estimation. The authors of [4] propose a compiler-assisted technique to rapidly estimate without simulation. However, this approach is developed for the FPGA based processors. Oyamada et al. [5] present an integrated approach for system design and performance analysis. An analytic approach based on neural networks is used for high-level software performance estimation. This approach takes about 17 s to estimate the performance of an MPEG4 encoder application. A hybrid simulation method is introduced in [6] which also uses a cache simulator to measure memory access delay. [9] presents a complementary method for increasing the accuracy of approaches that are annotating timing information into source code by mapping binary representation to source level. This approach requires the source code and the binary-level CFG. In [7], an estimation approach is proposed for transaction level. One drawback of this work is that the mapping between the C processes to PEs should be determined before using this estimation approach. These approaches are suitable for estimating the performance of a PE, but efficient design space exploration requires faster retargetability.

Javaid et al. [8] propose two estimation mechanisms whose goal is to minimise the estimation time. Though the approach is retargetable for pipelined MPSoCs, the performance estimation of individual component of design space is yet not retargetable. Mohanty and Prasanna [10] present a mechanism for DSE using interpretive simulation which requires specific inputs to the proposed model.

We base our work on [1] for DSE as it is retargetable and does not involve simulating the target application across the design space. However, the estimation accuracy of this approach is largely dependent on the weight table entries of PEs in the design space.

3   Retargetable Profiling

Retargetable profiling [1] is a high-level estimation technique, which is divided into two stages - Profiling and Retargeting.

In the profiling stage, the system specification is instrumented and simulated to gather basic block execution counts. Static analysis then computes the number of operations executed (distinguished by type) for each data-type executed and stored in the form of specification characteristic table. This specification characteristic table has the format same as weight table of a PE. Note, the profiling stage is done only once per application.

In the Retargeting stage, the designer decides the mapping of behaviour to a PE. Performance of executing the behavior on the selected PE is estimated by multiplying specification characteristics (obtained from profiling) with delay values stored in the weight table of that PE. The total performance (E) of that PE is computed through a matrix multiplication and sum.

$$E = \sum_{OpType} \sum_{DataType} (F_{OpType.DataType} \times W_{OpType.DataType}) \qquad (1)$$

where $W_{OpType.DataType}$ is the weight (i.e. clock cycles) and $F_{OpType.DataType}$ is the occurrence frequency of each operation type $OpType$ of data-type $DataType$. Since retargeting consists of a pure static approach, it avoids the time-consuming steps of simulation and profiling.

With its extremely fast estimation speed, retargetable profiling is very suitable for DSE. However, it requires a tedious manual step of extracting the weight table information (execution delay for each operation and datatype combination) from the data sheet of each PE. Considering that the IP vendors have their unique way of representing this information, data collection can be time-consuming. Furthermore, dedicating only one table for each processor limits the designer to one configuration in terms of compiler optimizations and hardware configurations. This limitation makes the design space too simplistic. Moreover, some affecting elements are unknown, such as details of pipeline and data forwarding, because the vendors often do not release this information. This poses many challenges to manually define weight tables. This paper, introduces a framework for automatically generating the weight tables by calibration.

4   Weight Calibration (WeiCal)

This section proposes a technique for calibrating PE weight tables. It automatically populates the weight tables using a training set of benchmarks and a Linear Programming Formulation (LPF). This methodology expands flexibility of the retargetable profiling approach [1], and can increase the accuracy by implicitly considering more architectural features.

4.1 An Overview of the Framework

As shown in Fig. 1, WeiCal generates weight tables for PEs according to a set of training benchmarks. Every benchmark is captured in *SpecC* language (based on ANSI-C) and then profiled with *SCProf* profiler [1] to determine the application computation demand. It includes the frequency of all operation types for each data type for the whole application. Each benchmark is also executed on a real processor (Processing Element (PE)) to obtain accurate benchmark execution cycles. An LP formulation is constructed using the benchmark characteristics and measured execution cycles. Solving this linear system yields the weight table for the PE.

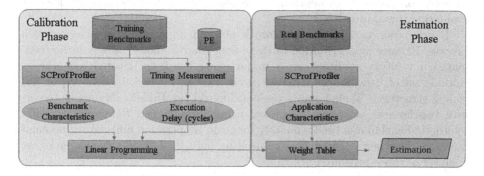

Fig. 1. Framework flow

4.2 Linear Programming Formulation (LPF)

This section describes the LPF to obtain weight tables. For each benchmark i on a particular PE, (B_i) specifies the measured execution time (cycles). D_{ij} denotes the computational demand of benchmark i as determined by profiler. For ease of explanation, we fold every combination of operation-type and data-type into one index j. W_j denotes the weight of one operation and datatype combination. An equation is generated for each benchmark which includes the weights of each operation-data-type combination, occurrence frequency of each combination and total execution time. The number of equations would be equal to the number of benchmarks available. The weights in each equations are the unknowns, which will be solved by LPF. However, as not all factors impacting the performance can be measured, the linear equation system cannot be accurately solved. To allow for some error in the estimation of each benchmark, we introduce a Calibration Fudge factor (CF). Finding the weights with the overall least absolute error (CF) will yield the most accurate estimation. The LPF is as follows:

Minimise:

$\Sigma_i |CF(i)|$

Subject to:

$Benchmark1 : D_{11}.W_1 + D_{12}.W_2 + ... + D_{1M}.W_M + CF_1 = (B_1)$

$Benchmark2 : D_{21}.W_1 + D_{22}.W_2 + ... + D_{2M}.W_M + CF_2 = (B_2)$

...

$BenchmarkN : D_{N1}.W_1 + D_{N2}.W_2 + ... + D_{NM}.W_M + CF_N = (B_N)$

where N is the number of benchmarks and M is the number of operation type and data-type combinations. Each benchmark is represented by one equation. Adding benchmarks will increase information for the LP Solver to find the weights of that PE, to then produce a more realistic weight table leading to a better future estimation.

5   Implementation

This section presents the benchmarks, tools, PEs and metrics that are used for evaluating the approach.

Benchmarks used in the framework play an important role in estimation process. Balance in distribution of these benchmarks allows more accurate estimation for future applications. A major effort has been devoted to gather a suitable set of benchmarks that can cover most of operations, data types and coding structures. Table 1 shows the benchmarks. In Table 1, *Randomly Generated* benchmarks have been generated using the modified *Randprog* tool [15]. Synthetic benchmarks predominately focus on a operation and data-type combination. They are only used for calibration only. The *WCET* benchmarks are a subset of those presented in [16].

Table 1. List and categories of benchmarks

Source	Names of benchmarks
MiBench [12] & DSP-Stone [13]	AES whetstone bcnt blit bubblesort cnt crc crc2 edn fft1 fir2 gamma hanoi heapsort linpack lms lms2 ludcmp matmult matrix basicmath ndes nsichneu peakSpeed1 prime queens v42 wavelt
Randomly Generated	frand1 frand10 frand12 frand13 frand16 frand17 frand18 frand19 frand2 frand20 frand3 frand4 frand6 frand8 frand9 rand3 rand5 rand6 rand7 rand8 rand9
Synthetic	synadddouble synaddfloat synaddlonglongint syndivdouble syndivint syndivlonglongint synmindouble synminfloat synminint synmulfloat synmulint synmullonglongint synmuldouble synaddint synminlonglongint syndivfloat
WCET	adpcm crc2 edn fft1 fir2 lms ndes nsichneu qurt

We used the *SCProf* [1] profiler to extract application demand and *gcc* to compile the benchmarks for real hardware. We used the open source SCIP solver [17] to solve LPF. We have applied WeiCal to two different processors (Blackfin527 [14] and ARM9 [11]), with various hardware configurations (SRAM and SDRAM with Blackfin527 [14]) and compiler optimizations (O0, O1, O2, O3 with ARM9 [11]).

Table 2. Grouping of operations and data types for dimensionality reduction

Groups	Pristine entries in original weight table
constant	constant
array access	array access, content of
function call	function call, return
post increment	post increment, pre increment, post decrement, pre decrement
not	bitwise not, logical not
multiply	multiply, multiply/assignment
divide	divide, modulo, divide/assignment, modulo/assignment
add	add, subtract, add/assignment, subtract/assignment
branch	if, if else, for, while, do while, default, switch, case, break, continue
shift left	shift right, shift left
equal	all compare operations
or	bitwise or, logical or, exclusive or, and, logical-and
assignment	all possible assignment operations
int	unsigned long int, unsigned char, char, unsigned short, pointer, bool short, unsigned int, long int, unsigned long
long long int	long long int, unsigned long long int
float	float, unsigned float
double	double, long double, unsigned double

As metrics, we mostly use absolute error, comparing real execution cycles with estimated cycles. However, absolute accuracy may not always be required. During DSE, different design alternatives are compared. In this setting, the correctness of a relative comparison is sufficient. *Fidelity* quantifies the correctness of a relative comparison.

The dimensions of the weight table and specification characteristic table are defined by the number of possible operations (number of rows) and datatypes (number of columns). The SCProf profiler distinguishes 55 operations and 16 datatypes. This leads to 880 different pairs of operations over datatypes. In order to estimate 880 weights (execution delays), the LP formulation needs at least 880 training benchmarks. It is challenging to collect such a large number of suitable benchmarks. In addition, it would lengthen the LP solver run-time. To reduce the number of required benchmarks, we reduce the dimensionality of the weight table by grouping similar operations and datatypes based on architectural assumptions. Table 2 summarizes our assumptions. Overall, we group all operations into 12 different operation groups and all datatypes into 4 datatype groups. This dramatically reduces the of combinations from 880 down to 48 combinations of operations and datatypes.

6   Validation Through Synthetic Model

Any estimation approach is limited by the number of observable features (profiling restrictions), and by the complete availability of processor performance information (limited micro-architectural knowledge). To initially validate and optimise our approach under known conditions, we employ a synthetic model. We designed a statistical model which produces synthetic PEs and synthetic benchmarks to be used in WeiCal. Using synthetic model increases visibility over real measurements and processors. Each processor is modelled by a set of elements that contribute to delay in execution (such as execution of an operation, cache hit and cache miss). To mimic the effect of partial observability by the profiler, we declare some of these effects as observable, while other effects as non-observable. The number of training benchmarks and non-observable elements are varied to study their impact on the estimation accuracy. In order to realise the non-observable elements, their effect was deliberately included when calculating the measured execution time. However, the occurrence of non-observable elements in benchmarks is hidden from the profiler. In result, the profiler counts only the observable elements, while the timing measurement includes delay (cycles) due to observable as well as non-observable elements. The LPF will attribute the effects of non-observable elements to the observable elements. As such, the number of cycles will increase for each observable feature. This is similar to other models which for example fold memory access delay statistically into operations.

Processor P is modelled as

$$P = [W_k][W_u] \tag{2}$$

where $[W_k]$ is the set of delays for known elements and $[W_u]$ is the set of delays of unknown elements. The particular values for $[W_k]$ and $[W_u]$ are randomly chosen (linear distribution) during the generation of a processor model.

Similarly, a synthetic benchmark is defined as recurrence of elements known and unknown to the Profiler.

$$B = [R_k][R_u] \tag{3}$$

where $[R_k]$ is the set of recurrence for known elements and $[R_u]$ is the set of recurrence of unknown elements. The particular values for $[R_k]$ and $[R_u]$ are randomly chosen (linear distributed) during the generation of a benchmark.

The delay of a specific synthetic benchmark i on a particular synthetic PE j is defined as

$$(Delay)_{ij} = [R_k]_i[W_k]_j + [R_u]_i[W_u]_j \tag{4}$$

Figure 2 shows the effect of non-observable elements evaluated by changing the ratio of observable elements to non-observable elements in the synthetic model. The total number of elements was constant (60), while varying the non-observable elements as 2%, 25%, 40% and 60%. The non-observable elements was set to contribute 15% of the total computation demand.

In the upper left graph of Fig. 2, the mean estimation error quickly converges to 2% when the number of training benchmarks reaches 60. With 25% non-observable elements, the mean estimation error stays at 12% with more than 60 training benchmarks (upper right). When non-observable elements increase to 40% or even 60%, both the average and absolute estimation error are high. The estimation error is no longer improved with more than 60 training benchmarks.

It indicates that the number of training benchmarks need to be necessarily larger than the number of elements in order to converge the estimation error. However, even a large number of training benchmarks does not improve the accuracy of the weight table and corresponding estimation when the non-observable elements are more than 40%. At least 50 training benchmarks are required for the estimation error to converge. The number of training benchmarks should be greater than the number of weights in the weight table for correct estimations.

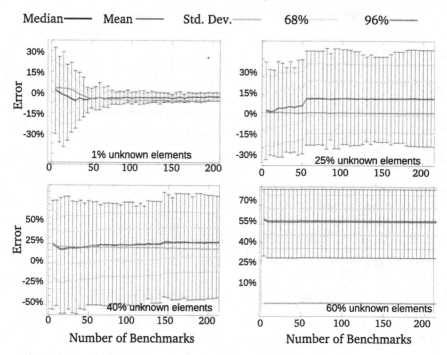

Fig. 2. Effect of number of benchmarks on average error

The synthetic model allowed us to evaluate the effect of the non-observable elements and training benchmarks on the estimation error. The estimation accuracy improves with fewer non-observable elements. It is impossible to achieve a meaningful estimation with non-observable elements over 40% of all (observable and non-observable) architectural elements. Furthermore, the estimation error converges when the training benchmarks is slightly more than the desired observable elements. Adding more training benchmarks does not further improve the accuracy largely.

7   Experimental Results

The efficiency of our approach affects the high-level design decisions. On one hand, accuracy is desired to correctly guide the DSE. On the other hand, performance estimation should be fastest to evaluate many design combinations.

Accuracy is evaluated is terms of absolute error and fidelity. In order to measure estimation error, we excluded one benchmark from the training benchmarks and used it as a target application to determine estimation accuracy. The procedure was repeated through all the real benchmarks. Real and synthetic benchmarks were used for calibrating the weight tables. However, only the real benchmarks were used as test applications as they better reflect the characteristics of an actual workload. The results are aggregated in Fig. 3.

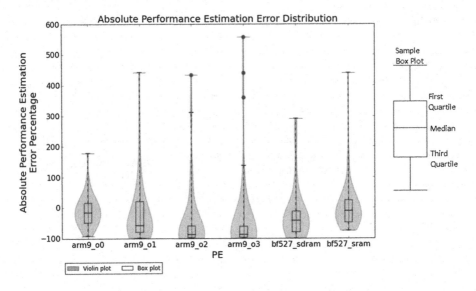

Fig. 3. Estimation error on real platforms

Figure 3 shows the median, quartiles, minimum and maximum of the estimation errors among all benchmarks across all PEs. The box plot shows these static quantities, while the violin plots show the distribution of estimation error across the benchmarks. Figure 3 also shows the effect of compiler optimizations and hardware configurations on the estimation error. The majority of benchmarks have an estimation error close to median (−6%) for Blackfin with SRAM. Moving from SRAM to SDRAM deteriorates the median to −30%. Most accurate results are achieved with low optimization. The ARM9 with O0 has the median at −11% with most of the benchmarks having an estimation error close to median. As the optimization increases, the association of source code with the execution time reduces. This is due to the weak correlation between source-level C code and binary at higher optimization levels. With an increased optimization to O1 for ARM9, the median is at −57%. WeiCal is able to distinguish between various software and hardware configurations. Some applications do not perform well in this approach in terms of the estimation accuracy. This is the cost being paid for estimating at the highest level of abstraction. In some configurations, WeiCal has a higher absolute error than what was reported in [1] as we are now using more complex processors, memory hierarchies and compiler optimizations.

In early DSE, fidelity (i.e. relative comparison) is sufficient and absolute accuracy is less important. In order to analyse fidelity, we describe fidelity matrix, which shows the fidelity between all the possible pairs of PEs from the design space. Table 3 presents the fidelity matrix. To further analyse fidelity, we plot also fidelity over the measured performance gap between the investigated PE configurations. Fidelity depends on closeness between real performance of PEs being compared.

Table 3. Fidelity matrix

	BF527 SRAM	BF527 SDRAM	ARM9 O0	ARM9 O1	ARM9 O2	ARM9 O3
BF527 SRAM	100%	90%	89%	76%	80%	80%
BF527 SDRAM	-	100%	76%	90%	93%	92%
ARM9 O0	-	-	100%	94%	96%	100%
ARM9 O1	-	-	-	100%	57%	61%
ARM9 O2	-	-	-	-	100%	55%
ARM9 O3	-	-	-	-	-	100%

Table 3 shows that performance estimation using calibrative weight tables has high fidelity with average fidelity being 82%. Fidelity increases when performance gap between the compared PEs is larger. The estimated comparison of ARM9 O0 with its higher optimization counterparts is correct in more than 94% of the cases.

In addition to accuracy, the value of estimation methodology also depends on the time it takes for making an estimation. A separate aspect is the duration for generating a weight table (i.e. performance of WeiCal). The weight table is determined only once in the lifetime of a PE and is less important. Hence, calibration takes place only once. We have automated executing benchmarks on target PEs and measuring execution duration (clock cycles). The average time it takes to load each benchmark is 2.5 s. The LPF took 0.6 s to generate the weight table for 48 given equations (48 benchmarks). The calibration phase took nearly 120 s in addition to the actual execution time of all benchmarks on the hardware.

Conversely to calibration, the estimation in retargeting to different PE configurations occurs very frequently during DSE. Thus, its performance is highly critical. Estimation is merely a matrix multiplication of the PE weight table and application profile table. As the dimensions of weight table and application profile table are fixed, the estimation time is independent of the application size and

PE complexity. On a single core of 3.1 GHz i5-3450 Intel host, 25 million estimations/second can be obtained regardless of application size and PE complexity. Additionally, as the estimation is only a matrix multiplication, it's parallelization has been studied a lot. The average error of 24% is acceptable for early DSE where fidelity and high speed of estimation are more prominent factors.

8   Conclusion

Rapid estimation with sufficient fidelity is essential for DSE. In this context, retargetable source-level profiling [1] is a promising approach. It profiles a specification once to determine the specification computation demand. Then, estimating the application's execution time is as simple as a matrix multiplication of the specification computational demand and weight table capturing the PE's computation supply. However, this approach heavily relies on the quality and availability of weight tables.

The work presented in this paper proposes a calibration-based framework to automatically determine a processor's weight table(s). It avoids the manual and error-prone process of manual capturing processor characteristics (execution time). In particular, it mitigates the challenge of limited visibility of the source-level profiling (i.e. C statements) and the associated challenge of attributing non-visible characteristics into the accounted operations.

We devised a synthetic model in order to validate the approach and analyse the bounds. We measured efficiency of the WeiCal using 49 benchmarks (mainly MiBench and DSP Stone) on ARM9 and Blackfin BF527 processors and considered memory configurations (SRAM and SDRAM) and software optimizations (O0, O1, O2 and O3). With the weight table approach 25 million estimations/second can be performed on a single core of 3.1 GHz i5-3450 Intel host. The average estimation error was 24%. However, the approach offers higher fidelity especially with larger performance gap between (e.g. above 94% fidelity for comparing ARM0 at O0 with other optimizations). The high estimation speed with good fidelity makes this methodology an ideal cornerstone for an automated DSE.

References

1. Cai, L., Gerstlauer, A., Gajski, D.: Retargetable profiling for rapid, early system-level design space exploration. In: Proceedings of the 41st Annual Design Automation Conference, DAC 2004, San Diego, CA, USA, pp. 281–286 (2004). ISBN 1-58113-828-8
2. Lattuada, M., Ferrandi, F.: Performance modeling of embedded applications with zero architectural knowledge. In: IEEE/ACM/IFIP International Conference on Hardware/Software Codesign and System Synthesis (CODES+ISSS), pp. 277–286 (2010)
3. Wang, Z., Herkersdorf, A.: An efficient approach for system-level timing simulation of compiler-optimized embedded software. In: 46th ACM/IEEE, Design Automation Conference, pp. 220–225 (2009)

4. Aung, Y.L., Lam, S.-K., Srikanthan, T.: Compiler-assisted technique for rapid performance estimation of FPGA-based processors. In: IEEE International SOC Conference (SOCC), pp. 341–346 (2011)
5. Oyamada, M., Wagner, F.R., Bonaciu, M., Cesario, W., Jerraya, A.: Software performance estimation in MPSoC design. In: Asia and South Pacific Design Automation Conference Proceedings of the 2007, pp. 38–43 (2007). ISBN 1-4244-0629-3
6. Gao, L., Karuri, K., Kraemer, S., Leupers, R., Ascheid, G., Meyr, H.: Multiprocessor performance estimation using hybrid simulation. In: 45th ACM/IEEE Design Automation Conference, pp. 325–330 (2008)
7. Hwang, Y., Abdi, S., Gajski, D.: Cycle-approximate retargetable performance estimation at the transaction level. In: Design, Automation and Test in Europe, DATE 2008, pp. 3–8 (2008)
8. Javaid, H., Janapsatya, A., Haque, M.S., Parameswaran, S.: Rapid runtime estimation methods for pipelined MPSoCs. In: Design, Automation Test in Europe Conference Exhibition, pp. 363–368 (2010)
9. Stattelmann, S., Bringmann, O., Rosenstiel, W.: Fast and accurate source-level simulation of software timing considering complex code optimizations. In: Design Automation Conference (DAC), 2011 48th ACM/EDAC/IEEE, pp. 486–491 (2011)
10. Mohanty, S., Prasanna, V.K.: Rapid system-level performance evaluation and optimization for application mapping onto SoC architectures. In: 15th Annual IEEE International ASIC/SOC Conference, pp. 160–167 (2002)
11. Samsung Electronics: 32 bit CMOS Microcontroller User's Manual. S3C2440A, July 2004. Rev. 1
12. Guthaus, M., Ringenberg, J., Ernst, D., Austin, T., Mudge, T., Brown, R.: MiBench: a free, commercially representative embedded benchmark suite. In: IEEE International Workshop on Workload Characterization WWC-4, pp. 3–14, Dec 2001
13. Zivojnovic, V., Martinez, J., Schlager, C., Meyr, H.: DSPstone: a DSP-oriented benchmarking methodology. In: The International Conference on Signal Processing Applications and Technology, pp. 715–720 (1994)
14. Analog Devices: Blackfin Embedded Processor. ADSP-BF527 (2013). Rev. D
15. Eide, E., Regehr, J.: Volatiles are miscompiled, and what to do about it. In: EMSOFT (2008)
16. Gustafsson, J., Betts, A., Ermedahl, A., Lisper, B.: The malardalen WCET benchmarks - past, present and future. In: WCET 2010, Brussels, Belgium, pp. 137–147 (2010)
17. Achterberg, T.: SCIP: solving constraint integer programs. Math. Program. Comput. 1, 1–41 (2009)

Low Latency FPGA Implementation of Izhikevich-Neuron Model

Vitor Bandeira[1]👤, Vivianne L. Costa[1,2], Guilherme Bontorin[1(✉)],
and Ricardo A. L. Reis[1]

[1] Universidade Federal do Rio Grande do Sul PGMicro/PPGC – Instituto de
Informática, Porto Alegre, Brazil
{vvbandeira,gbontorin,reis}@inf.ufrgs.br
[2] Universidade Federal do Paraná PPGMNE, Curitiba, Brazil
vlcosta@ufpr.br

Abstract. The Izhikevich's simple model (ISM) for neural activity
presents a good compromise between waveform quality and computational cost. FPGAs (Field Programmable Gate Array) are powerful, flexible, and inexpensive digital hardware that can implement such model.
In this paper, we present a highly combinational, low latency implementation of ISM for FPGA. In the absence of official benchmark to
compare different implementations, we propose two different metrics to
compare the technical literature with our implementation. In this benchmark, we can implement a system that, when compared to the literature,
has almost 1.5 times the number of digital neurons (DN), and latency
more than 56 times smaller. This shows that our implementation is best
suited for hybrid network systems and presents a fair performance for
only-artificial networks.

1 Introduction

The human brain has about 10^{11} neurons, and each one can have more than 10^4
synaptic connections with others neurons [8]. As the most inspiring and powerful
computing machine we know at present, it is normal to try breaking the code
and understand how it works. We believe its computer capacity comes from a
three-level complexity: (a) the number of adaptable cells, the neurons; (b) the
capability of configurable connections, the synapses; and (c) the waveform that
is at the same time robust against noise and capable of encoding information,
the spike or action potential.

Considering the waveform, the literature presents various spike models, each
one with respective biological plausibility and computational complexity. The
Izhikevich's Simple Model (ISM) [9] presents one of the best compromises
between waveform quality and computational cost at the moment. It is composed of a system of two ordinary differential equations of the first order that
can be easily digitalized. Regarding capability of configuration connections and
the number of cells, it is important to find hardware that can at the same time be

© IFIP International Federation for Information Processing 2017
Published by Springer International Publishing AG 2017. All Rights Reserved
M. Götz et al. (Eds.): IESS 2015, IFIP AICT 523, pp. 210–217, 2017.
https://doi.org/10.1007/978-3-319-90023-0_17

powerful, flexible, and inexpensive. FPGAs (Field Programmable Gate Array) seem to fill all these requirements as reprogrammable digital circuits.

Some papers describe different implementations of ISM in FPGA [1,4–6,10,11]. They differ from how serial or parallel the computations are implemented and the number of pipeline stages used. Our implementation is highly combinational and present low latency.

No other paper before has proposed any benchmark. To compare our work with others, we propose two different metrics. The first one is neural lattice network. It estimates the maximum number of cells we can simulate in a single hardware.

The second metric we propose is the latency of one neuron. It is the time a variation on the input takes to propagate to the output. This metric has a direct correlation to how parallel an implementation is. Depending on the application, this performance can or cannot be important. Hybrid neural networks, like [2], are an example of systems where such performance is fundamental. These are systems where the whole network is composed of the real-time communication between an artificial and a living part. Low and reliable latency is fundamental to ensure the real-time communication integrity between networks. As biological neurons have latency slower than digital ones, we expect to reuse the hardware, virtualizing a greater number of neurons.

In Sect. 2, we review the simple model proposed by Izhikevich and adapt its equation for digital computing. Section 3 presents the hardware implementation of the neuron and shows a lattice network for comparison reasons. Section 4 shows the hardware results of the implementation to compare it to current literature. Section 5 concludes with the potential of this work and comments about future projects.

2 Izhikevich's Simple Model

2.1 Equations Model

Ensuring some biological plausibility, the ISM reduces the Hodgkin-Huxley model in two-dimensional system of ordinary differential equations [9]:

$$\frac{dv}{dt} = 0.04v^2 + 5v + 140 - u + I \tag{1}$$

$$\frac{du}{dt} = a(bv - u) \tag{2}$$

with the auxiliary after-spike resetting:

$$v \geq 30mV \implies \begin{cases} v \leftarrow c \\ u \leftarrow u + d \end{cases} \tag{3}$$

where v is the membrane potential of the neuron and u is the membrane recovery variable, both in millivolts (mV); t is the time in milliseconds (ms); I is the total

Table 1. Parameters for each neurocomputational feature and injected current used in the implementation

| | | Neural behaviour | | | | | |
		Tonic spiking	Phasic spiking	Tonic bursting	Phasic bursting	Mixed mode	Spike-frequency adaptation
Parameters	a*	0.015625	0.015625	0.015625	0.015625	0.015625	0.0078125
	b*	0.15625	0.1953125	0.15625	0.1953125	0.1953125	0.1953125
	c	−65	−65	−50	−55	−55	−65
	d*	4.6875	4.6875	1.56125	0.0390625	3.125	6.25
Input	I*	10.9375	5	11.71875	4.6875	9.375	23.4375

injected currents in nanoamperes (nA); a, b, c, and d are parameters to set the desired waveform or the neuronal activity.

The parameter a describes the time scale of the recovery variable u. The parameter b represents a sensitivity of the recovery variable u to the subthreshold fluctuations of the membrane potential v. The parameter c describes the after-spike reset value of the membrane potential v. The parameter d represents after-spike reset of the recovery variable u. Different choices of the parameters a, b, c, and d result in different intrinsic firing patterns.

2.2   Change of Variables

To facilitate the model implementation in a digital circuit, it is possible to rewrite Eqs. (1) to (3) as:

$$h\frac{dv}{dt} = \frac{1}{32}v^2 + 3.90625v + 109.375 - u^* + I^* \tag{4}$$

$$h\frac{du^*}{dt} = a^*(b^*v - u^*) \tag{5}$$

$$v \geq 30mV \implies \begin{cases} v \leftarrow c \\ u^* \leftarrow u^* + d \end{cases} \tag{6}$$

where $h = 0.78125$, $u^* = hu$, and $I^* = hI$; the parameters a, b, and d are replaced by a^*, b^*, and d^*, respectively, each one also multiplied by h. This transformation is suggested in [4] and [1], but both neglect the factor h.

The new system of differential Equations (4) to (6) ensures the same behavior of Eqs. (1) to (3). We can solve by Euler's Method [3], a numerical method of the first order, which produces accurate results. This approach results on:

$$v_{n+1} = v_n + \Delta t\left[\frac{1}{32}v_n^2 + 3.90625v_n + 109.375 - u_n^* + I_n^*\right] = v_n + \Delta t.kv \tag{7}$$

$$u_{n+1}^* = u_n^* + \Delta t\left[a^*(b^*v_n - u_n^*)\right] = u_n^* + \Delta t.ku \tag{8}$$

where Δt is the time increment of the Euler's Method. Moreover, in Eq. (7) we also approximate $3.90625v \approx 4v$ [4]. kv and ku are used further in the implementation and they represent the variation for each iteration.

The parameters in Table 1 are adapted from the original publication [9] considering the factor h, and it depends on the type of the simulated neuron. The choice of parameters is beyond the scope of this paper, as it is a current research topic. The input current is set to an appropriated input to reveal a realistic behavior.

In the next section, we show the methodology for ISM implementation on FPGA.

3   Neuron Implementation

3.1   One Neuron

For our implementation, we use combinational logic for the most of the circuit. The circuitry is as parallel as possible, optimized for latency rather than the area without the reuse of hardware. Figure 1 presents a single neuron, and Fig. 2 the computation for the new value of v, u^* as well as the activity log. For the calculation of the next v and u^*, we opted for two parallel operations, one for the case with a spike and other without a spike and select between them afterward.

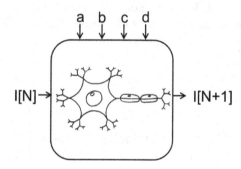

Fig. 1. Implementation of one neuron

Each neuron receives the parameters (a^*, b^*, c, d^*) from a top module and stores locally the initial values for v and u^*. We use an 18-bit fixed point two's complement representation: 1 sign bit, 9 bits for the integer part and 8 bits for the fractionary part. This representation is better suited for digital implementations than floating point, and 18 bits uses more efficiently the available hardware without compromising the accuracy as presented on [1].

The initial values of v and u^* are, respectively -70 mV and -15.63 mV. The time incremental is $\Delta t = h = 0.78125$ ms (milliseconds). The parameters and injected currents are exhibited in Table 1.

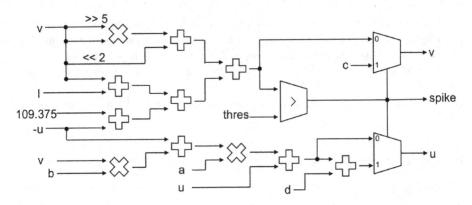

Fig. 2. Schematics of one neuron, the operations to compute Eqs. (4) to (6). All variables and parameters in this figure already account for the variable change presented in Sect. 2.

3.2 Network for Tests and Metrics

We have chosen a lattice network: one neuron is directly connected to the next, by $I_{[N]}$ and $I_{[N+1]}$, Fig. 3. Even though this has low biological meaning, it can be used estimate the maximal number of neurons that can be implemented on a single FPGA chip.

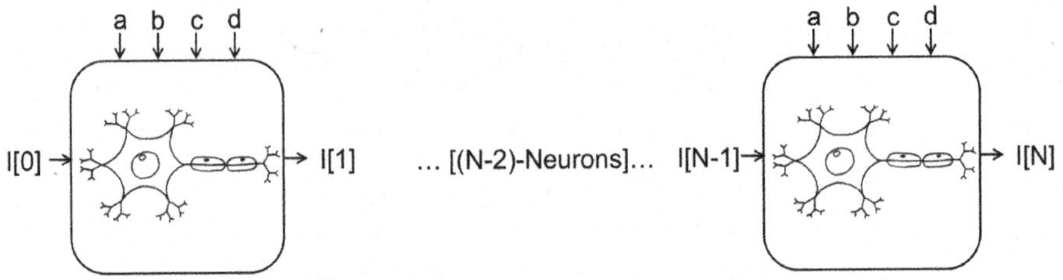

Fig. 3. Schematics of the lattice network used.

We use an Altera's DE4 Board (EP4SGX230KF40C2) to estimate the number of cells that we could implement, and measure latency. Figures 4 and 5 represent about 200 ms in biological time and about 1.8 ms in FPGA with a 250-MHz clock. The maximum and minimum tensions are, respectively, +32 mV and -70 mV. Table 1 contains the parameters used for the implementation as well as the input current. These results were obtained with the SignalTap II, provided in the Quartus II software, and will be presented in the next section.

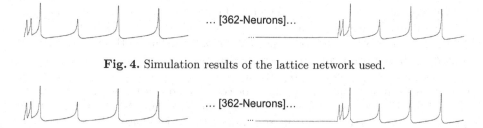

Fig. 4. Simulation results of the lattice network used.

Fig. 5. Measurement of the lattice network used.

4 Results

Figure 4 shows the simulation of our Verilog description of lattice network using ModelSim^{TM}. Figure 5 shows the measurement of the lattice network on the FPGA, with only the first and last neuron being presented. The data for Fig. 5 was obtained using the SignalTap II tool from Quartus II Software. This tool implements a circuit on the FPGA that acquires data directly on the logic circuits and then send it through a JTAG connection to the computer. The data can be displayed and handled on SignalTap II or exported to other software. Only one neuron activity is shown, but we have tested the activity of the six neurons presented in Table 1.

Table 2. Comparison of our implementation with literature

Ref	Digital neurons	HW Use		Time performance			Representation (bits)		FPGA	
		FF	LUT	Clock (MHz)	Pipeline Stages	Latency (ns)	Total	Integer Decimal	Vendor	Family
[5]	32	28%	44%	50	0	320	-		Xilinx	Spartan
[4]		64%	78%	40	5	150	18	10.8		
[1]	1	1%	1,5%	84.81	7	94.33				Virtex-4
[10]	25	79%		198	23	121.21	44	32.12		
[6]	32	32%	36%	110.47	6	63.37	18	9.8		Virtex-5
[11]	256	3.39%		307	96	315.96	32	-		
		7.04%		214	147	453.27	64			
This	364	93%		250	0	8	18	10.8	Altera	Stratix IV

With a lattice network, we can fit 364 digital neurons (DN) on an FPGA. This is 1.5 times more than previous from the literature, [11], which presented 256 DN (Table 2). Our estimative is from a lattice network, but this number alone is expressive. And it is important to estimate how many realistic DN we can implement in a realistic physical network.

We consider that there is no coherence of network implementations and available data in the literature since each paper implements a different network. Therefore, we do not compare values for virtual neurons at the network level. Indeed, we have not found any paper comparing it either.

There is much evidence of biological data from experiments indicating that the information in brain structures can be coded, among other ways, in the time interval between spikes [12]. Because of this, we have considered paramount to our implementation to have a high precision on the spike timestamp, which is the instant that the spike occurred. That is achieved with low latency and reliable system.

The latency is the time that the cell takes to provide a valid output from a variation on the input. We have shown that our latency (8 ns) is more than 56 times smaller than the literature, the best comparison being with [11] (453.27 ns), Table 2.

The pipelines presented in the literature do not show a parallel load, causing to have a bigger latency. And also it implies an approximation of the spike timestamp as high as the pipeline extension. We suppose that such an approximation do not interfere with their applications [1,4,6,10,11], but the same cannot be said for all applications.

5   Conclusion

In this paper, we presented a highly-combinational low-latency implementation for Izhikevich's Neuron Model in FPGA. This approach is better suited for hybrid network applications as it has the best latency in the literature, Table 2. Some other implementations can be better suited for emulation of networks purely artificial with less precision in spike timestamp, as they use fewer resources than ours.

We could also implement more DN in a single FPGA board than the literature when we consider our lattice network. Although as in many cases with bioinspired circuits, these implementations are very particular, and a fair comparison between two different networks is near impossible.

Future works include: (a) to implement a network with more biological meaning; (b) to reuse logic blocks and to implement a pipeline for some calculations to achieve a better speed without compromising latency; (c) to use precomputed values in auxiliary shared memory to reduce computation time and latency; and (d) to explore the parallelism technique for multiple virtual neurons, increasing the maximum size of a network in a single FPGA chip.

As our application is to study and interface with natural living neural networks, the FPGA implementation is preferable for it has easier configurability, reconfigurability, and test. Other implementations such as artificial networks implemented on a full-custom analog [7], or digital integrated circuits may be interesting to implement the short-term objectives (a) through (d) are achieved. Such long-term implementation can improve power consumption, timing performance, and area occupation at the expense of configurability.

Acknowledgment. This work is funded by the following agencies: Federal Agency for Support and Evaluation of Higher Education of Brazil (CAPES), the National Council for Technological and Scientific Development (CNPq), and the Foundation for Research of the State of Rio Grande do Sul (FAPERGS). The authors thank the Macnica-DHW Ltda for the FPGAs boards and technical support.

References

1. Ambroise, M., Levi, T., Bornat, Y., Saighi, S.: Biorealistic spiking neural network on FPGA. In: 47th Annual Conference on Information Sciences and Systems (CISS), pp. 1–6, March 2013

2. Bontorin, G., Renaud, S., Garenne, A., Alvado, L., Le Masson, G., Tomas, J.: A real-time closed-loop setup for hybrid neural networks. In: 29th Annual International Conference of the IEEE Engineering in Medicine and Biology Society, EMBS 2007, pp. 3004–3007, August 2007

3. Burden, R.L., Faires, J.D.: Numerical Analysis, 9th edn. Brooks/Cole Publishing Company, Boston (2011)

4. Cassidy, A., Andreou, A.: Dynamical digital silicon neurons. In: IEEE Biomedical Circuits and Systems Conference, BioCAS 2008, pp. 289–292, November 2008

5. Cassidy, A., Denham, S., Kanold, P., Andreou, A.: FPGA based silicon spiking neural array. In: IEEE Biomedical Circuits and Systems Conference, BIOCAS 2007, pp. 75–78, November 2007

6. Cheung, K., Schultz, S., Leong, P.: A parallel spiking neural network simulator. In: International Conference on Field-Programmable Technology, FPT 2009, pp. 247–254, December 2009

7. Indiveri, G., Horiuchi, T.K.: Frontiers in neuromorphic engineering. Front. Neurosci. **5**, 118 (2011)

8. Izhikevich, E.M.: Neural excitability, spiking and bursting. Int. J. Bifurcat. Chaos **10**(6), 1171–1266 (2000)

9. Izhikevich, E.M.: Simple model of spiking neurons. IEEE **14**, 1569–1572 (2003)

10. Rice, K.L., Bhuiyan, M., Taha, T., Vutsinas, C.N., Smith, M.: FPGA implementation of Izhikevich spiking neural networks for character recognition. In: International Conference on Reconfigurable Computing and FPGAs. ReConFig 2009, pp. 451–456, December 2009

11. Thomas, D.B., Luk, W.: FPGA accelerated simulation of biologically plausible spiking neural networks. In: Pocek, K.L., Buell, D.A. (eds.) FCCM, pp. 45–52. IEEE Computer Society (2009)

12. Wennberg, R., Velazquez, J.L.P.: Coordinated Activity in the Brain: Measurements and Relevance to Brain Function and Behavior. Springer, New York (2009). https://doi.org/10.1007/978-0-387-93797-7

Reconfigurable Buffer Structures
for Coarse-Grained Reconfigurable Arrays

Éricles Sousa(✉)⬤, Frank Hannig⬤, and Jürgen Teich⬤

Hardware/Software Co-design, Department of Computer Science,
Friedrich-Alexander-Universität Erlangen-Nürnberg (FAU), Erlangen, Germany
{sousa,hannig,teich}@cs.fau.de

Abstract. Coarse-Grained Reconfigurable Arrays (CGRAs) have emerged as a powerful solution to speedup computationally intensive applications. Heterogeneous MPSoC architectures containing such reconfigurable accelerators have the advantage of providing high flexibility, power-efficiency, and high performance. However, CGRAs may suffer from a data access bottleneck. To mitigate this problem, we present a reconfigurable buffer architecture for CGRAs. Here, the buffers can be configured at runtime to select between different schemes for memory access, i.e., addressable RAMs or pixel buffers. We showcase the benefits of our approach by prototyping a heterogeneous MPSoC architecture containing a RISC processor and a class of CGRA called Tightly Coupled Processor Arrays (TCPAs). The architecture is prototyped in FPGA technology. For basic image processing algorithms, we demonstrate that our proposed buffer structures for system integration allow to increase the memory bandwidth utilization and allow for a performance improvement of up to 7% in comparison to state-of-the-art solutions for image processing.

1 Introduction

Semiconductor technology has already hit the *power wall* and is not far away from hitting the *utilization wall* [1]. These effects are caused by shrinking technology, which continuously leads to higher energy densities. However, chips can only handle a limited power budget. As a consequence, the potentially available chip area might not be fully utilized or at least not simultaneously. Thus, these days, energy efficiency has become more important than pure computing power. This means, that in order to scale computing performance in the future, systems' energy efficiency has to be significantly improved. The design of embedded systems containing heterogeneous hardware and customized resources, such as accelerators dedicated for one application domain, is a promising solution to address this challenge.

In this realm, CGRAs are appealing by providing programmability with the potential for high computational throughput and at the same time high energy efficiency [2]. There are many possible ways of integrating such reconfigurable

M. Götz et al. (Eds.): IESS 2015, IFIP AICT 523, pp. 218–229, 2017.
https://doi.org/10.1007/978-3-319-90023-0_18

accelerators into System-on-Chip (SoC) designs. For instance, they can be tightly coupled with a processor and the communication can be realized by a specialized interface or via a shared register file. An alternative is to share the last level cache of a CPU. In this case, a dedicated controller for the shared cache (e.g., shared L2 cache) is needed for connecting CPU and accelerator. However, this approach requires cache coherency models and protocols that need to be adapted according to the targeted application. Apart from these system integration options, it is also possible to connect a hardware accelerator to a shared bus or NoC. Here, the communication with the rest of the system could be realized by message passing, for example, using DMA transfers to/from a local accelerator memory. Although this solution scales very well, the overhead for accessing shared resources may compromise the performance of such accelerators. As a solution for this challenge, we propose to use a very flexible buffer structure that can be configured at runtime either as addressable RAM or pixel buffer as first presented in [3].

In this paper, we propose to use such buffers for coupling a RISC processor directly to the border processing elements of a class of CGRAs called TCPAs (tightly coupled processor arrays [3]). We are using an edge detection algorithm as a case study to demonstrate how the image processing throughput can thereby be increased up to the memory bandwidth available in the system. In the remainder of this paper, we first compare our solution with the state-of-the-art solutions in literature. Then, the target class of TCPA accelerators is presented in Sect. 3. Section 4 describes in detail our proposed system integration of a TCPA to a RISC processor and its implementation as an FPGA prototype. Experimental results on memory bandwidth and performance improvements are provided in Sect. 5. Finally, we conclude our work in Sect. 6.

2   Related Work

Often, there is only a fine line between on-chip processor arrays and coarse-grained reconfigurable architectures (CGRA) since the provided functionality is similar. CGRA examples include architectures such as PACT XPP [4] and ADRES [5], both of which are arrays that can switch between multiple contexts by runtime reconfiguration. Whereas ADRES is a CGRA that is tightly coupled with a VLIW processor, PACT's XPP architecture provides a column of RAMs at two borders of the array, which can be configured to two different modes: addressable or streaming mode. However, except one simple counter per buffer, the architecture does not provide any sophisticated address generators. Thus, if complex buffer addressing schemes are required, the PEs of the array have to be involved in the task of address computations. In [6], the authors propose a generic VHDL template based on a full buffering approach which allows a fast and efficient parallel and pipelined processing of 2-D stencil code applications. This approach is limited to regular window-based applications and the stencil mask has to move always in the same scanning order. In order to cover different applications, Liang et al. [7] describe different kinds of buffering schemes such as full buffering, partial buffering, packing, and buffering with packing. However, at runtime, there is no possibility to switch between these configurations and the selection of the buffer operation has to be defined as a parameter at synthesis time. In the area of high-level synthesis, there exist two tools, ROCCC [8], which provide so-called *smart buffers*, and PARO [9], which allows to generate dedicated pixel buffers automatically. Unlike all aforementioned research works, the reconfigurable buffer structure introduced in [3] is able to adapt according to different application requirements.

3   Accelerator Architecture

A TCPA [10] as shown in Fig. 1 denotes a class of CGRAs being highly parameterizable. The heart of this accelerator consists of a massively parallel array of tightly coupled Very Long Instruction Word (VLIW) Processing Elements (PEs) complemented by peripheral components such as I/O buffers as well as several control, configuration, and communication companions. Some parameters, such as number of PEs, interconnect topology, number of functional units as well as the register organization within the PEs, are defined at synthesis time, whereas other parameters such as programmable delays between neighbor processors and inter-PE interconnect can be reconfigured at runtime. Each PE at the boundary can read/write data directly from/to a local buffer (denoted I/O buffer in Fig. 1) connected to it and each PE can exchange data with its neighbor PE in a single clock cycle. A TCPA can exploit a parallel and direct PE-to-PE communication, as long as input data is available as well as space is available for accepting processed output data at the surrounding I/O buffers of the array. Through the VLIW nature of each PE and the parallel and synchronous execution of mainly loop nest iterations, a TCPA nicely exploits both instruction and loop-level parallelism while achieving a much higher energy efficiency compared to general purpose Commercial Off-The-Shelf (COTS) embedded processors [11]. TCPAs can be integrated into SoC designs, e.g., using a bus-based interconnect architecture, shared registers, or a shared data cache. Thus, they can be used as accelerators in different platforms in order to speedup computationally intensive applications. The building blocks of a TCPA are briefly described in the following.

Processor Array: Before synthesis, the rows and columns defining the total number of PEs of an array need to be specified. The array may be even configured to have regions of heterogeneous PEs. For instance, some of the processors at the borders might include extra functionality for the purpose of address generation. However, in the rest of the paper, we consider only homogeneous arrays.

Array Interconnect: The PEs in the array are interconnected by a circuit-switched mesh-like interconnect, which allows data produced in one PE to be used already in the next cycle by a neighboring PE. An interconnect wrapper encapsulates each PE and is used to describe and parameterize the inter-PE network topology. The wrappers are arranged in a grid fashion and may be customized at compile time to have multiple input/output ports in the four

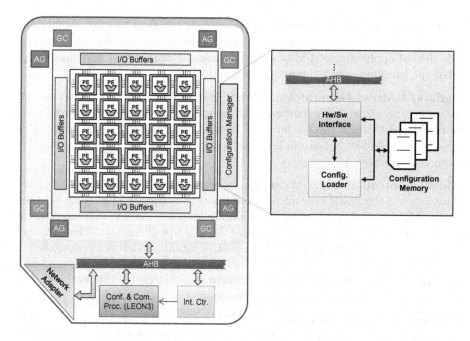

Fig. 1. An abstract architectural view of a TCPA is shown on the left. The abbreviations AG and GC stand for address generator and global controller, respectively. On the right side is the configuration manager (CM) shown that provides the interface to reconfigure the entire TCPA architecture.

directions, i.e., north, east, south, and west. Using these wrappers, indeed different topologies like a 2-D mesh, but also other topologies such as torus or 4-D hypercube can be implemented and changed dynamically. Thus, the array interconnect can be reconfigured to support different applications. To define all possible interconnect topologies, an adjacency matrix is defined for each interconnect wrapper in the array at compile time. Each matrix explains how the input ports of its corresponding wrapper and the output ports of the encapsulated PE are connected to the wrapper output ports and the PE input ports, respectively. If multiple source ports are allowed to drive a single destination port, then a multiplexer with an appropriate number of input signals is generated. The select signals for such generated multiplexers are stored in configuration registers and can therefore be changed at runtime [12]. Two different networks, one for data and one for control signals, can be defined by their data width and number of dedicated channels in each direction. For instance, two 16-bit channels and one 1-bit channel might be chosen as data and control network, respectively.

Processor Element: A PE itself is again a highly parameterizable component with a VLIW (very long instruction word) structure. Different types and numbers of functional units (e.g., adders, multipliers, shifters, logical operations) can be instantiated as separate functional units, which can work in parallel. We call the processing elements *weakly programmable* [12] since the functional units have only a reduced, domain-specific instruction set, which is tailored for a specific field of applications. Additionally, the control path is kept very simple (no interrupt handling, multi-threading, instruction caching, etc.).

Buffers/Address Generators: As the PEs are tightly coupled, they do not have direct access to a global memory. Data transfers to and from the array must be performed through the border PEs. Instead of using FIFOs, the border PEs are connected to highly adaptable surrounding I/O buffers that are explained in more detail in Sect. 4.

Global Controller: Due to the regularity of the considered loop programs, and since most of the static control flow information is needed in all PEs that are involved in the parallel computation of a given loop nest, we can move as much as possible of the *common* control flow out of the PEs to a global controller (GC) per application. The GC generates branch control signals, which are propagated in a delayed fashion over the control network to the PEs where they are combined with the local control flow (program execution). Moreover, this orchestration enables the execution of nested loop programs at *zero-overhead loop*.

Configuration and Communication Processor: The admission of an application on the processor array, as well as the communication with a network via a network adapter (NA), and TCPA programming is managed by a companion RISC processor (LEON3 in Fig. 1) that is named configuration & communication processor (CCP). In consequence, the companion handles resource requests and initiates appropriate DMA transfers via the NA to fill and flush the I/O buffers around the array.

Configuration Manager: The Configuration Manager (CM) holds configuration streams for the TCPA. This includes both the assembly codes to be loaded into the PEs as well as interconnect reconfiguration. Since TCPAs are coarse-grained reconfigurable architectures, the size of their configuration streams normally amounts to a few hundred bytes, which enables ultra fast context switches in the system. The configuration loader transfers a configuration stream to the PEs via a configuration bus. It is possible to group a set of PEs in a rectangular region to be configured simultaneously if they receive the same configuration, thereby reducing significantly the configuration time. As also depicted in Fig. 1, the CM is mainly composed of three parts, a hardware/software interface, configuration loader, and configuration memory. The interface decodes the commands sent from a CCP, which can read or write into a configuration memory that stores the interconnection configuration as well as the binary code for all PEs. Once the configuration memory is populated, the configuration loader starts to configure the interconnection topology between the PEs. Afterwards, each PE is loaded with its assembly (binary) code, and finally, the CM issues a reset to trigger the start of parallel computation on the configured array.

4 Reconfigurable Buffer Structures

TCPAs are envisioned to be used as programmable accelerators in MPSoCs and are very suited for domain-specific computing from the areas of signal, image, and video processing, as well as other streaming processing applications. Based on the inherent algorithmic nature of an application and the chosen paralleliza-tion strategy (e.g., pipelining, loop partitioning), different I/O and buffering approaches might be appropriate. For example, consider an one-dimensional dig-ital signal processing application for a continuous audio signal where input data (audio samples) are streamed into a filter, are processed and after some ini-tial latency filtered data are streamed out. For such 1-D applications, streaming buffers (e.g., a FIFO) at the input and the output would be ideally suited in order to decouple the filtering from the rest of the system. Especially in case of systems that are comprised of buses or NoCs, which do not offer any guaranteed service, asynchronous streaming buffers are vital in order to increase performance and quality.

For two-dimensional image processing (e.g., edge detection, Gaussian filter-ing) or linear algebra algorithms (matrix-matrix multiplication, LU decompo-sition, etc.), the requirements are quite different. In this case, the data often already resides somewhere in the system—e.g., in the main memory—and has to be transported to the accelerator before it can be computed. If large problem instances have to be computed, partitioning techniques [13,14] are used to break down the data into several smaller chunks, which have to be transported and processed one after the other in the accelerator. Data locality is a key concept for efficient execution (performance, energy consumption) in such cases. Thus, the amount of reads and writes to the main memory has to be minimized as much as possible, and redundant data copies should be avoided in order to increase energy efficiency. For instance, when blocking is applied to map stencil computations to multiple processors that can process the input data independently in parallel, border problems may occur, i. e., input data on the border area is needed in two partitions. The size of this overlap region varies according to the window size of the local operator. For a window with $w \times w$ pixels, the total of data that overlaps into neighboring regions is equal to the kernel radius, $r = \left\lfloor \dfrac{w}{2} \right\rfloor$. Yet, because the pixels are shared in two directions, the overlap area is twice the radius r of the window, i.e., $2r$. Thus, when an input image of size $W \times H$ is partitioned in M horizontal tiles, the total of data shared between all partitions is given by Eq. (1)

$$T_{overlap} = 2r \cdot W \cdot (M - 1) \tag{1}$$

In the case where only N vertical tiles are computed in parallel, Eq. (1) can be rewritten by replacing the terms W and M by H and N, respectively.

Moreover, the additional overhead for transferring all the border elements from the local memory to the input buffers is defined by Eq. (2)

$$Overhead = T_{overlap} \cdot L, \tag{2}$$

where L is the latency to copy these data from the local memory to the input buffers. To avoid this additional overhead, a hardware mechanism is desirable that does not affect the performance and does not require any data copies.

In order to fulfill the aforementioned demands, we propose a highly adaptable architecture, which can be configured to either work as addressable memory banks (RAM), provide data in a streaming manner, or function as buffers customized for stencil operations. Figure 2(a) presents an overview of the proposed I/O buffer architecture, which uses dual-ported RAMs (DPRAMs) as interface for data transfer and clock domain transition between the local bus (AHB[1]) on the top and the processor array on the bottom. To reduce the amount of connectors to the AHB, several DPRAMs may be wrapped as a single buffer, where the individual RAMs are associated to the most significant bits of the target address, presented by the AHB. The connection between the DPRAMs and the processor array can be established in several ways, as each of the RAM components has a discrete data channel to the TCPA. To increase the storage capacity, the address space of DPRAMs can be combined, as it is shown for combinations of two and four DPRAMS in Fig. 2(b) and (c), respectively. Although Fig. 2(a) shows the read and the write direction between the buffer and the TCPA, the two subsequent figures (b) and (c) omit the write direction from the array to the buffer for better visibility. Data reads and writes between the DPRAMs and the TCPA are generated by a single address generator (AG) for the buffer, which can be configured to follow arbitrary addressing schemes, for instance, to facilitate dense or sparse stencil operations. Depending on the configuration, the most significant bits of the address, generated by the AG are used to select between concatenated memories. Data partitioning onto neighboring processing elements and loop-carried data dependencies between iterations may introduce offsets between computations [15], however, the addressing scheme for data access remains the same, thus it is sufficient to delay the values generated by the AG through the use of configurable shift registers (CSRs). Instead of enabling every part of the CSR individually, the amount of necessary control logic can be greatly reduced by following a logarithmic scheme, which also reduces the energy consumption.

In addition to the so far introduced capabilities, it is very often necessary to propagate entire image lines between neighboring processing elements for computation. To reduce memory transfers into the buffers over the local bus, also a chained buffer is supported, referred to as *pixel buffer*. The key idea is to initially fill the buffers from the local bus and to pass data from one buffer to the next as it is read out. Operating the buffers in this way only requires a single port to maintain data streaming to the buffer. However, the contents can be fed to the array via individual ports in parallel. For instance, three interlinked buffers provide also three output ports to the TCPA, whereas new data will only be written to the first buffer in the sequence. Since the two ports of the DPRAM also provide Y clock transition between the bus and the TCPA, the bus-side port of the memory must provide a means to switch between the bus

---

[1] *Advanced High-performance Bus* (AHB) is a bus protocol introduced by ARM Ltd. as part of the *Advanced Microcontroller Bus Architecture* (AMBA) for SoC designs.

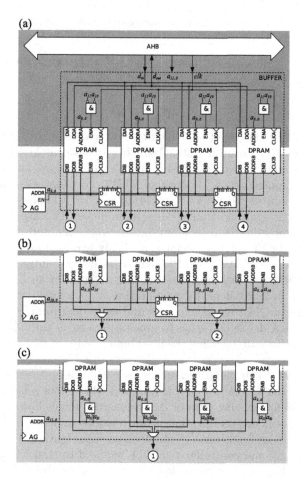

Fig. 2. In (a), (b), and (c), a reconfigurable I/O buffer architecture is shown which may be configured into different modes and trade-off the buffer sizes with the number of available independent ports to the processor array [3].

and TCPA clock domain. Despite of the individual representations shown above, the buffer architecture is a combined implementation, which allows to select one of the introduced modes.

5   Experimental Results

In order to demonstrate the concepts and benefits of our proposed I/O buffer architecture, the TCPA shown in Fig. 1 has been synthesized on a Kintex-7 FPGA prototyping platform. The architecture consists of a RISC processor and a TCPA, both connected through an AMBA bus. An SRAM of 256 MB is also available and used to store the input image frames arriving over the network adapter (NA) as shown in Fig. 1. The RISC processor is a LEON3, which is a

Table 1. Resource utilization of our reconfigurable buffer structure on a Kintex-7 FPGA.

Component	Slice register	LUT	DPRAM
Reconfigurable buffer	825	1,658	5

synthesizable VHDL model of a 32-bit processor compliant with a SPARC V8 architecture and can run up to 120 MHz. This processor is highly configurable at synthesis time and is particularly suitable for SoC designs. In our prototype, the TCPA is composed of a 5×5 array of VLIW processing elements operating at 60 MHz. The considered target application is a 5×5 Laplace operator used to detect the vertical and horizontal edges in an image. This algorithm is widely used as a pre-processing step in many image processing and computer vision applications. In the prototyped architecture, only five read ports are necessary to deliver data to the TCPA. Each PE computes one convolution coefficient and the last PE in the last row also performs the addition of all convolved values and outputs the final result of the computation.

We assume two DMA engines to read and write data from/to buffers. Using the addressable RAM, the DMA has to provide data to all individual channels of the input buffer. Instead, by using the pixel buffer, only the first channel receives data and automatically delivers the pixel values to adjacent channels.

To achieve similar granularity and access pattern as succeeded in the pixel buffer, the addressable RAM would require a double buffer scheme to hide the additional access for copying data of the consecutive image lines that are swept by the scanning window. This option is not considered, because the implementation of a double buffer scheme would demand more hardware resources. Furthermore, an additional controller would be required to transfer data from the main memory. Therefore, we use a blocking operation for the addressable RAM. Hence, the input image is divided into 5 horizontal tiles and each tile is individually processed by a group of 5 PEs. On the other hand, using the pixel buffer the input data is a steady stream. In both buffer schemes, the number of hardware resources is the same. Table 1 presents the resource utilization of one reconfigurable buffer structure that has 5 I/O channels. Since the accelerator is connected to a shared bus, it is possible to minimize the communication latency by transferring the input data simultaneously along with computation in an overlapping fashion. Thus, the input buffer can constantly deliver data. The output results are displayed by using a dedicated connection to a DVI interface. Hence, the AMBA bus is not involved in this operation and these two processes do not compete with each other. However, if there is any other application using the bus at the same time as the DMA attempts to read data from the local memory, it would result in a bus contention and the system performance would be affected.

Before starting the computation on the TCPA, it is necessary to define the mode of operation of all input and output channels of the reconfigurable buffer. For that, we use the LEON3 to load a configuration data into the buffer structure.

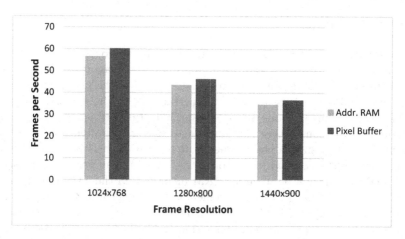

Fig. 3. Average performance of a 5×5 Laplace operator running on an FPGA-based TCPA implementation at 60 MHz and using different buffer schemes.

Unlike [6,7], our proposed work has the possibility to change the mode of operation at runtime. The reconfiguration overhead is equal to 840 cycles, i.e., 7 μs, since the bus operates at 120 MHz. For measuring the system performance, we consider three different frames sizes, i.e., 1024×768, 1280×800, and 1440×900. For evaluating the performance, we first configure the input buffers as addressable RAM and observe the average throughput obtained from the TCPA. In the second experiment, we configure the input buffers to work as a pixel buffer. In both cases, the channel size is equal to the width of the input image. Thus, it is possible to perform the kernel computation of entire lines without fetching new data from the global memory. Figure 3 presents the average performance in frames per second by taking into account the reconfiguration overhead for switching between the different buffer schemes. There, we observe that although the addressable RAM can be very customized for irregular memory access, it does not propagate the input data to adjacent input PEs, which share data in their borders.

By applying Eq. (1), we conclude that these additional data amount to 16, 20, and 22.5 KB for the three different frame sizes, i.e., 1024×768, 1280×800, and 1440×900, respectively. The latency for transferring data from the SRAM to input buffers corresponds to 8 cycles per transfer and using Eq. (2), we observe that the performance loss depicted in Fig. 3 corresponds exactly to the time for copying the pixels located at the border of the image. However, by using the pixel buffer, it is possible to achieve higher performance. This is because it is designed for increasing data locality by means of propagating the input data to different channels. Thus, we can avoid to provide redundant data copies to the input buffers and consequently may increase the memory bandwidth utilization, in this example up to 7%.

6 Conclusion

This paper presents a reconfigurable buffer structure for coarse-grained reconfigurable arrays. In addition to traditional address-based memory banks, the buffer architecture can deliver data in a streaming manner to the processing elements of the array. Moreover, to minimize data transfers to the buffers, the design contains an interlinked mode which is especially targeted at 2-D kernel computations. For demonstrating the advantages of our reconfigurable I/O buffer structure, we synthesized a heterogeneous architecture consisting of a RISC processor and a tightly coupled processor array (TCPA). The processor is used for starting DMA transfers between a SRAM memory and the TCPA composed of a 5 × 5 array of VLIW processing elements. The target application chosen for performance evaluation of different I/O buffer modes is an edge detection algorithm that is widely used in computer vision and embedded applications. In the case of such stream-based applications, the pixel buffer mode outperforms the addressable RAM mode. As image lines will be needed in subsequent steps of the image kernel computation, the feedback concept reduces the amount of required memory transfers to the buffers to a minimum by propagating the image data from one memory to the next. Therefore, by means of selecting the right buffer configuration, a considerably higher performance may be achieved. In the case of an input frame resolution of 1024 × 768, the performance could be increased by 7%. Due to the higher data locality, the TCPA was able to compute 60 frames per seconds, while the reconfiguration overhead was only 7 μs. By performing such an ultra-fast reconfiguration, the overhead for switching between the different buffer schemes can be neglected.

However, the addressable RAM mode of operation can be more efficient in the case of partial buffering or non-raster scanning. As a future work, we intend to analyse not only the power efficiency of our approach, but also the system performance by considering different window sizes, partitioning schemes as well as scenarios of concurrent applications competing for shared resources such as in invasive computing [16].

Acknowledgment. This work was supported by the German Research Foundation (DFG) as part of the Transregional Collaborative Research Centre "Invasive Computing" (SFB/TR 89) and Research Training Group 1773 "Heterogeneous Image Systems". The first author is also grateful to the Brazilian National Council for Scientific and Technological Development (CNPq) for supporting his research.

References

1. Goulding-Hotta, N., Sampson, J., Venkatesh, G., Garcia, S., Auricchio, J., Huang, P., Arora, M., Nath, S., Bhatt, V., Babb, J., Swanson, S., Taylor, M.: The Green-Droid mobile application processor: an architecture for silicon's dark future. IEEE Micro **31**(2), 86–95 (2011)
2. Yongjun, P., Park, J., Mahlke, S.: Efficient performance scaling of future CGRAs for mobile applications. In: International Conference on Field-Programmable Technology (FPT), pp. 335–342 December 2012

3. Hannig, F., Schmid, M., Lari, V., Boppu, S., Teich, J.: System integration of tightly-coupled processor arrays using reconfigurable buffer structures. In: Proceedings of the ACM International Conference on Computing Frontiers (CF). ACM (2013)
4. Baumgarte, V., Ehlers, G., May, F., Nückel, A., Vorbach, M., Weinhardt, M.: PACT XPP - a self-reconfigurable data processing architecture. J. Supercomput. **26**(2), 167–184 (2003)
5. Bouwens, F., Berekovic, M., De Sutter, B., Gaydadjiev, G.: Architecture enhancements for the ADRES coarse-grained reconfigurable array. In: Proceedings of the International Conference on High Performance Embedded Architectures and Compilers, pp. 66–81 (2008)
6. Schmidt, M., Reichenbach, M., Fey, D.: A generic VHDL template for 2D stencil code applications on FPGAs. In: Proceedings of the International Symposium on Object/Component/Service-Oriented Real-Time Distributed Computing Workshops, pp. 180–187 (2012)
7. Liang, X., Jean, J., Tomko, K.: Data buffering and allocation in mapping generalized template matching on reconfigurable systems. J. Supercomput. **19**(1), 77–91 (2001)
8. Guo, Z., Buyukkurt, B., Najjar, W.: Input data reuse in compiling window operations onto reconfigurable hardware. In: Proceedings of the 2004 ACM SIGPLAN/SIGBED Conference on Languages, Compilers, and Tools for Embedded Systems (LCTES). ACM, pp. 249–256 (2004)
9. Hannig, F., Ruckdeschel, H., Dutta, H., Teich, J.: PARO: synthesis of hardware accelerators for multi-dimensional dataflow-intensive applications. In: Woods, R., Compton, K., Bouganis, C., Diniz, P.C. (eds.) ARC 2008. LNCS, vol. 4943, pp. 287–293. Springer, Heidelberg (2008). https://doi.org/10.1007/978-3-540-78610-8_30
10. Hannig, F., Lari, V., Boppu, S., Tanase, A., Reiche, O.: Invasive tightly-coupled processor arrays: a domain-specific architecture/compiler co-design approach. ACM Trans. Embed. Comput. Syst. (TECS) **13**(4s), 133:1–133:29 (2014)
11. Kissler, D., Strawetz, A., Hannig, F., Teich, J.: Power-efficient reconfiguration control in coarse-grained dynamically reconfigurable architectures. J. Low Power Electron. **5**(1), 96–105 (2009)
12. Kissler, D., Hannig, F., Kupriyanov, A., Teich, J.: A highly parameterizable parallel processor array architecture. In: Proceedings of the IEEE International Conference on Field Programmable Technology (FPT). IEEE, pp. 105–112 (2006)
13. Teich, J.: A compiler for application specific processor arrays, ser. Reihe Elektrotechnik. Shaker (1993). https://books.google.de/books?id=WqOGAgAACAAJ
14. Teich, J., Thiele, L., Zhang, L.: Scheduling of partitioned regular algorithms on processor arrays with constrained resources. In: International Conference on Application-Specific Systems, Architectures, and Processors (ASAP), pp. 131–144, August 1996. https://doi.org/10.1109/ASAP.1996.542808
15. Hannig, F., Dutta, H., Teich, J.: Mapping a class of dependence algorithms to coarse-grained reconfigurable arrays: architectural parameters and methodology. Int. J. Emb. Syst. **2**(1/2), 114–127 (2006)
16. Teich, J.: Invasive Algorithms and Architectures. IT-Inf. Technol. **50**(5), 300–310 (2008)

Author Index

Printed in the United States
By Bookmasters